The Impact of Alfred Marshall's Ideas

The Impact of Alfred Marshall's Ideas

The Global Diffusion of his Work

Edited by

Tiziano Raffaelli

Professor of the History of Economic Thought, University of Pisa, Italy

Giacomo Becattini

Emeritus Professor of Political Economy, University of Florence, Italy

Katia Caldari

Assistant Professor, University of Padua, Italy

Marco Dardi

Professor of Economics, University of Florence, Italy

Edward Elgar
Cheltenham, UK • Northampton, MA, USA

Published by
Edward Elgar Publishing Limited
The Lypiatts
15 Lansdown Road
Cheltenham
Glos GL50 2JA
UK

Edward Elgar Publishing, Inc.
William Pratt House
9 Dewey Court
Northampton
Massachusetts 01060
USA

A catalogue record for this book
is available from the British Library

Library of Congress Control Number: 2006011133

ISBN 978 1 84720 512 4

Printed and bound by MPG Books Group, UK

Contents

Contributors

Lluis Argemí, University of Barcelona, Spain (d. 4 March 2007)
Roger E. Backhouse, University of Birmingham, UK
Bradley W. Bateman, Denison University, Ohio, US
Anthony Brewer, University of Bristol, UK
Michal Brzezinski, University of Warsaw, Poland
Volker Caspari, Technical University Darmstadt, Germany
Carlo Cristiano, University of Pisa, Italy
Marco Dardi, University of Florence, Italy
Robert W. Dimand, Brock University, Canada
Irina Eliseeva, Saint Petersburg State University of Economics and Finance, Russia
Anthony M. Endres, University of Auckland, New Zealand
Guido Erreygers, University of Antwerp, Belgium
Riccardo Faucci, University of Pisa, Italy
Mauro Gallegati, Polytechnic University of Marche, Italy
Peter D. Groenewegen, University of Sydney, Australia
Harald Hagemann, University of Hohenheim, Germany
Tore Jørgen Hanisch, University of Agder, Norway
Arnold Heertje, University of Amsterdam, The Netherlands
Andrea Maneschi, Vanderbilt University, Tennessee, US
Steven G. Medema, University of Colorado, Denver, US
Nita Mitra, University of Calcutta, India
Robin Neill, University of Prince Edward Island, Canada
Mikio Nishioka, Doshisha University, Kyoto, Japan
Michel Quéré, CNRS, France
José Reis, University of Coimbra, Portugal
Bo Sandelin, University of Gothenburg, Sweden
Arild Sæther, University of Agder, Norway
Paul B. Trescott, Southern Illinois University, Carbondale, US
Keith Tribe, University of Sussex, UK
Alberto Zanni, University of Florence, Italy

Introduction

This volume developed as a nearly spontaneous sequel to the *Elgar Companion to Alfred Marshall* (ECAM), edited in 2006 by T. Raffaelli, G. Becattini and M. Dardi. The main aim of that book was to highlight the new trends in the interpretation of Marshall's thought, the origins of which can be traced back to the 1970s and J.K. Whitaker's publication of a number of early manuscripts, at that time scarcely known, as well as to the revival, in the studies of industrial districts by G. Becattini and his school, of a Marshallian approach to industrial economics. Since these initial developments, an increasing number of scholars from various parts of the world have carried out a process of historical revision from which a radically new reading of Marshall has emerged, as we think is made clear in the numerous contributions to the ECAM.

What was missing from that volume was a systematic country-by-country study of the impact of Marshall's ideas over the course of the last century. In fact, some of the entries included in the present volume had originally been commissioned for the ECAM, and were already available at the moment of publication in 2006 (a delay for which we again apologise to the authors). But the editors came to realise that the picture at that time assembled was far from complete, and that the world's reception of Marshall's economic thought was a topic that was large and interesting enough to merit a separate volume. Relevant contributions already received were thus set aside temporarily, additional contributions were commissioned, and so, with time, the present volume took shape.

For the sake of clarity, a few words on the premises upon which our project has been built, and on the extent to which we feel that our aims have been achieved, are in order. By 'reception' on a national basis we mean, somewhat in line with reception studies in literary theory, something quite different from a mere assessment of the open-field performance of Marshall's economics in the race with those competing lines of thought that crowded the area of economic research in his and in later times. The justification for focusing the study on national boundaries and on the ability – or lack of ability – of Marshall's thought to cross them and fertilise the spaces beyond lies in an interest in what happens when different cultures come into contact with each other. There is a phase of such contact in which the collision between, on the one hand, mutual understanding based on common premises and needs, and on the other the biases or incomprehension generated by different local traditions and habits of thought, has the power of shaping the ensuing course of the history of ideas. That phase should be, in our view, the core object of reception studies. While in the history of ideas as normally understood we tend to arrange our evidence according to a conceptual grid, here we have to follow an essentially 'local' criterion since our primary interest is in the context-specific factors – the organisation of cultural and academic institutions, the prevailing social and economic concerns and, through these, the deep-lying preconceptions and intellectual habits of entire populations – which act as filters with respect to the inflow of foreign ideas. The latter are stopped at the border or let in depending on an implicit collective judgement based on multiple criteria, among which the purely intellectual ones do not always play a decisive role. We feel that Marshall, himself an admirer of Montesquieu and convinced that the proof of good theories lies in their ability to respond to the demands of actual human societies, would have approved of this kind of approach.

For sure, we had no intention of developing this point of view into a 'reception theory' in the way that some literary theorists have done, but we did feel that it could throw light on deeper issues of a more general nature than merely a geographical survey of Marshall's fortunes. It is a fact that the main trends of economic thought over the last two-and-a-half centuries are, by and large, the product of a tiny part of the world – an intellectual workshop concentrated in a small bunch of European countries, later extended to include the US, which started to rise to their present dominant position only from the interwar period onwards. Why this is so is a complex question to which many answers can be given, starting from those that point to the obvious parallels with the colonisation process – primarily a fact of economic and military power – waxing and waning over the course of the past two centuries. But a part at least of the explanation must have to do also with the degree of universality of those theories that demonstrate a capacity to transcend their origins and to elicit a response in minds trained in alien traditions. 'Universality' in this sense is not necessarily a matter of scientific truth, which in economics is never beyond dispute. Rather, it seems to depend on the ability to propose a game in which others will desire to participate, so to speak, at first sight, lured into it by an appeal so basic that there is very little need to specially adapt the rules in light of exotic customs. Passive learning alone will not make for a good reception. There must be active involvement, and this in turn requires that the proposed theories are perceived as still not settled, half-way puzzles whose pattern is already discernible and interesting enough to invite continuation. The outcome, it is worth noting, is not necessarily convergence to a common way of thinking; reception may lead to the emergence of a dominating orthodoxy, but it may also lead to an increasing variety of approaches. In the case of Marshall's reception, as we shall see in a moment and as this volume as a whole bears out, diversification largely outweighs conformity to an orthodoxy.

While several schools of European and American economic thought have been largely successful in gaining wide reception, Marshall's specific record is somewhat mixed. It is precisely this fact that makes his case particularly interesting. Aspects of Marshall's thought came to be embodied in the nascent neoclassical paradigm and so participated in the process of global diffusion of the latter that has occurred over the past century. Other aspects were at first overlooked and soon forgotten, but this was not forever. In fact some of these elements resurfaced much later in particular countries and then spread out along well-defined regional lines contributing to the preservation of a certain economic pluralism. To add to the complexity of the case, there is the further peculiarity that some of Marshall's economic ideas had an indirect and almost underground diffusion by way of cognate disciplines such as political science, urban planning, sociology, demography, rural studies and so on.

The project of reconstructing this far from linear story in all of its ramifications proved to be more arduous than expected, however, and this volume must be seen as only a first step towards its accomplishment. There is, first of all, the fact that large sections of the world are missing due to our inability to find collaborators. To mention some of the most glaring absences: the whole of Latin America as well as South Africa, a country with close links to British economic culture (where, by the way, the distinguished Marshall scholar H.M. Robertson spent his entire academic career). In view of the recent growth of Islamic economics, we also regret the total omission of Muslim countries.

Secondly, and in our view more importantly, we realise that many of the national cases considered properly required a full investigation of the social and cultural circumstances of the country, of all the relevant political events and of the alternative economic theories, both domestic and imported, locally competing with Marshall's: actually a job for a team of collaborators, each team in turn needing co-ordination with others in order to form large-scale views of entire cultural and linguistic areas. The cost of managing a web of teams like this exceeded our resources, would have required far more time to produce, and would have resulted in a much larger volume. Our contributors, almost always working single-handedly in the face of complex national realities, have done their best to deal with at least the academic part of the story, rarely attempting forays into social and cultural history. While we believe that they have made a good job given the limited resources at their disposal, we have to admit that what we are able to offer here is at best an approximation to our idea of a satisfactory and complete reception study of Marshall's economic thought. We hope that the very incompleteness and imperfection of this collection may serve as a stimulus for further studies in this direction.

With regard to each country included in the survey, we have asked our contributors to organise their exposition around three main questions: (1) When and how did Marshall's economic writings – or their translations – spread throughout the country? (2) What was their impact on the state of economic ideas in the country and on their subsequent evolution? (3) Which aspects of Marshall's approach were most widely accepted and developed, and which were rather criticised or ignored?

While Part II of the volume refers to Marshall's domestic reception, Parts III to V correspond to the three groups into which we have classified the overseas countries included within the survey, that is: (1) English-speaking countries, (2) continental Europe, (3) Asian countries, the latter group limited to the three largest: China, India and Japan. The final Part VI is devoted to three case studies of economists whose attitude towards Marshall appears to have exerted a certain influence upon the reception of his thought, but who could not be included readily in any specific national area because they spent most of their academic careers outside their country of origin. These are the cases of the Italian Vilfredo Pareto, the Austrian Joseph A. Schumpeter and the Romanian Nicholas Georgescu-Roegen.

Part I is introductory. It contains two brief essays that take stock of, respectively, past and current interpretations of Marshall's position in the history of economic thought. Brewer's survey ends with Blaug's 1962 textbook on the history of economic thought and summarises what may be considered the 'old view' of Marshall that had emerged by the end of the first half of the twentieth century. This mid-century state of the art provides the starting point for Groenewegen, who focuses on the relationship between the publication of a large body of previously little-known materials, including Marshall's correspondence, and the revival of Marshall studies that began in the 1970s and which has generated deep changes in the way his work is now perceived and evaluated (in this connection, it is probably unnecessary to remind readers of the existence of a monumental repository of secondary literature on Marshall up to 1995, the eight volumes of Wood 1982 and 1995).

Alfred Marshall, founder of the Economic Tripos in Cambridge, promoter of the *Economic Journal*, member of key governmental commissions (Depression of Trade, Gold and Silver, Indian Currency, Labour, the Aged Poor) and witness for others, was the leading British economist of the post-Millian age. It seems appropriate that the Indian scholar N. Jha chose to title his survey of British economic thought, as illustrated by the pages of the *Economic Journal* in the years from 1890 to 1915, 'The age of Marshall' (Jha 1973). And yet, Marshall's influence in his own university of Cambridge lost motive power soon after his death, and his direct legacy – embodied primarily in the person of A.C. Pigou – soon gave way to the 'new' Cambridge school that arose around J.M. Keynes, P. Sraffa, R. Khan, Joan Robinson and the other members of the Cambridge 'circus' in the 'years of high theory'. Many of Marshall's pupils had their own careers outside Cambridge, scattered in different places (Leeds, Manchester, Birmingham,

Oxford), and their work was relegated to what appeared to be a secondary line in industrial economics. The first monograph published by the Oxford University Institute of Statistics in 1945, *Small and Big Business* by Joseph Steindl, it may be recalled, seemed to toll the death knell for the whole of Marshall's theory of the firm and industry (Steindl 1947).

Curiously, then, the influence of Marshall's legacy was more long lasting abroad than at home. In English-speaking countries, not only were his main books part of many university syllabuses for a long time (for example, Australia, New Zealand), but also aspects of his approach and theory deeply affected the trend and character of 'local' economics. For instance, Marshall's ideas on the scope and method of economics, on the role of biological thinking in economics, and on applied economics were fundamental reference points for many economists in New Zealand, whereas Marshall's monetary theory was especially emphasised in Australia.

The case of the US constitutes of course a separate chapter among the English-speaking countries. In the pluralistic scenario of the early twentieth century up to the 1930s, before, that is, the US had emerged as the leading world centre for the development and dissemination of economic theory, Marshall's thought could play an active role in enhancing differences and stimulating new lines of research. As the century wore on, however, the intellectual vitality of American academia and (we may add) the influx of numbers of refugee scholars from continental Europe quickly turned the perception of Marshall's work from that of a point of contemporary reference to a thing of the past with 'no more than historical interest'. Yet pluralism remained an essential component of the American scenery, so that an important Marshallian enclave could continue to thrive in Chicago and fuel the economic debate for a long time to come.

Remaining in North America, the proximity of Canada to Harvard and Chicago, in addition to the important role played in the US by institutionalism (and, through it, by the German historical school), seems to have played a role in preventing Marshallian writings and thought from spreading widely in that country, despite the presence at McGill University for a certain period of A.W. Flux, a direct pupil of Marshall's.

With regard to non-English-speaking countries, the situation is more complex. Language barriers hampered the direct diffusion of Marshall's writings, rendering the process generally slower and more difficult. A complete list of the first translations of Marshall's works into foreign languages, even limited to the *Principles* alone, is unfortunately unavailable and proved to be very difficult to reconstruct (as a tip for future researchers willing to face this daunting task, we suggest that an investigation in the archives of the former Macmillan and Co., now Macmillan Publishers, would probably be more rewarding than a country-by-country survey). In the group of non-English-speaking countries we may distinguish two alternative scenarios: (1) countries in which there was already an important alternative economic tradition that served to obstruct the spread of Marshall's economics; and (2) countries in which peculiar characteristics of culture and sensitivity fostered the diffusion of Marshall's thought.

In the first group we find France, with a clearly deep-rooted Walrasian and general equilibrium tradition; the German-speaking countries and Poland, with the role of alternative tradition played first by the Historical and then by the Austrian schools; and Sweden, with its national tradition of theoretical economics. In these countries Marshall's writings and thought had a rather weak influence, often circumscribed within a short period of time (such as the interwar period in Poland) or limited to the role played by individual scholars (such as A. Lowe in Germany or N.G. Pierson in early twentieth-century Holland, at that time a country under the theoretical influence of Germany).

In China, partly because of the State censorship that for a long time took Marshall for a representative bourgeois economist, his thought had apparently almost no influence, although some of his books were translated and used as textbooks in certain universities. More recently, in the wake of China's opening to the Western world, the main reference for economic studies has been the US.

In the second group we have Italy where, despite a strong presence of the Pareto–Walrasian tradition, a large number of economists diffused Marshall's writings (M. Pantaleoni to begin with, followed among others by R. Dalla Volta, M. Fanno and F.M. Vito), although in some cases in a form mixed with Walrasian elements (or example, U. Ricci), Belgium (E. De Laveleye, M. Ansiaux) and Norway (T.H. Aschehoug, P.T. Aarum, R. Frisch), where Marshall's books were widely known and the *Principles* used as a textbook. In Norway, the most appreciated aspects of Marshall's thought were his method of analysis, and his analysis of production with particular regard to cost of production, the role of time and increasing returns.

Perhaps the most remarkable instance in this second group of countries is Japan, where Marshall, considered to be half-way between the classical tradition (J.S. Mill) and the German historical school, exercised a very deep influence. In particular, Marshall's methodology (period analysis and *cæteris paribus*) was widely praised.

In all these countries Marshall's influence was far from constant over time. With the consolidation of a compact, increasingly formalised and systematised hardcore of theoretical foundations in the second half of the twentieth century, his thought seemed to be relegated to an uninspiring periphery. But the essays collected here bear witness to a widespread if recent revival of Marshallian ideas in countries of both groups. The first case is that of Italy, where the 1970s saw a convergence of lines of research in industrial economics and in the history of economic thought that resulted in a reappraisal of Marshall centred on the concept of the industrial district. This event might be described as a merger of Marshall's ideas on industrial organisation with the Italian tradition of *economia civile*. The second interesting case is France, where, after a long period during which Marshall's thought was neglected, life was finally breathed into his notion of internal and external economies thanks to the contributions of F. Perroux, while industrial district analysis began to flourish in the wake of its rediscovery in Italy. Similar processes took place in Portugal and Spain. Finally, Japan has recently witnessed the re-evaluation of some aspects of Marshall's thought, especially with regard to industrial economics and social and political issues.

The case of Spain, which we feel to be one of the missed opportunities of this volume, deserves a few words of explanation. Early in 2003, while still planning the entries for the ECAM, we asked Lluìs Argemì, professor at the Universitat de Barcelona, for an entry on the diffusion of Marshall's thought in Spain. In due time he sent us a draft of the first part of the essay, and requested a meeting to discuss it before engaging in the second part. At that moment we were busy dealing with an ECAM which by then was growing in size beyond all our expectations, and the *rendezvous* was postponed several times. Unfortunately, in March 2007 Professor Argemì suddenly died. We tried in vain to find someone to revise and complete the draft that he had left, and so have decided, in the end, to publish it as it is. We apologise for the partial coverage of a country so important as Spain, particularly because the post-1950 period that is left out is certainly the most interesting part of the story (for in these years several Catalan economists engaged in studies of Spanish industrial districts played a constructive role in the generation of a new interest in Marshallian thought). In partial reparation, we inform readers that a substantial piece on Marshall in Spain can be found in the introduction by Professor Juan Velarde Fuertes to a recent reprint of a 1948 Spanish translation of the *Principles* (Velarde Fuertes 2005). Also J. Trullén (2009) is of some interest in this connection.

The three 'personalised' chapters in Part VI are intended to meet a possible objection and to repair an omission in the ECAM. Certainly the reception of the thought of an important author in foreign countries is always swayed, at least in part, by chance factors, such as for example the presence of other eminent and locally influential actors with whose thought the work of the former may harmonise favourably or clash disgracefully for totally idiosyncratic reasons. When the characters in question play their roles, be they supportive or oppositional, in well-defined national contexts, as was the case for example with Pantaleoni in Italy (supportive) and Walras in France (oppositional), these factors are easily captured in a country-by-country survey such as the present one. But important actors risk slipping past without being noticed when particular biographical circumstances lead them to spend their life and exert their influence in trans-national environments. An outstanding example is Sraffa, a Cambridge-based Italian economist who certainly played a large part in the decline of Marshallian economics in most European countries soon after Marshall's death. Sraffa's case was always known to be important and consequently received dedicated treatment in the ECAM, but other similar cases escaped the editors' attention at the time, and did not fit perfectly into the national format of the first three parts of this volume. This is why we planned this special section with three chapters devoted to, respectively, Pareto, Schumpeter and Georgescu-Roegen. Their role in the story of the reception of Marshall turns out to have been a mixed one. Their attitudes went through phases that reflect their own personal evolution: Pareto distancing himself progressively from Marshall while Schumpeter and Georgescu-Roegen ended up recognising some common ground, albeit with some circumspection and always with qualifications. None of the three had the spirit of a follower, but the three chapters do point to a common element – the presence within each of a few Marshallian seeds, each of which sprouted into different varieties of economic plants.

The survey conducted in this volume suggests to us a final consideration concerning the very nature of Marshall's overall contribution to economics. The kind of reception that his thought encountered seems to indicate that its strongest point was not 'universality' in the sense mentioned above – the ability to design an intellectual game attractive to a wide range of minds and characters – rather, its strongest point arose from the forceful utilitarian inclination that led him to conceive of theories as 'adaptive toolboxes', operative implements for practical men involved in problematic situations, no matter whether they were economists, politicians or businessmen. In the guise of a universal doctrine the appeal of Marshallian economics quickly waned, displaced from the central economic canon by theoretical engines of more sophisticated design that appeared to provide a more adequate interpretation of what Marshall himself had called the 'firm backbone' of the discipline. But as a practice-oriented doctrine it held out against all rivals and met with wide and renewed acceptance, especially when and wherever attention was turned to issues of social and industrial organisation. After all is said and done we may very well conclude that Marshall's contribution to what was to become the internationally-established economic mainstream was comparatively minor; but not so the impulse that he gave to the study of local circumstances as the only way to bring general economic principles to bear on the solution of factual problems. This is a major methodological contribution, and one that is definitely not neutral with respect to the contents of economic theory; for it presupposes that the economic principles themselves are given an inherently flexible formulation, that they are open to continuous negotiation with novelty, and that they are conceived not as cornerstones of a fully-fledged paradigm but as evolutionary instruments by means of which human societies can learn how to deal with changes either of the endogenous sort or those deriving from external sources.

The recent Marshallian revival, as witnessed by the publication of archive material that has widened our understanding of his work, the blossoming of essays and books devoted to his thought and culminating in the ECAM, and indeed also illustrated by this volume, is evidence of the enduring appeal of Marshall's work. This revival may also be taken as a sign of an implicit request for more variety in the way economic theories are designed; a request fully in line with the evolutionary spirit (remember the *Principles*, V, IV, §3, 'the tendency to variation is a chief cause of progress') which animated the whole of Marshall's thought. And indeed, after the long period of relative stability that marked the heyday of general equilibrium theory, today's economics is undergoing considerable change. New developments in economic and social science inspire new readings of Marshall's work; while the latter, in turn, has proved to be capable of inspiring and accompanying ever-newer research programmes. These processes are emblematic of what Marshall himself defined as a classical author: '[A] classical author ... has stated or indicated architectonic ideas in thought or sentiment, which are in some degree his own, and which, once created, can never die but are an existing yeast ceaselessly working in the Cosmos' (Marshall to Bonar, 27 September 1898, in Pigou 1925, p. 374).

Giacomo Becattini, Katia Caldari, Marco Dardi and Tiziano Raffaelli

REFERENCES

Jha, N. (1973), *The Age of Marshall: Aspects of British Economic Thought 1890–1915*, London: Frank Cass.
Pigou, A.C. (ed.) (1925), *Memorials of Alfred Marshall*, London: Macmillan.
Steindl, J. (1947), *Small and Big Business: Economic Problems of the Size of Firms*, Oxford: Basil Blackwell.
Trullén, J. (2009), 'National industrial policies and the development of industrial districts: Reflections on the Spanish case', in G. Becattini, M. Bellandi and L. De Propris (eds), *A Handbook of Industrial Districts*, Cheltenham, UK and Northampton, MA, USA: Edward Elgar, pp. 726–38.
Velarde Fuertes, J. (2005), 'Prólogo, o Marshall y las economistas españoles', in A. Marshall, *Principios de economia*, Fundación ICO, Madrid: Sintesis.
Wood, J.C. (ed.) (1982), *Alfred Marshall: Critical Assessments*, 4 vols, London: Croom Helm.
Wood, J.C. (ed.) (1995), *Alfred Marshall: Critical Assessments*, 2nd series, 4 vols, London: Routledge.

PART I

'Conventional' and 'new' views of Alfred Marshall

1. Alfred Marshall's place in the history of economic thought: the 'conventional' interpretation

Anthony Brewer

By the time of Marshall's death he was the grand old man of British economics. The subject was dominated by his students, or by those who had been taught by his students. He did not have quite the same standing outside Britain but was without question a major figure. The assessment of his legacy was largely in the hands of writers who were themselves working within a 'Marshallian' research programme. Not surprisingly, they focused on those aspects of his work which were most familiar to them, those which had been built on by his pupils and successors – it was, one could say, an assessment of Marshall through Pigovian spectacles. In recent years, historians of economics have emphasised evolutionary, institutionalist, and cognitive aspects of Marshall's thought, dealt with in many chapters of the *Elgar Companion to Alfred Marshall*. The focus here will be on the 'conventional' interpretation of his work which became established by the mid-twentieth century.

The construction of Marshall's posthumous reputation and his place in the history of economics began soon after his death. Keynes (1924) anticipated many of the themes of subsequent assessments. He made very strong claims. 'As a scientist [Marshall] was, in his field, the greatest in the world for a hundred years' (Keynes 1924, p. 140). At the same time, there is a curiously defensive tone about much of the memoir. It is not simply that Keynes knew that others might not rate Marshall so highly, but that he could see good reasons for their scepticism.

The core of the problem, as Keynes and many others since have seen it, was the long wait before the *Principles* came out in 1890. Before that date Marshall had published little, and by the time it appeared most of the major elements on which he built his system had been published by others, sometimes many years earlier. A sceptic might well claim that Marshall had done no more than to synthesise existing ideas in a successful textbook. In some areas, the case is still worse. Marshall did not give a systematic exposition of his monetary theory until he published *Money, Credit and Commerce* in 1923, at the very end of his life. In Keynes's view, his powers were failing by then and the result was a 'mere shadow of what he had it in him to bring forth twenty or (better) thirty years earlier'. The sceptical response is obvious: why should we credit Marshall for what (we are told) he might have written but did not? If the result of delay was (in Keynes's words) a 'jejune treatment, carefully avoiding difficulties and complications' (Keynes 1924, p. 163) then that is how it should be judged.

Keynes's reply to the sceptics has two elements, which are not always clearly separated. First, there is the issue of priority, linked to Marshall's delay in publishing. Marshall made a number of more or less explicit claims to subjective priority and his supporters have often implied that if he had published promptly his priority would have been clear. Second, there is the evaluation of the substance of his work. In Keynes's often quoted words: 'Jevons saw the kettle boil and cried out with the delighted voice of a child: Marshall too has seen the kettle boil and sat down silently to build an engine' (Keynes 1924, p. 155). If the second part of this were accepted, then Marshall would deserve credit as the creator of an 'engine of polished steel' (Pigou 1925, p. 86).

There is no real issue over priority. The credit for any new idea goes to the person who publishes first, or otherwise puts it in the public domain. Ideas which are kept secret are of no scientific value. By that simple standard, the major theoretical developments in late nineteenth-century economics were first published by others, though Marshall often improved on them and added much in detail. Schumpeter (1954, pp. 838–40) settled the basic question long ago. The issue of priority, or originality, would not have bulked so large in the literature if Marshall himself had not repeatedly sought to minimise his debt to others, claiming to have developed ideas independently even though he was not first to publish. These claims may be relevant from a biographical viewpoint but not in terms of the wider history of economics.

There is a complication. Marshall's unpublished ideas filtered out through his teaching, private conversations, and correspondence long before they became fully public, a fact which helps to account for the pattern and timing of his influence and reputation. As Keynes (1924, p. 149) remarked: 'those economists all over the world who know Marshall only by his published work may find it difficult to understand the extraordinary position claimed for him by his English contemporaries and successors'. To the extent that Marshall's ideas came into wider use before he published them himself, they become part of the public and objective history of the discipline. The issue of priority becomes a little blurred, though the major issues of priority turn on how far Marshall had got in the late 1860s and 1870s, before his return to Cambridge and before he built up his body of disciples there. There has been much detailed work on the development and dissemination of particular parts of Marshall's work but it has not changed the main outlines of the picture.

Why was Marshall so slow to publish? His reasons may be of no more than biographical interest, but a fair amount of ink has been devoted to them. Keynes (1924, pp. 170ff.) started the ball rolling, giving what he saw as good and bad reasons for delay. For Marshall economics 'is not a body of concrete truth but an engine for the discovery of concrete truth' (ibid., p. 171). It was not the engine itself but its application to real problems that mattered, and he was reluctant to publish the analytical framework or elements of it on their own. He aimed to write comprehensive treatises, but was not capable of doing it quickly. His health and other pressures on his time did not help. Among bad reasons, he was too afraid of being wrong, too easily upset by controversy, and he undervalued pure economics because of his desire to tackle subjects directly linked to human wellbeing.

Turning to the substance of Marshall's work, it is clear that he had a massive influence, though the exact character of his contribution is harder to specify. The claim that he was the most important economist of his generation cannot be based on any single original analytical idea. Was he simply an expositor and synthesist who shaped the ideas of others into a palatable form, or did he really construct an 'engine' which was more than the sum of its parts? His disciples were sure of the answer; Pigou, for example, asserted that Marshall 'built a structure as different from anything known before as a modern locomotive is from Stephenson's "Rocket"' (Pigou 1925, p. 87; a locomotive of Pigou's time was still a steam engine similar in principle to the Rocket but massively more powerful and effective).

Keynes's list of the main contributions to knowledge in the *Principles* is a starting point. Other lists would differ somewhat. I will provide a shortened version of Keynes's list, and then comment on it.

1. Replacing one-sided cost or demand-based price theories with a theory treating both equally. 'After Marshall's analysis there was nothing more to be said' (Keynes 1924, p. 182).
2. Demand/supply equilibrium extended 'to discover a whole Copernican system, by which all the elements of the economic universe are kept in their places' (ibid., p. 183), using the principle of substitution at the margin and bringing wages and profits into the general analysis of demand/supply equilibrium.
3. The explicit introduction of time into the analysis using the concepts of the long and short run.
4. Consumer surplus.
5. The analysis of monopoly and increasing returns.
6. The notion of elasticity.
7. The historical element in the *Principles*.

This is a mixed bag. Items (1) and (2) summarise a revolution in economic thinking that took place in the later nineteenth century, but to credit it all to Marshall is clearly going too far. The 'Copernican ... general theory of economic equilibrium' (ibid., p. 183) should be credited to Walras, not Marshall. Item (3) points to the distinctively Marshallian and widely-used short-run/long-run distinction. It is rather characteristic of Marshall in that it is in fact a rather artificial special case – it is very rare for there to be one group of freely variable inputs while another group remain rigidly fixed – but it proved such a valuable aid to thought that it became second nature for generations of economists. Items (4) and (5) cannot be said to be original to Marshall, and the notion of elasticity (6) is a notational convenience rather than a theoretical advance. Item (7) is an oddity. Keynes himself describes the historical aspect of the *Principles* as a not-very-satisfactory compromise, and it is hard to see that it had an important influence.

Schumpeter's comment on the first six items in Keynes's list seems to hit the mark. 'Not one of them can be accepted without qualifying reference to the work of others, though in conjunction and as elements of a general treatise for a wider circle of readers, they were of course new enough' (Schumpeter 1954, p. 839 n.).

That said, it is clear that Marshall did create an ensemble, an 'engine' that was more than the sum of its parts. Several generations of economists thought of economics in essentially Marshallian terms, albeit a Marshall tidied up and formalised by Pigou and others. Anyone who has studied, or taught, in an introductory economics course, has almost certainly been exposed to a recognizably Marshallian system, though perhaps a little less so now than a few decades ago. Think, for example, of the partial equilibrium analysis of the competitive firm and industry – marginal and average cost curves, price equals marginal cost, long-run adjustment through entry and exit and so on. Even the way we always draw diagrams with price on the vertical axis comes from Marshall.

Gerald Shove's much cited essay of 1942 exemplifies the strongest form of the Cambridge Marshallian view. He rejected any suggestion of a compromise between classical and marginal economics, arguing instead for a direct line of descent from Ricardo and John Stuart Mill to Marshall, and thus to Marshall's Cambridge followers. Marshall himself had rejected any assessment of his work as a compromise or synthesis, though Pigou (1925, p. 87) was less worried by it.

The core of Shove's argument is a claim that Marshall's work grew 'naturally ... out of an attempt to test, and fill the gaps in, Ricardian doctrines by the use of a mathematical apparatus' (Shove 1942, p. 296). 'It is of the true Ricardian stock' (ibid., p. 295). He picked four places where Ricardo was in need of generalisation, supplied by Marshall (ibid., pp. 296–9). (1) If (marginal) costs vary with output, demand equations are needed to complete the system. (2) Technical coefficients in production are not fixed but depend on input prices and on the scale of output. (3) Ricardo assumed subsistence wages but by Marshall's time it was clear that this would not do. (4) A further relation between the supply of capital (or its evolution over time) and the return to it is needed. 'All of these gaps (except perhaps the second) would leap to the eye of anyone trying to "translate" Ricardo's doctrines into differential equations' (ibid., p. 299).

This is clearly a 'Whig' interpretation of history, with the past as an imperfect version of the present and the present (Cambridge, 1942) as the inevitable result of the elimination of the errors of the past. Shove's aim was to argue for a direct line from Ricardo to Marshall, with no compromise or synthesis, but there is an obvious problem. The 'gaps' did indeed leap to the eye of a Cambridge-trained economist of Shove's generation, but there are other readings of Ricardo. If the gaps, and the way of filling them, were indeed so obvious, why was it that no-one had done so in more than 50 years between the publication of Ricardo's *Principles* and the start of Marshall's reworking? If it was all so obvious, what was Marshall's distinctive contribution?

Shove was aware of the problem and tried to convey the magnitude of Marshall's achievement while still insisting on its Ricardian ancestry. The unifying idea of 'the balance at the margin' with 'the principle of substitution acting everywhere as a master key' is 'entirely foreign to Ricardo's way of thinking: and to Mill's. If the Ricardian analysis was our starting point, by the end of the journey we have entered a new world' (Shove 1942, pp. 303–4). But if it is admitted that to see these particular gaps and to 'generalise' Ricardo in this particular way was far from automatic, one has to ask whether Marshall may have consciously or unconsciously followed Jevons or others. The picture of Marshall as author of a compromise or synthesis could re-emerge.

Keynes and Shove exemplify the view of Marshall developed in by Marshall's pupils. In recording and defending Marshall's contribution, they were defining and promoting the school of thought to which they themselves belonged. By the years after World War II, the subject had moved on and discussion of Marshall's contribution became less partisan, without the defensive air of the earlier Cambridge writings.

As general equilibrium became increasingly central to economic theory in the middle and later twentieth century, Marshallian partial equilibrium analysis could be seen as a side-shoot from a continental general equilibrium tradition. As economics became more formal and mathematical, not only Walras but also Edgeworth and Pareto came to be seen as figures rivaling Marshall in importance. Schumpeter's magisterial *History of Economic Analysis*, for example, is shaped by his view of Walrasian general equilibrium as the centrepiece of (static) economic theory (see Duval 2002). Book V of the *Principles* 'is the classic masterpiece of … partial analysis' but 'the wider conception of the general interdependence of all economic quantities' is formulated 'embryonically but still explicitly' in the notes. 'It seems fair, therefore to list Marshall also among the builders of the general-equilibrium system' (Schumpeter 1954, p. 836). Schumpeter praised the 'tremendous wealth of analytical and factual detail, ... a vast structure ... analytically chiseled into shape by an artist in neat and economical conceptualisation' (ibid., p. 835). Marshall was a great economist, not merely a technician and a historian (ibid., p. 836), but Walras was the greatest of all, at least as far as pure theory is concerned. Beside Walras's system, most theoretical writings of the period 'look like boats beside a liner' (ibid., p. 827).

By the later twentieth century it had become possible to recognise the historical importance of the Marshallian school without any need to take a partisan position. For example, Mark Blaug's *Economic Theory in Retrospect* ([1962] 1996), perhaps the best known general treatment of the history of economics since Schumpeter, has nearly a hundred pages on 'Marshallian economics', discussing Marshall but also work in the tradition he started. Other standard histories accord Marshall a similar position, while also recognising the importance of other traditions such as that stemming from Walras.

REFERENCES

Blaug, M. ([1962] 1996), *Economic Theory in Retrospect*, Cambridge: Cambridge University Press.
Duval, N. (2002), 'Schumpeter on Marshall', in R. Arena and C. Dangel-Hagnauer (eds), *The Contribution of Joseph Schumpeter to Economics*, London and New York: Routledge, pp. 66–85.
Keynes, J.M. (1924), 'Alfred Marshall, 1842–1924', *Economic Journal*, **34**, 311–72, reprinted in J.M. Keynes (1961), *Essays in Biography*, London: Mercury Books, pp. 125–217.
Pigou, A.C. (ed.) (1925), *Memorials of Alfred Marshall*, London: Macmillan.
Schumpeter, J.A. (1954), *History of Economic Analysis*, London: Allen & Unwin.
Shove, G.F. (1942), 'The place of Marshall's *Principles* in the development of economic theory', *Economic Journal*, **52**, 294–329.

2.   Recent Marshallian scholarship: an overview

Peter D. Groenewegen

It was really only after Marshall's *Principles of Economics* lost its status as a major current text in economics sometime during the early 1950s that Marshall's work began to be systematically treated in the history of economic thought literature. An early example is Hutchison's *Review of Economic Theory 1870–1929* (Hutchison 1953, Chapter iv). At the outset, Hutchison drew attention to the fact that Alfred Marshall, and above all his *Principles of Economics*, were the most written about part of his subject matter, especially during the 1920s and 1930s. This included the valuable study of Marshall's production and distribution theory as part of the formative period 1870–1900 which Stigler (1940) examined for his PhD thesis. Regrettably, this work also set a trend in portraying Marshall as mistakenly ignoring the theoretical neatness of static perfect competition analysis, particularly in the context of Marshall's discussion of internal and external economies.

Hutchison explained this large Marshall literature by both Marshall's 'high standing' and by 'the wealth of original and fertile ideas in his work'. Hutchison's chapter on Marshall commenced with a biographical sketch, largely based on Keynes's 1924 obituary article, and then looked in turn at Marshall and economic history, partial analysis and competitive industry, statics and dynamics, long and short periods, the distribution of national income, general overproduction, fluctuations and money, and economic and industrial policy. This drew on all of Marshall's published work, including that gathered posthumously in Pigou's *Memorials*. It is undoubtedly the most thorough early account of Marshall's economics before the availability of new Marshall material from the mid-1970s. The chapter on Marshall was also the longest by far in Hutchison's valuable study of the development of modern economics.

Another 1950s text, Lekachman (1959), gave considerable space to Marshall's views in its chapter on 'The new economics from the 1880s'. This subdivided discussion of Marshall's economics into a systematic treatment of Marshall's contributions to theory and secondly his development of an 'armoury of tools'. Lekachman highlighted the modernity of Marshall's value and distribution theory in terms of supply and demand, despite the lip-service it paid to classical predecessors, his emphasis on the problem of time, his implicit denial of the practical relevance of general equilibrium analysis, his development of a theory of the firm and industry, his contribution of the distinction between internal and external economies, the tax/bounty welfare argument which merged this with notions of consumer surplus, while the concept of elasticity is hailed as the major tool which Marshall developed, even if it did not originate with him. Among Marshall's monetary contributions, Lekachman listed his restatement of the quantity theory in Cambridge cash-balance form, his distinction between real and money rates of interest, and his invention of the chain index number. Apart from the discussion of the monetary contributions, Lekachman's treatment concentrated on Marshall's economic work in the *Principles*.

Another major text, Blaug ([1962] 1996) presented Marshall as one of the founders of the marginal revolution, and then exhaustively discussed Marshallian economics, broadly interpreted, in two long chapters: 'Utility and demand', 'Cost and supply', rather than investigating what Marshall had actually said on these topics. Fortunately, the second of these chapters contains a reader's guide to Marshall's *Principles*, but even this is occasionally interrupted by comparisons (for example, that of Walras and Marshall on stability conditions). Blaug's discussion concludes with an assessment of the greatness of Marshall's contribution but this did not really go beyond the *Principles*. This text, according to Blaug, 'must be considered one of the most durable and viable books in the history of economics' (ibid., p. 405), partly because it provided solutions to old problems, and partly because it stimulated many future generations of economists. However, Blaug's concentration on the *Principles* in its final four editions as the 'only' book by Marshall, allows him to suggest misleadingly that Marshall was responsible for side-tracking monetary issues in economics. Blaug also insisted that Marshall's *Principles* is 'unsatisfactory' because it is ambivalent about the value of its theoretical subject matter, hides the diagrams and the mathematics, and fails to live up to its evolutionist and 'economic biology' claims. Blaug's treatment never explicitly recognises that Marshall's original plan for the *Principles* had been much broader, and initially intended as a two-volume work. Only much later did it become a 'volume of foundations' to be supplemented by three companion volumes (on *Industry and Trade*, on *Money, Credit and Commerce* and on *Economic and Social Progress*). Blaug's account cannot therefore be described as a genuinely historical appraisal of Marshall's economic work, interesting and insightful though it is from its more limited perspective in assessing Marshall's theory against the background of later analytical developments in mainstream economics.

The interpretation of Marshall in the history of economics greatly advanced from the end of the 1970s as a result of three factors. First was the immense editorial work by J.K. Whitaker and others to bring the riches of Marshall's unpublished papers to a wider readership. The last include the publication of Whitaker's (1975) edition of the early economic writings, the edition of Marshall's *Lectures to*

Women (Raffaelli, Biagini and McWilliams Tullberg 1995), an edition of official papers additional to those collected by J.M. Keynes in 1926 (Groenewegen 1996), the early philosophical writings (Raffaelli 1994), and finally the splendid three-volume edition of Marshall's correspondence and associated material (Whitaker 1996). Publications of these writings enabled contrasts to be drawn between the ·old and the young Marshall, and allowed study of the evolution of his economic ideas from the 1860s to the 1920s. It thereby greatly enriched the interpretative Marshall literature from the 1980s as compared with that of the 1920s and 1930s so largely devoted to the *Principles*. Secondly, there were important biographical contributions which corrected the many false trails and dubious facts emanating from Keynes's 1924 obituary, brilliantly written though it was. These include work by Coase on Marshall's ancestry and family (Coase 1994), Whitaker's investigation of Marshall's Bristol and Oxford (Whitaker 1972) period, and Denis O'Brien's essay on Marshall (1981) – not all of them strictly biographical – to culminate in Peter Groenewegen's lengthy biographical study (Groenewegen 1995) which placed Marshall's life and work in full historical context. Third, and perhaps the most important, was the impetus given to Marshall studies internationally by the many Marshall conferences and publications arranged during 1990 to commemorate the centenary of publication of the *Principles of Economics*. Such events were organised by the Royal Economic Society; the Economics Department of the Universities of Ancona, Florence and Pisa; Rita McWilliams Tullberg and some other members of the Economics Faculty at Cambridge University (McWilliams Tullberg 1990); the Scottish Economic Society; the American Economic Association; the History of Economics Society; *Économie Appliquée*; Japanese Economics Societies; and, on a much smaller scale, in many other parts of the world (for reviews of these meetings, see Becattini 1991; Groenewegen 1991; Whitaker 1991). Taken together, these three factors considerably broadened the Marshall research agenda, and vastly extended the scope of the material for appreciating his intellectual labours in economics and associated fields by historians of economics. A number of major samples of this vast Marshall literature need to be given.

Over the years 1986 to 1990, David Reisman published a three-volume appreciation of Marshall's economics (Reisman 1986, 1987, 1990). The first of these discussed Marshall's analytical apparatus as demonstrated by the contents of his *Principles*. The second volume examined Marshall's policy analysis under the heading 'progress and politics', dealing in turn with human betterment, its relation with growth and collective action (subdivided rather anachronistically into 'micro- and macro-economic policy'), as part of the mission of the economist. The third instalment of this Marshall trilogy investigated that mission as exhibited chronologically at Cambridge, Bristol, Oxford and again at Cambridge, and in his various writings with special reference to the *Principles*. Reisman's contribution was essentially a survey and summary of Marshall's published economic writings, rather than a biographical treatment of his life and work.

The published proceedings (Whitaker 1990) of a conference at Cambridge organised under the auspices of the Royal Economic Society included 12 studies (not all of them presented at the actual conference) on Marshall's life and work by leading scholars. Stigler assessed the place of Marshall's *Principles* in the development of economics; R.C.O. Matthews discussed Marshall's view on the labour market; Laidler looked at Marshall and the development of monetary theory; Creedy at Marshall on international trade; Loasby assessed Marshall's views on firms and markets; O'Brien his work on economics in relation to the classical economists; Collard presented an overview of post-Marshall Cambridge economics; Whitaker discussed the implication of the non-appearance of *Principles* Volume II; Bliss discussed Marshall and capital theory; Dasgupta some price theory aspects of Marshall's period analysis; Peter Newman looked at the great barter controversy and John Chipman concluded the volume with an interpretation of Marshall's consumer surplus analysis. In short, both conference and book were rich and rewarding tributes paid by the Royal Economic Society to one of its founders.

A second conference on Marshall organised at Cambridge had a biographical as well as analytical agenda (McWilliams Tullberg 1990). After a prologue by Sir Austin Robinson on Cambridge economics in the post-Marshall period, Coase presented his detailed research on Marshall's family and ancestry; Whitaker surveyed Marshall's theories of competitive price; Dimand looked at Marshall's notions of general equilibrium value and distribution theory; Mirowski raised the mechanics of Marshall's supply and demand apparatus; Groenewegen reviewed Marshall's taxation economics; Phyllis Deane looked at Marshall on free trade; Gallegati discussed the spread of Marshall's economics in Italy until 1925; Coats discussed Marshall and ethics, and John Maloney 'Marshall and business', perhaps the other side of the coin.

The two-volume proceedings of the Marshall centenary conference at Florence (Dardi, Gallegati and Pesciarelli 1991–92) fully reveals the breadth of Marshall studies as they developed during the Marshall year. After an opening lecture by John Whitaker on 'Marshall's *Principles* after one hundred years' 25 additional papers were presented. These were published in three sub-sections: 'Development of the Marshallian vision: philosophy, ethics and industrial society'; 'Historical context and connections'; and, perhaps the most important, a 'Re-examination of some strands of Marshall's theory'. Most of the contributors were Italian, closely followed in numbers by economists from the English-speaking world (United Kingdom six; United States one, Australia two) and by one representative each from Sweden, Israel, France and Germany. A truly international gathering therefore paid tribute to Marshall's work at Florence.

The first section of the published conference volumes started with Raffaelli's insightful discussion of the analysis of the human mind in Marshall's early philosophical writings; and continued with Groenewegen's critical assessment of Marshall as historian of economics; Dardi's detailed review of the concept and role of the individual in Marshall's economics; Loasby's splendid characterisation of what made institutions efficient for Marshall; Pesciarelli's investigation of the role of the entrepreneur in Marshall's growth theory; Becattini's thorough survey of 'Market and communism' in Marshall's thought, with special emphasis on Marshall's views on 'utopias' and 'character'; Matthews and Supple on Marshall's economic history and its stress on 'economic freedom' and concluded with McWilliams Tullberg on Marshall's effective denial of a role for women in advancing economics. It provided therefore a rich blend of examining Marshall the economist, the philosopher, the historian, the social and political thinker, and the man.

Part II provided overviews of the historical context of Marshall's work in his early years (Butler); Marshall's strong advocacy of economic studies as an essential part of the university curriculum (Kadish); the Marshall Library and its development from 1903 to 1944 (Ross); Marshall's lectures to women by one of their editors (Biagini); the view of the *Principles* by the third generation of Cambridge economists (Harcourt); Sraffa's 1925 critique of Marshall's theory (Roncaglia) and a view of Pareto on Marshall (Zanni). The last two contributions of Part II can be seen as preparing the way for the re-examinations of Marshall's theory presented in Part III. These dealt with the role of demand (Caravale); time (Gay, Kregel and Maricic); credit, confidence and speculation (Gallegati); increasing returns and competition (Marchionetti); land tenure and progress (Cecchi) and capital theory (Cavalieri) in Marshall's economics. It is not difficult to agree with the proposition that the 1990 evaluations of Marshall's work were far more wide reaching in their scope than the textbook treatments of Blaug and Lekachman, and the vast Marshall literature of the 1920s and 1930s.

There is also a somewhat ironical twist associated with the centenary celebrations of Marshall's *Principles* in 1990. Far from only considering Marshall's book as an icon in the development of economics for much of the late nineteenth and early twentieth centuries, or treating the intricacies and minutiae of Alfred Marshall's life and work, many of the contributions to these conferences demonstrated the richness of the Marshallian terrain, the still very substantial scope for correcting misrepresentations of Marshall's economics and, above all, showed the continuing relevance of the Marshallian legacy in economics for today. As a recent far from just historical study of Marshall's economics (Arena and Quéré 2003) demonstrates, that legacy can stand continuing revisitations before it is fully exploited. Hence assessing Marshall's role in the development of economics is an ongoing, practical exercise for economists and not just an antiquarian endeavour for historians of economics past, present and future. A major recent contribution to Marshall scholarship is *The Elgar Companion to Alfred Marshall* edited by Tiziano Raffaelli, Giacomo Becattini and Marco Dardi (2006). Its contents will not only greatly assist future Marshall scholarship to an inordinate extent; these contents in themselves reflect the high state of contemporary Marshall scholarship in many parts of the world.

REFERENCES

Arena, R. and M. Quéré (eds) (2003), *The Economics of Alfred Marshall. Revisiting Marshall's Legacy*, London: Palgrave.

Becattini, G. (1991), 'Four meetings about Marshall: Reports, impressions, reflections', *Marshall Studies Bulletin*, **1**, 5–20. Online: http://www.dse.unifi.it/marshall/welcome.htm.

Blaug, M. ([1962] 1996), *Economic Theory in Retrospect*, 5th edn, Cambridge: Cambridge University Press.

Coase, R.H. (1994), *Essays on Economics and Economists*, Chicago: Chicago University Press.

Dardi, M., M. Gallegati and E. Pesciarelli (eds) (1991–92), 'Alfred Marshall's *Principles of Economics* 1890–1990', *Quaderni di storia dell'economia politica*, **9** (2–3), **10** (1).

Groenewegen, P.D. (1991), 'The Marshall centenary as seen in the East and South', *Marshall Studies Bulletin*, **1**, 25–30. Online: http://www.dse.unifi.it/marshall/welcome.htm.

Groenewegen, P.D. (1995), *A Soaring Eagle: Alfred Marshall 1842–1924*, Aldershot, UK and Brookfield, US: Edward Elgar.

Groenewegen, P.D. (ed.) (1996), *Official Papers of Alfred Marshall. A Supplement*, Cambridge: Cambridge University Press.

Hutchison, T.W. (1953), *A Review of Economic Theory (1870–1929)*, Oxford: Clarendon Press.

Lekachman, R. (1959), *A History of Economic Ideas*, New York: McGraw Hill.

McWilliams Tullberg, R. (ed.) (1990), *Alfred Marshall in Retrospect*, Aldershot, UK and Brookfield, US: Edward Elgar.

O'Brien, D.P. (1981), 'A. Marshall, 1842–1924', in D.P. O'Brien and J.R. Presley (eds), *Pioneers of Modern Economics in Britain*, London: Macmillan, pp. 36–71.

Raffaelli, T. (ed.) (1994), 'Alfred Marshall's early philosophical writings', *Research in the History of Economic Thought and Methodology*, *Archival Supplement*, **4**, 53–159.

Raffaelli, T., G. Becattini and M. Dardi (eds) (2006), *The Elgar Companion to Alfred Marshall*, Cheltenham, UK and Northampton, MA, USA: Edward Elgar.

Raffaelli, T., E.F. Biagini and R. McWilliams Tullberg (eds) (1995), *Alfred Marshall's Lectures to Women*, Aldershot, UK and Brookfield, US: Edward Elgar.

Reisman, D. (1986), *The Economics of Alfred Marshall*, London: Macmillan.

Reisman, D. (1987), *Alfred Marshall. Progress and Politics*, London: Macmillan.

Reisman, D. (1990), *Alfred Marshall's Mission*, London: Macmillan.

Stigler, G.J. (1940), *Production and Distribution. The Formative Period*, New York: Macmillan.

Whitaker, J.K. (1972), 'Alfred Marshall: The years 1877 to 1885', *History of Political Economy*, **4**, 1–61.

Whitaker, J.K. (ed.) (1975), *The Early Economic Writings of Alfred Marshall, 1867–1890*, 2 vols, London: Macmillan.

Whitaker, J.K. (ed.) (1990), *Centenary Essays on Alfred Marshall*, Cambridge: Cambridge University Press.

Whitaker, J.K. (1991), 'Reflections on the centenary year', *Marshall Studies Bulletin*, **1**, 21–4. Online: http://www.dse.unifi.it/marshall/welcome.htm.

Whitaker, J.K. (ed.) (1996), *The Correspondence of Alfred Marshall, Economist*, 3 vols, Cambridge: Cambridge University Press.

PART II

The home reception

3.   Marshall at Cambridge

Carlo Cristiano*

In the 50 years that followed his inaugural lecture in 1885, the place that Marshall occupied in Cambridge economics underwent a series of modifications. At every turn, the change reflected the evolution of the Marshallian school, from the publication of *Principles*, through the era of Pigou and the 'years of high theory' (Shackle 1967), to the Keynesian revolution of the 1930s. This chapter is an overview of this period from the standpoint of the reception of Marshall's thought by his pupils and the second generation of Cambridge economists.

CAMBRIDGE IN THE 'AGE OF MARSHALL'

The years 1885–1914 are known as the 'Age of Marshall' (Jha 1973). This is also the period in which Marshall won his battle for the establishment of an independent economic Tripos (Tribe in this volume; Groenewegen 1988) and in which the Marshallian 'old school' of economics (Becattini 1990, 2006) was created, put in motion, and delivered into the hands of A.C. Pigou and a few other pupils.

When Marshall was in direct control at Cambridge, the guidelines that he imposed gave centre stage to industrial economics, encouraged applied research, and banished pure theory nearly altogether. Becattini (ibid.) noticed that this choice was not obvious, for his school was filled with high-ranking mathematicians; yet Marshall actively impeded any digression in the direction of excessively abstract reasoning, and oriented his fellow workers towards more concrete issues.

The circumstances of the day favoured such an approach. Many of the most highly-debated issues in British policy during this period, and especially those connected with fiscal policy and industrial relations, were a good opportunity for application of economic analysis, which, as Keynes would remind students in the introduction to the Cambridge economic handbooks, was intended 'as an engine for the discovery of concrete truth'. As Whitaker (1990) has shown, however, the same circumstances also contributed to the definitive abandonment, in 1907, of the projected second volume of *Principles*, marking a watershed in Marshall's authorial biography. From this date onwards, Marshall proceeded very slowly to the publication, first of all of *Industry and Trade* (1919), and then *Money, Credit and Commerce* (1923), while an intended final volume on 'Economic progress' was put off to the post-war years, and so ended up as the 'book that never was' (Groenewegen 2005). Had all these books come into being, and had they been published at an earlier point in Marshall's career, the Professor would very likely have had a much more profound influence upon his pupils.

While we may speculate as to the possible effects of Marshall's slow rate of literary production, what can be said with certainty is that the conceptual apparatus of Volume I of *Principles* was developed in Cambridge and found a plurality of applications in several different aspects of the British economy. The school produced works on local development (Chapman 1904), combination (Macgregor [1906] 1938), cooperation (Fay 1908), industrial relations (Pigou 1905; Layton 1914), prices and distribution (Pethick-Lawrence 1899; Bowley 1900; Layton 1912). Moreover, at the end of the period, the profound but hitherto unpublished Marshallian tradition of analysis of the quantity theory of money and the trade cycle, which had been revived by Keynes's work as a lecturer on money and finance, bore fruit in two important works: Keynes's *Indian Currency and Finance* (1913), which focused on a highly-debated aspect of the pre-war gold standard, and Robertson's *A Study of Industrial Fluctuations* (1915).

Within the limits imposed by Marshall, a variety of experimental approaches were developed. C.P. Sanger's 'The fair number of apprentices in a trade' (1895), which appeared in the *Economic Journal* of December 1895, was an early application of sophisticated analysis to a very concrete issue, intended to illustrate the powers of advanced academic research to the sceptical 'practical man'. Pethick-Lawrence's *Local Variation in Wages* (1899) was the result of field research which attempted to provide new empirical evidence that would aid a better understanding of the theory of distribution, while at the same time using this theory in the collection and interpretation of the new data. Bowley's (1900) and Layton's (1912) analyses of British prices from 1820 onwards were more conventional works, both surveying the same subject from a statistical and historical perspective.

Major works on core industrial issues were Chapman (1904) and Macgregor ([1906] 1938). Chapman's 'morphology' of the Lancashire cotton industry is a case study on local development. Neither a simple piece of economic history nor a mere empirical illustration of *Principles*, Chapman's book shed light on the background of Marshall's analysis of localisation and also upon his generalisations as to the entrepreneurial functions of a 'merchant and organiser of production' and a 'leader of *men*' (Marshall 1920, p. 297). Considered in retrospect, Chapman provided a clear example of an industry in which there are significant economies that are external to the firm but internal to the industry, precisely the case that Sraffa (1926) would later label as irrelevant because unrealistic. While complementing Chapman's *Lancashire*, Macgregor's *Industrial Combination* nevertheless developed in the opposite direction. More focused on theory, Macgregor began from Marshall's definition of the representative firm but proceeded to explore the conditions under which combination could turn out to be 'the "representative method" of the twentieth century'. A keynote of Macgregor's variations upon Marshall's evolutionary themes is the ever-greater prominence he gave to non-casual, deliberate change; a view that would give him an advantage in the post-war debate on 'rationalisation' during the Lancashire crisis, when the issue at hand concerned the lack of coordination among individual businesses.

This bird's-eye view is sufficient to show that, just as was the case with mathematical economics, the Cambridge school as Marshall left it had the potential to become a great centre for industrial studies. Nevertheless, there is no evidence that Marshall ever attempted precocious specialisation. Rather, with the limited (at least in quantity) human capital he had at his disposal, he organised a division of labour that could cover a wide area, ranging from economic history (Clapham, Meredith, Fay) to money and finance (Keynes), while at the same time maintaining a focus on industry (Becattini 2006). And with Chapman and Macgregor quickly moving to other universities, industrial economics soon became but one of several subjects taught and developed within the Cambridge school.

The industrial economist who remained at Cambridge after Marshall's retirement was Layton, who imparted neither continuity nor originality to the subject. As Layton himself admitted, he was uninterested in advancing any part of analysis, and his main concern was to keep in touch with a changing reality by way of the continuous collection and organisation of empirical data. This research agenda clearly emerges in *Prices*, as well as in his second book, *The Relations of Capital and Labour* (1914), in which Layton demonstrated great continuity with Marshall (Groenewegen 2007), but no innovation. As a potential research leader, therefore, Layton was not very promising. Nonetheless, there is evidence that Marshall really appreciated the work he did as a teacher (Whitaker 1996, III, p. 362), and his final departure from Cambridge (and from academic economics) in 1914 was another blow to a field of study that had been extremely important in the early stages of the school.

The departure from Cambridge of Layton, as well as of Chapman and Macgregor, had significant long-period consequences. Marshall bequeathed to the Cambridge school two great books and a handful of pupils, and the pupils, as well as the books, could be expected to provide the vehicles upon which his influence was carried forward into the twentieth century. An important albeit a negative factor, then, in the transformation of the 'old school' into a 'place' in economics (Marcuzzo, Naldi and Sanfilippo 2008) was that the two men who took the lead in the teaching of economics at Cambridge immediately after Marshall's retirement were not industrialists. These men were Keynes and Pigou (Groenewegen 1995b), the fathers of, respectively, Cambridge macroeconomics and welfare economics. The study of the economics of industry was continued at Cambridge in the works of Robertson, A. Robinson and a few others, but nobody emerged in this period as the school's representative in this field, which subsequently experienced little continuity in either teaching or research.

CHANGE IN 'CHROMOSOMES'

After Marshall, and before the emergence of Keynes as the dominant figure at Cambridge, the chief representative of the school was obviously Pigou, whom Marshall had chosen – some might have said imposed – as his successor. As the new professor, he was regarded as an authority. Indeed, as the emerging theorist of the school it was Pigou who, in the conceptual setting of his *Wealth and Welfare* (1912), first tried to readapt Marshall's analysis. Indeed, as both the new professor and the leading theorist, he would later come to be considered as a kind of authorised translator of Marshall's 'old style' economics. Yet Pigou did not act passively, merely aiming to be the repository of Marshall's legacy and the continuer of his tradition, but rather worked actively as an innovator and, therefore, should be seen as a strong filter that stood between Marshall and the second generation of Cambridge economists.

Becattini (1990) has suggested that, at a certain time, the 'chromosomes' of the Cambridge school must have undergone a process of alteration. Such an interpretation certainly fits with the changes that occurred when, within the new theoretical environment that he was creating, Pigou introduced increasing/decreasing return industries and external economies. Moreover, adaptation entailed severe selection. Other key genetic strands of Marshall's industrial analysis, such as the representative firm and the life-cycle hypothesis, almost disappeared from view. Not surprisingly, another useful hint towards a solution of Cournot's dilemma, the idea of a downward sloping demand curve for each firm (the solution that was indicated by Sraffa and which Joan Robinson developed), was completely ignored by Pigou. Until 1928, when Allyn Young reopened the field of industrial organisation and pointed to it as the place wherein a solution to the dilemma could be found, Pigou's choices imposed (or, at least, authorised) a very restrictive view of Marshall. Looking ahead, this would give Sraffa an advantage in the debate of the 1920s, in which the theory of value was treated independently of the fundamental link that Marshall saw, and always tried to emphasise, between this theory and the analysis of industrial organisation.

But at this date the 'controversy on costs' was yet to come, and Pigou in these years had other priorities. Welfare economics was the territory he was intent upon exploring, building on the work of both Marshall and Sidgwick, and trying to give it a new practical dimension.

Pigou and Marshall shared a common view of laissez-faire as an imperfect system, a deeply felt concern for the condition of the lower classes and a strong belief that economics had much to say on this social issue, but the ways in which they proceeded from these broad presuppositions were difficult to reconcile. Different – even opposing – interpretations of their work converge on the same conclusion: Marshall simply could not approve of what his disciple was doing. For Backhouse (2006), while utilitarianism in itself was but a secondary line in Marshall's thought, Pigou took utilitarianism to such radical consequences pertaining to redistribution that even Sidgwick could not accept them. Complementing Backhouse's account, Medema (2006) emphasises Marshall's distinction between the static and more operational dimension of welfare economics, which Pigou developed, and a 'larger, more abstract, and overarching concept' of welfare. This latter dimension of Marshall's thought, which has recently been investigated by Dardi (2010), is 'dynamic-evolutionary-biological' and focused on the 'progress of the individual', but disappeared from view in Pigou's development of welfare economics.

Dardi has shown us how Marshall both included and subordinated utilitarianism, which he did not so much reject as redeploy within economic analysis. Utilitarianism, for Marshall, became an ethically neutral criterion of rational behaviour, deployed within a wider evolutionary framework the superior logic of which curbed and placed limits upon the practical relevance of welfare economics. For Dardi, this redeployment of utilitarianism leads to the same conservative view, in this case based on the predictable consequences of redistribution on incentives, that for Backhouse marks the fundamental difference between Pigou and Sidgwick. Marshall's evolutionary outlook, however, posed other, more fundamental obstacles in the path of Pigouvian welfare economics. For Marshall, the qualitative consequences of redistribution for consumption, and, through these consequences, the impact that redistribution has upon people's character and upon their capabilities, comes prior to any statical comparison in terms of welfare. By contrast, throughout his life Pigou emphasised the beneficial effects of income redistribution in the presence of poverty (Pigou 1951, p. 294). This was not inconsistent with Marshall's own view, but Pigou was determined to carry it very much further than his master would have been comfortable with.

In seeking a more operational welfare economics, Pigou (1912) derived private and social marginal net products from Marshall's consumers' surplus, reformulated the laws of returns in terms of a 'rigid relation' between the supply curve of an industry and the curve of marginal supply prices – a new analytical tool which, for Marshall, had 'no reality' (Bharadwaj 1972, p. 33) – and transformed Marshall's tentative conclusions as to the doctrine of 'maximum satisfaction' (Marshall 1920, p. 470) into a new theory of taxation.

On this last move, Pigou's chain of reasoning is definitely too long and straightforward by Marshall's standards (Pigou 1912, pp. 172–9). The cost of production of each additional unit of the product is its supply price, that is, the marginal supply price, a 'perfectly rigid relation' connects the curve of marginal supply price to the supply curve, and it follows directly from this relation that the supply price exceeds/falls short of the marginal supply price in increasing/decreasing return industries. Therefore, other things being equal, marginal net products of increasing return industries are expected to be above average (and vice versa), and this provides the theoretical justification for a scheme of taxes and bounties on decreasing/increasing returns industries. Before coming to this conclusion, Pigou did admit that a problem of reconciling increasing returns with competitive conditions might emerge, but – he argued – the 'difficulty is apparent rather than real. Provided that certain external economies are common to all the suppliers jointly, the presence of increasing returns in respect of all together is compatible with the presence of diminishing returns in respect of the special work of each severally' (ibid., p. 177).

This particular element of the Cambridge 'chromosome' was of great importance. In the debate that followed, and even today, this solution of the 'reconciliation problem' (or 'reconciliation exercise' – another name for Cournot's dilemma) is commonly rejected on the ground that it is hardly 'realistic' (Marchionatti 2001). The common objection, recurring in Young (1913) and Sraffa (1926), is that it is very difficult, if not impossible, to find an industry in which economies exist which are external to each firm but internal to the industry. Writing for an Italian audience, Becattini (1986) suggested that, as a matter of fact, industries of this kind are not so difficult to imagine, the Italian industrial districts being a good example. Moreover, and as noted above, the same could be said also of the Lancashire cotton industry, which Chapman (1904) investigated and Marshall often referred to. Pigou, however, presented his external–internal economies as a merely formal solution, providing neither an empirical foundation for his solution, nor any reference to localisation as an alternative to big business.

Even within the school, Pigou received criticism on this point. Robertson (1924, p. 23) protested that the emphasis on external economies excluded from view all cases in which increasing returns depend on unexploited internal economies. Moving further in this direction, one solution could have been to make reference to the different versions of the life-cycle hypothesis (Marshall 1920, [1919] 1927) or, more generally, to make use of Marshall's own suggestions as to how to deal with increasing returns within the static framework. This would have entailed the abandonment of any rigid functional connection between quantities and costs (Marshall 1920, p. 319), a qualitative distinction between the causes of increasing return and those of decreasing return (ibid., p. 805), an empirical verification that internal economies had not yet led to monopoly, and finally the adoption of the representative firm as the proper unit of analysis (ibid.; on this latter point see also Loasby 1978, pp. 7–9). But Pigou never moved in this direction.

Obviously, the issue is not whether or not Pigou was 'guilty' of not having followed a path that Marshall had indicated. But it is important to catch the drift of the change that was in process of occurring, because Pigou's choices had consequences for the intellectual relationship that he was responsible for creating, not just between Marshall himself and what was to become Marshallian orthodoxy at Cambridge, but also for the relationships that would soon come into being between this orthodoxy and ongoing debates in Europe and the US. The attacks on the Cambridge position by Young, and later by Frank Knight, for example, originated with their reception of Pigou (1912, 1920; see Marchionatti 2001, pp. 50–55); while Sraffa (1925) showed that the representation of variable costs as a functional relation was a worldwide phenomenon, and Sraffa's own criticisms (1925, 1926) concerned Pigou as well as Marshall (Marchionatti 2001), sometimes confusing the one with the other (Raffaelli 2001).

As it so happened, a theory of value which was originally part and parcel of a wider conceptual apparatus, and which owed much of its heuristic value to the adoption of a very particular and even personal methodology, was going to be discussed, and subsequently rejected, by a new scientific community, made up of both Cambridge economists and outsiders. These economists met Marshall on their (still quite long) journey to the construction of a standard methodology that would provide for the investigation of but a limited region of the whole field that had been covered in *Principles* and *Industry and Trade*; a newly restricted area that now centred upon value theory, and in which industrial analysis was admitted only as an ancillary, and primarily empirical, field of study.

DISMANTLING MARSHALL'S THEORY OF VALUE

Pigou's treatment of variable costs was a prelude to future developments at Cambridge. After initial warning signs in the US, a first ripple appeared to disturb the tranquil surface of Cambridge orthodoxy in 1922, when Clapham published his article on 'empty boxes'. This was soon followed by Robertson's 1924 criticisms of Pigou's definitions as too abstract for the very concrete tasks that they were called upon to perform; a criticism that encompassed the problem of allowing internal economies into theory. But these criticisms proved to be but preliminary skirmishes, with the main attack coming from Sraffa (1925, 1926) and aimed not merely at a few chapters in books by Pigou, but at the whole of Marshallian value theory.

The manner in which Marshall's value theory was dismantled during the 1920s has become a well-known story, and one that has remained a matter of both research and controversy for a long time. Schumpeter (1954), Samuelson (1967), Shackle (1967), Blaug (1968) and Moss (1984) are among those who celebrate the abandonment of Marshall's value theory, while Andrews (1951), Becattini (1962), Loasby (1978), Abouchar (1990) and Hart (2003) adopt the opposite point of view. In this literature it is worth singling out Becattini (1986) and Prendergast (1992), who explore the conceptual barriers that separated Marshall and Sraffa, thereby providing an analysis that becomes pivotal in Marchionatti's (2001) important reconstruction and interpretation of the whole debate.

In the context of this chapter a few key moments in this story warrant particular attention, for they illustrate how, even before their capitulation to Sraffa, many Cambridge Marshallians showed little awareness of (or, perhaps, little willingness to accept) some of the core foundations of Marshall's economic analysis. One clear illustration of this disposition is illustrated in the way that, despite the care with which Marshall had insisted upon a strong relation between the analyses of industrial organisation in Book IV and of value theory in Book V of *Principles*, Sraffa encountered no resistance when he imposed the theory of value, and this alone, as the battleground. In the same way, he met scarcely any opposition in imposing an interpretation of this theory in which partial equilibrium analysis was not an analytical tool but a representation, which he found unsatisfactory, of the economy as a whole and the way it works.

Marshall's partial equilibria are mental experiments, imaginary situations in which one set of quantities at a time is allowed to change, while all other forces are momentarily bound in the pound of *cæteris paribus*. By definition, this is not a perfect representation of the economic system. Yet if only an approximation to real conditions, partial equilibria are not arbitrary representations. Rather, they reflect a particular characteristic of the economy (one that Herbert Simon would convey through his image of the world as 'empty') that was of primary importance for Marshall.

Where general equilibrium theory provides a snapshot of all economic interconnections, Marshall developed a different method of understanding economic life. In his view, provided that not all interconnections have the same force, partial equilibrium analysis can be employed in the study of more or less complete adaptation to local changes. The resulting technique reflected an idea of a hierarchy of relevance determined by proximity in time and space, which Marshall thought to be strongly supported by empirical evidence and, therefore, 'realistic'. Nonetheless, Sraffa succeeded in imposing a position in which the apparatus of general equilibrium analysis was to be adopted, not because it was a more powerful tool, but rather because it provided a better representation of reality.

Once this position was tacitly accepted as defining the ground of the argument, Sraffa's conclusion that Marshall's theory of value was compatible with variable costs only in a very limited range of situations appeared devastating. Subsequently, two possible ways out of this blind alley were proposed within the pages of the *Economic Journal*. One route, indicated by Young (1928) and Schumpeter (1928), consisted of pursuing dynamics rather than statics, and was followed in Cambridge by Shove (1930). The other path built on the second part of Sraffa (1926), where it was suggested, as a solution to Cournot's dilemma, that each firm faces a downward sloping demand curve – thus picking up Marshall's idea of a 'particular' market for each firm (1920, p. 458). Moving well beyond Sraffa's original intentions, this development proved to be the first step towards Joan Robinson's theory of imperfect competition.

En route to Robinson's theory, the representative firm was declared useless by Robbins (1928) and substituted with Pigou's equilibrium firm – a firm that is in equilibrium when the whole industry is in equilibrium. According to Moss's (1984) reconstruction of events, Pigou's equilibrium firm was the second step leading to the theory of imperfect competition. The third and last step was taken when every firm was assumed to be an equilibrium firm.

Moss describes this series of steps as leading not only to a theory of imperfect competition, but also to a theory of perfect competition. His view seems to be correct, because, at least in Marshall, there is no theory of perfect competition. As Marshall wrote on a page of an essay that Maynard Keynes had written for him during his 1905 'apprenticeship', perfect, or 'automatic', competition 'belongs to the mathematical world on the other side of the looking glass' (Raffaelli 2000, p. 143; see also Marshall [1919] 1927, p. 397). Subsequently, a new, standardised way of theorising took the place of all the apparently inexplicable idiosyncrasies of Marshall (Samuelson 1967).

As a by-product of this transformation, a new and rather stylised image of Marshall emerged. Prior to this, however, and as remembered by Austin Robinson (1990), the official portrait of 'Marshallian orthodoxy' looked like the uncritical reception of the thought of a man of the past. This made the task that Sraffa set for himself much easier. But Robinson's recollections of Cambridge immediately after the war provide other, more practical explanations of how it was that Sraffa entered into the Cambridge mind like a hot knife through butter. The image of a school made up of only six teachers, with Pigou alone capable of teaching advanced economics, and all based upon the text of *Principles*, stands in stark contrast with the cosmopolitanism and the sophistication revealed by the wide range of references found in Sraffa's article in the *Annali*.

All this was but a passing interlude. Within a few years, a new scientific community had mushroomed around Keynes, the Robinsons and Sraffa. Nevertheless, in the early 1920s Marshall's school was a quite weak creature. Perhaps too weak to undertake the difficult task of trying to understand 'what Marshall really meant'. This work of interpretation was performed piecemeal, and very quickly, along the way. And it was done on the restricted ground that Sraffa had imposed and, since 1912, Pigou had indirectly and inadvertently authorised.

The proposed readings of Marshall were always very selective, and often distorted. For instance, the 1898 article on 'Distribution and exchange', which could have provided a privileged perspective upon Marshall's own views concerning the aims and limited scope of the static apparatus, passed altogether unnoticed. And even key passages in Book V of *Principles* were ignored, as happened when Robbins asked himself why Marshall resorted to the representative firm. His answer was not taken from the text of *Principles* (Book IV, Chapter xiii; Book V, Chapter xii; Appendix H). Instead, it came out of a secondary work by Robertson, thereby illustrating that Robertson himself took not the slightest notice of the introduction of a biological idea of equilibrium within the static theory of value, nor of the methodological link between Books IV and V (Robbins 1928, p. 391). In the same vein, dealing with Cournot's dilemma, Sraffa made no reference to the life-cycle hypothesis and the representative firm. Indeed, Sraffa went even further, proclaiming an interpretation of the evolution of Marshall's thought, from *The Economics of Industry* to *Principles*, in which Marshall was accused of having deliberately hidden a fundamental inconsistency in his theory of value by means of the 'unrealistic' concept of internal–external economies (Prendergast 1992).

As Prendergast has suggested, Sraffa was far from convinced that any non-casual relation could exist between the quantity produced and costs, but he took for granted that, if one did exist, a functional relation should represent it. Thus, while Marshall dedicated much of his work to a study of how relations between costs and quantity occur in practice, Sraffa could not see how such a relation, if it ever existed, could be expressed by means of a functional connection without incurring inconsistencies. On top of fundamental ideological incompatibility (Becattini 1986), a dialogue that began from opposite presuppositions and which had no chance of direct intercourse was not the road to mutual comprehension.

Schumpeter's 1928 *Economic Journal* article, 'The instability of capitalism', provided a further disruptive interpretation of the 'received view' of Marshall, in this case one that originated from outside of Cambridge and was external to the costs controversy. Pushing increasing returns and internal–external economies onto the side of dynamics, but not ignoring Marshall's own *penchant* for economic biology, Schumpeter tried to impose his own view of economic development as a discontinuous evolutionary process. In this perspective, Marshall's biological metaphors were to be removed, not because they were incompatible with the framework of both static and dynamic theory, as Marshall himself (1898) had admitted, but because they suggested an incorrect interpretation of economic change. Schumpeter saw creative destruction and forced savings, imposed by the entrepreneurs and bankers of his *Theorie der wirtschaftlichen Entwicklung*, where Marshall had seen the virtue of parsimony and a linear, cumulative idea of evolution (Raffaelli 2003, p. 119). Indeed, albeit only implicitly, Schumpeter did even more than this: for Marshall's positive outlook, in which human beings are capable of creating their own future, was now eclipsed by Schumpeter's more deterministic and more pessimistic attempt to forecast the inescapable destiny of capitalism.

In this not very encouraging context, Allyn Young (1928) offered a contribution that, for a moment at least, seemed to lead the whole debate back to the starting point and once more onto a Marshallian track. Not that this article was a defence of Marshall. But with his attempt to find a dynamic way out of the static blind alley – a prospective solution conjured up in the image of a 'moving equilibrium' – Young reopened many of the old drawers that had been so abruptly closed. Thus Young rehabilitated Marshall's distinction between external and internal economies as a valuable conceptual solution to the Cournot problem, and also reaffirmed, on the basis of both empirical evidence and common sense, that the box of increasing return industries was not so empty as Clapham had suggested. In addition, and in implicit continuity with Marshall (1898, 1920, p. 319), Young argued that reasons for variation in costs are both 'qualitative' and 'quantitative', that such variations depend on changes in both technology and organisation, and that no functional relation may represent these causal connections. This re-introduced into the debate the study of technical and organisational conditions, along with the Smithian framework of *Principles* (Book IV). The idea that Young put forward was that each industry, and not only the single firm, faces a downward sloping demand curve. 'Smith's theorem' – that 'the division of labour is limited by the extent of the market' – reconciled unexploited internal economies with competitive conditions.

Though stimulating, Young's article did not change the underlying direction of Cambridge value theory. In 1933, J. Robinson imposed a new static standard with her theory of imperfect competition, which, together with Chamberlin's monopolistic competition, succeeded in ejecting the concept of industry outside of the sphere occupied by the theory of value, where it remained until the publication of Andrews (1951) and Becattini (1962). It would now be many years before Marshall would to be reappraised and interpreted as providing a key step towards evolutionary economics (Metcalfe 2006) and as a precursor of non-Coasian, capability-based theories of the size and boundaries of the firm (Langlois 2006). Nevertheless, much of what at the time was ignored or dismissed by value theorists, and which Young partially resurrected, must have sounded very familiar to those who, working in parallel to the mainstream at Cambridge and elsewhere, had continued to develop industrial economics on a sound Marshallian basis.

MARSHALLIAN INDUSTRIAL ECONOMICS IN THE 'YEARS OF HIGH THEORY'

The *tour de force* in high theory reinforced, though perhaps did not create *ex novo*, a common wisdom concerning the Marshallian legacy. According to this standard interpretation, a sporadic yet never interrupted parallel development of Marshallian industrial analysis at Cambridge and elsewhere, was dismissed as non-theoretical descriptive work, and so its contributions passed almost unnoticed. Yet as Raffaelli (2004) has shown, the 'old school' works by Chapman (1904) and Macgregor ([1906] 1938), were followed in the interwar

years by the contributions of Robertson in 1923 – of which Robertson (1928) is
a revised version – Lavington (1927), A. Robinson (1931) and Sargant Florence
(1933), and were far from devoid of any theoretical meaning. This literature,
of which Marshall's *Industry and Trade* remains the masterpiece, shared a
common conceptualisation of industry based on Marshall's own dialectical and
evolutionary 'analytical matrix' (Groenewegen 1995a, p. 710). In this literature
many avenues of research that pure theory progressively abandoned, alongside
a few others that only properly developed after the publication of *Industry and
Trade*, contributed to a shared conception of industry and of the firm.

The divergence between pure theory and industrial analysis was strikingly
illustrated by the way that the idea that the extent of the market is limited
for both the individual firm and the industry was introduced as a novelty in
the context of value theory. For such an idea recurs as a commonplace in the
industrial economics literature, in which the reciprocal influences between
technical and organisational conditions and the extension of particular and
general markets were continuously discussed.

Following Marshall ([1919] 1927), the second generation of Marshallian
industrialists began to consider the limited extent of markets from the point
of view of standardisation. Robertson (1928, p. 7) integrated this concept
into the dialectic between 'differentiation' and 'integration', which derives
from *Principles* and which he now adapted to the analysis of the 'structure of
industry'. Robertson's book expressed the author's dissatisfaction with Pigou's
missed explanation of the relation between internal economies, increasing
returns and business size. But, following the general trend, Robertson kept the
two sides of the question neatly separated. In fact, this way of doing economics
was not very Marshallian. Nevertheless, it prevailed.

It is not, therefore, so surprising to find that Chapter ii of Robertson's *The
Control of Industry*, published in the Cambridge handbooks series, explained
the limit to the growth of the firm by means of the industrialists' formulation.
Following the analysis of the American case put forward in *Industry and
Trade*, in which large and homogeneous markets permit a high level of product
standardisation and the adoption of large-scale production, Robertson's
explanation of the limits to the growth of firms in different industries is couched
in terms of the degree of standardisation, which itself is 'conditional on the
growth of communications and the widening of markets' (ibid., p. 20). The
main advantage of large-scale production is the reduction of costs that only a
'large firm' – one that can introduce 'more highly specialised machinery, and
keep it occupied more continuously than a small' (ibid., p. 21) – can obtain.
For Robertson, however, the 'economies of large-scale government rather than of
large-scale technique dictate the size of the modern business unit' (ibid., p. 25).

This statement was important, and potentially innovative, because it indicated
at least the possibility that larger managerial structures could be more efficient

than privately-owned firms. Robertson, however, in true Marshallian fashion, did not mean that there was an absolute advantage on the side of big business, or that the industrial world was moving towards generalised bureaucratisation – as Schumpeter (1928) was at that time suggesting. Rather, he explained, 'the battle between the large firm and the small is not one which is ever fought to a definite finish', and furthermore, the advantages that could be reaped from large-scale technique and management varied from one industry to another.

On this last point, not all the Marshallians travelled in the same direction, but all of them employed the same conceptualisation, of which Lavington (1927) epitomised the essential logic. Derived from Chapters iii–iv of Book II of *Industry and Trade*, Lavington's scheme considers standardisation from the point of view of a theory of business organisation in which the focus is on the limited power of the individual mind in coordinating complex processes. This is a typically Marshallian notion, associated with the trade-off between the advantages of specialisation on the side of production and coordination costs on the side of management.

Leaving aside the 'desire for monopoly', and taking as given the 'effective range of marketing' (that is, the extension of the market), Lavington's scheme runs as follows:

> The more restricted the variety of the process undertaken by a single business ... the simpler is the task of direction. The more simple the work of direction, the larger is the volume of output which can be efficiently controlled by a single mind. And the larger the volume of output, the greater is the scope for the major economies of modern technique: namely, those which arise from the higher specialisation of men and machines, more conveniently described in Dr. Marshall's phrase as *uniform continuous process*; and those associated economies which arise from the use of *powerful appliances of production*. (Lavington 1927, pp. 27–8, emphasis in original)

Were it for these two forces alone, the process would result in a continuous disintegration of activities. Integration, therefore, is the outcome of the technical relations between successive or adjacent stages in the processes of production. More specifically, 'standardisation' favours disintegration, extreme 'individuality' calls for complete integration, while problems of coordination, deriving from the 'technical interdependence of products, of production processes and of mental processes behind them' (ibid., p. 32), may be a further motive of integration.

Robertson and Lavington, therefore, focused on two aspects of the same issue. The latter took market extension as given, and investigated in the abstract the relative advantages and disadvantages of integration from the point of view of the power of an individual mind and, as a subordinate issue, of the technique of production; the former included market extension as a variable, and interpreted the consequences of its change on both business organisation and production technology. Together, Robertson and Lavington could provide a common ground for an analysis of business size in relation to managerial structures. But business size had to do with the forms of competition as well, and in this respect, a more pressing issue presented itself. For the moment at least, the problem was to cope with the crisis of the British industrial system, based on small-sized businesses.

The post-war industrial depression was a highly-debated issue throughout Britain and had a massive impact on Cambridge. The crisis of the textile industry, in particular, was, in itself, another blow for Marshall's vision, for which Lancashire was a vivid representation of 'automatic' cooperation within a localised industry. Now, together with coal-mining, the cotton-spinning industry had become one of the main fields of 'rationalisation', the new watchword and another name for 'enforced cooperation'.

Like Macgregor at Oxford, Marshall's pupils and followers at Cambridge joined in the rationalisation movement. In Keynes' opinion, the need to promote coordinated action within the highly-competitive and traditionally individual-istic Lancashire industry constituted one of 'The economic consequences of Mr Churchill', and represented a 'microeconomic case against laissez-faire' (Marchionatti 1995), the broader argument of which he outlined in a series of articles in *The Nation and Athenaeum* between 1926 and 1929. More abstractly, yet nevertheless with reference to the crises of the textile and coal-mining industries, Shove (1930) elaborated a theoretical argument in which the individual expectations of non-coordinated entrepreneurs under conditions of imperfect competition impeded the growth of firms' average dimensions. In itself, this was not a complete novelty (see Macgregor [1906] 1938). However, during the costs controversy and within a period of industrial distress, it opened up a promising field that was also explored by Richard Kahn in *The Economics of the Short Period*, a dissertation submitted for a fellowship at King's in 1929.

As Dardi has argued in his introduction to the Italian translation of Kahn's dissertation (Kahn 1983), while the theories of imperfect competition and un-employment would later become separate fields in the works of J. Robinson and Keynes, in *The Economics of the Short Period* they walked hand in hand as an adaptation of Marshall's industrial economics, providing a new conceptualisation with the potential of being developed into a theory of unemployment.

Probably influenced by Shove, whose pupil he had been, Kahn interpreted the crisis as a situation in which the rational behaviour of individual firms impeded those adjustments, belonging to Marshall's long period, that should have re-stored full employment. Kahn's argument was that entrepreneurs, acting as non-coordinated agents, do not expand their output capacity, and thereby reduce average costs, because this would entail a price-cut in order to attract customers from their competitors' particular markets. As the competitors' reaction to a first move cannot be predicted, imperfect competition becomes a strategic situation, resembling the prisoner's dilemma, in which it is perfectly rational to keep the maximum level of production for each unit at a constant level.

After 1929, Kahn followed Keynes onto another track. Consequently, it was only in the published work of Shove (1930) that the idea of a link between imperfect competition and uncertainty was revealed. In his paper, Shove outlined the same strategic situation described by Kahn. However, writing for the Symposium on 'Increasing returns and the representative firm', he employed this piece of analysis as a dynamic solution to the problem of reconciling increasing returns with competitive equilibrium, finding the key to solving this dilemma in the existence of unexploited 'economies of rationalisation' and 'concentration'.

Thus, while Khan's book remained unpublished, the idea of a sub-optimal stable equilibrium for a whole industry recurred in Shove (1930), and in fact also later in A. Robinson ([1931] 1935), taking shape as an alternative to Marshall's representative firm and hence as a new solution to the reconciliation problem, superseding the life-cycle hypothesis as it came to terms with the new circumstances of British industry. But it was never developed into a theory of unemployment.

Shove (1930) aimed to dispose of the representative firm while, at the same time, keeping alive the distinction between the conditions of equilibrium for the industry and for the individual firm. Whereas in Marshall the industry is in equilibrium even though the firms are located at different points along the cycle of growth–maturity–decay, for Shove the equilibrium of the whole industry is a state of affairs in which the aggregate output of an industry remains constant while the internal allocation of resources is allowed to change according to the shifting expectations of the entrepreneurs. This 'process of reshuffling' entails path-dependency and, at least in conditions of imperfect competition, non-optimality. Shove took the situation in the cotton-spinning and coal-mining industries as a representation of how this may occur in practice (Shove 1930, p. 98).

Following a similar route, A. Robinson's *The Structure of Competitive Industry*, another Cambridge economic handbook, offered a more general, up-to-date and systematic treatment of the subject, representing the most advanced thought in the Marshallian literature on business size and structure, and constituting a link between Marshallian industrial analysis and ongoing developments in the pure theory of imperfect competition (J. Robinson [1933] 1965, p. v).

Like Shove, A. Robinson dropped the life-cycle hypothesis – which Marshall had already expressed in the past tense in later editions of *Principles* (for example, 1920, p. 316), and relaxed in *Industry and Trade* ([1919] 1927, pp. 315–16) – and attempted a new interpretation of the reconciliation between unexploited economies and competitive conditions.

In Marshallian fashion, Robinson identified competitive conditions with the existence of special, but contestable, markets, one for each firm. This assumption was in continuity with Macgregor ([1906] 1938) and also Robertson (1928). Together with Shove (1930), Robinson here provided the ground for a theory of the growth of the firm in terms of the limited exploitation of internal and concentration economies under imperfect competitive conditions. Market imperfection, which imposes a cost in transferring customers from one firm to another (A. Robinson [1931] 1935, pp. 120–22), combined with the 'five forces' upon which the firm's efficiency depends (technical, managerial and financial forces; the influence of marketing; risk and fluctuations), generates a costly and discontinuous pattern of growth along which a firm, working below the level of maximum efficiency, is not 'automatically' led to the 'optimum size'. Efficiency remains a function of size, but the passage from a lower to a higher local maximum requires a period of transition through a local minimum of efficiency, thus momentarily increasing the costs of growth due to imperfect competition. Therefore, as with Herbert Simon's idea of 'satisficing instead of maximizing', each firm can only try to move from one local optimum to another, while the optimum that will prevail depends on specific conditions, to be judged case by case.

A very critical transition, and one that Robinson highlights, is the 'departure from individual management and a local market, in the direction of organised and coordinated management, and a national market' (ibid., p. 122). Robinson was a rather conservative Marshallian on this point, and though he admitted that management had been the major field of innovation in British industry over the last decade (ibid., p. 47), he nevertheless remained loyal to a faith in the 'flexibility' and 'energy' of small businesses (ibid., pp. 48–51), and of the primacy of individuals over organisation (ibid., pp. 51–53). Hence, while he saw no upper limit to the growth of technical efficiency, Robinson affirmed that the 'managerial optimum sets not only a lower but also an upper limit to the scale of operation' (ibid., p. 48).

This last position of Robertson collided with that developed in Sargant Florence's *The Logic of Industrial Organisation* (1933). As in Lavington's scheme, Florence argued that maximum technical efficiency is reached when the highest throughput is placed under a single managerial unit; but Florence's managerial unit was an 'organisation', not an individual. Moreover, he placed no upper limit upon the optimum managerial unit: '[i]n the assumption of the economic advantage in specialisation of men and equipment, and of long-run conditions when factors of production can be adjusted and reorganised, there is in my view no limit to the increase in the physical return obtainable by larger-scale operation' (Sargant Florence 1933, p. 24).

Florence's word may perhaps indicate that a new and rather Chandlerian change was occurring in the Marshallian chromosomes. When placed in the context of his book as a whole, however, it is clear that the significance of his statements should not be exaggerated. For Florence, the potential advantages of large-scale production remained far more important than those of large-scale organisation. Nevertheless, in the words that Florence employed to express his disagreement with A. Robinson, a potentially stimulating divergence took the form of an alarming fissure: '[a]part from economists', Florence (ibid., p. 116) argued, 'those who have made a special study of organisation come to the conclusion that no limit is set to the size of organisation if correct principles are adopted to enable the single leader to delegate control'. Such a distinction between students of economics and students of organisation was hardly compatible with Marshall's inclusion of organisation among the factors of production. However, the disagreement between A. Robinson, the representative of the Marshallian tradition at Cambridge, and Florence, who had graduated from Cambridge in 1914 and was now Professor of Commerce at Birmingham, resulted only in a sterile argument in the *Economic Journal* (see A. Robinson 1934; Sargant Florence 1934).

A more promising line of research was carried on at Oxford, where Macgregor continued his work on the evolution of business methods. Macgregor treated firms as complex agents in which adaptive behaviour in the long run and profit-seeking behaviour in the short run coexist, thereby paving the way for Andrews's empirical investigation during the 1940s. Andrews's own reconstruction of the research that led to his *Manufacturing Business* (1949) focuses upon the practical impossibility of basing Macgregor's line of research upon the new theories of imperfect and monopolistic competition and, therefore, the need to take a step back to long-since dismissed concepts, because '"Old Marshall" at least supplied an analytical framework within which everyday life seemed to take on an intelligible shape' (Andrews 1951, p. 140). But even though Andrews eventually found a way back to Marshall, Marshall's failure to pass on his broad methodological conceptions has become a commonplace among Marshallian students. This chapter has pointed to significant instances of such communication failures. There is substantial agreement within Marshallian scholarship, however, that on this score Maynard Keynes provided a significant exception. In the view of Marshall's biographer, Peter Groenewegen, while 'Pigou never absorbed Marshall's message on method, conceptualisation, the nature of abstraction, style, and vision', these are 'parts of Marshall's economic legacy that Keynes found attractive and emphasised, not only in his tribute to Marshall [in Pigou (1925)] but also in the practice of his own work' (Groenewegen 1995b, p. 140; see also Raffaelli 1998, 2003, Chapter vii; Becattini 1990, 2006).

WAS KEYNES A MARSHALLIAN?

The nature and extent of Marshall's influence upon Keynes is a tricky issue, because the answer to the question 'was Keynes a Marshallian?' has changed, from time to time, with the perspectives from which it has been asked; and, in one particularly important case, this question was not asked at all.

This last situation arose in the wake of the abundant flow of research on the philosophical foundations of the Keynesian revolution inaugurated by Roderick O'Donnell's 1982 dissertation (later published as O'Donnell 1989) and Carabelli (1988). The subsequent debate continued throughout the 1990s, and its fruit incorporated into the biographical portraits of Keynes by Skidelsky (1983) and Moggridge (1992). The reason why these authors have dispensed with the question of Marshall's influence altogether seems to be that, although the vocation of both Marshall and Keynes was philosophy, there is scarcely any link between the master's immersion in Darwin, Spencer and German idealism (Raffaelli 2003) and the pupil's reception of Moore's ethical intuitionism and the reading undertaken in preparation for the *Treatise on Probability* (Raffaelli 2006).

If we turn from general to social and political philosophy, thereby coming closer to economics, the conclusion remains more or less the same. It is certainly true that Marshall and Keynes shared a common view on capitalism as a transitory and perfectible product of history, but the same could be said of all the leading Cambridge economists (Becattini 1990); and it may also be added that, on this point, Keynes's vision always remained that of a 'civil servant' (A. Robinson 1972): a practical man in search of immediate solutions to urgent problems, as opposed to a social scientist scanning the horizon of history and trying to find the right direction towards the future.

Things change significantly, however, when the focus shifts, as in Groenewegen (1995b), from Keynes's youthful enthusiasm for Moore and his 'religion' (Keynes [1938] 1972) to his mature reflections of the 1920s and 1930s as to the nature of the economist's profession. Indeed, the negative answer as to the question of Keynes's Marshallianism may be transformed into a resolute 'yes' if one enters into the technicalities of the Keynesian revolution, as Clower (1989) and Leijonhufvud (1999) have done.

It goes without saying that any attempt to provide a synthesis of these conflicting perspectives has no chance of reaching a definitive conclusion. On the other hand, one does not need to paint a portrait of Keynes as a faithful Marshallian in order to accept the idea that, while moving from very personal and non-Marshallian philosophical presuppositions and practical exigencies towards a profound revolution in economic theory, Keynes reinterpreted or replicated some key aspects of Marshall's economic methodology and theory along the way.

A turn to Marshall between 1924 and 1926, during which period Keynes wrote his obituary memoir of Marshall and edited his *Official Papers*, is documented in Groenewegen (1995b) and reflected in *The End of Laissez-Faire* (Keynes, 1926), where Marshall is hailed as the representative of an economics profession now freed from the catechisms of Mrs Martineau and Mrs Marcet. The timing is significant here, for these were the years of the 'long struggle of escape' from economic orthodoxy the culmination of which was the writing of the *General Theory*. Thus, even though the figure of Marshall loomed large as a pillar of orthodoxy, Keynes nevertheless had no hesitation in identifying him as a hero who had fought against an earlier dogma of unscientific laissez-faire.

There are also other Marshallian clues in Keynes's late thinking. For example, the change of mind that convinced Keynes to abandon the objective explanation of the cycle incorporated in the *Treatise* equations is, at least superficially, a step back to the Cambridge version of the quantity theory of money, in which Keynes had been a firm believer in his youth, and in which individual decisions take the place of the impersonal velocity of circulation. Furthermore, as the famous twelfth chapter of the *General Theory* suggests, the emergence of speculation as a third and antisocial alternative to the old choice between consumption and the investment of savings in production is rooted in a historically-determined institutional context, in which investment is made liquid by a new separation between ownership and control, and by the existence of new organised investment markets; a good example of how, as Marshall had suggested, 'economic thought' depends on the 'economic structure' (Marshall 1920, p. 10).

These last detailed changes occurred after 1926, and were not necessarily occasioned by the turn to Marshall. They are, however, a fair representation of economics as an engine in continuous need of readaptation, as well as an anticipation of the close relationship between Marshall's price theory and Keynes's *General Theory* recognised by Clower and Leijonhufvud.

Replicating Marshall's *bricoleur* style of theorising, the Keynesian revolution entailed a complete revision of the theory of interest, but not the abandonment of Marshall's price theory. Quite the reverse: after having encouraged the process of dissolution of the Marshallian apparatus while acting as the co-editor of the *Economic Journal*, Keynes had no difficulty in framing his theory as a generalisation of the macroeconomic conclusions that can be derived from Marshall's micro-theory. On the one hand, as Clower recognises, Marshall's representation of the market adjustment process was the only one of which Keynes had a thorough knowledge. On the other, as both Clower and Leijonhufvud hold, this representation fitted Keynes's case much better than did that of Walras.

The compatibility between Marshall's analysis of the price mechanism and Keynes's theory depends on those characteristics of the partial equilibrium apparatus, intended as an analytical tool for the study of adaptive behaviour to local changes, that were lost after Sraffa (1926). As Leijonhufvud (1999, p. 23) explains, while Marshall's time-period analysis is made up of adaptations in which one quantity or price moves and then the others follow, the Walrasian concept of equilibrium requires the simultaneous consistency of all choices, expressed in quantities and prices. Therefore, while in a Walrasian setting, '"unemployment equilibrium" is a contradiction in terms since the equilibrium concept requires the consistency of all trading intentions from a Marshallian standpoint, there is no riddle' (ibid.).

Within this methodological continuity, however, the Keynesian revolution imposed a definitive departure from Marshall in regard to the question of the scope of economic research. In some way, this closed the circle, because after the dissolution of Marshall's value theory, and the reduction of industrial economics to the subordinated rank of a subsidiary field, the Keynesian revolution now developed a new field of macroeconomics, thereby providing a new area in which Cambridge could define its own identity – for instance, in opposition to the 'bastard Keynesians' – which had nothing to do with Marshall's research programme. If a link remained it was in methodology. But Keynes's method, as Marshall's method before it, has proved to work much better as a subtle subject matter for historians of economics to ponder and tease out the meaning of, than as a dominant and shared point of view, capable of being replicated in a standard version and thus rendered readily available to the members of a school.

NOTE

*   The author wishes to thank the editors of the book for their comments and suggestions on a number of specific points, and Simon Cook for stylistic assistance.

REFERENCES

Abouchar, A. (1990), 'From Marshall's cost analysis to modern orthodoxy: Throwing out the baby and keeping the bath', *Économie Appliquée*, **43**, 119–43.
Andrews, P.W.S. (1949), *Manufacturing Business*, London: Macmillan.
Andrews, P.W.S. (1951), 'Industrial analysis in economics – with a special reference to Marshallian doctrine', in P.W.S. Andrews and T. Wilson (eds), *Oxford Studies in the Price Mechanism*, Oxford: Oxford University Press, pp. 139–72.
Backhouse, R.E. (2006), 'Sidgwick, Marshall, and the Cambridge school of economics', *History of Political Economy*, **38**, 15–44.
Becattini, G. (1962), *Il concetto d'industria e la teoria del valore*, Torino: Bollati Boringhieri.
Becattini, G. (1986), 'L'interpretazione sraffiana di Marshall', in R. Bellofiore (ed.), *Tra teoria economica e grande cultura europea: Piero Sraffa*, Milano: Franco Angeli, pp. 39–57.
Becattini, G. (1990), 'Alfred Marshall e la vecchia scuola di Cambridge', in G. Becattini (ed.), *Il pensiero economico: temi, problemi scuole*, Torino: UTET, pp. 275–310.
Becattini, G. (2006), 'The Marshallian school of economics', in Raffaelli, Becattini and Dardi (2006), pp. 609–16.
Bharadwaj, K. (1972), 'Marshall on Pigou's *Wealth and Welfare*', *Economica*, **39**, 32–46.
Blaug, M. (1968), *Economic Theory in Retrospect*, Homewood: Irwin.
Bowley, A.L. (1900), *Wages in the United Kingdom in the Nineteenth Century: Notes for the Use of Students of Social and Economic Questions*, Cambridge: Cambridge University Press.
Carabelli, A.M. (1988), *On Keynes's Method*, London: Macmillan.
Chapman, S.J. (1904), *The Lancashire Cotton Industry*, Manchester: Manchester University Press.
Clapham, J.H. (1922), 'On empty economic boxes', *Economic Journal*, **32**, 305–14.
Clower, R.W. (1989), 'Keynes's *General Theory*: The Marshallian connection', in D.A. Walker (ed.), *Perspectives on the History of Economic Thought*, vol. 2, Aldershot, UK and Brookfield, US: Edward Elgar, pp. 133–47, reprinted in R.W. Clower (1995), *Economic Doctrine and Method. Selected Papers of R.W. Clower*, Aldershot, UK and Brookfield, US: Edward Elgar, pp. 284–98.

Dardi, M. (2010), 'Marshall on welfare, or: the "Utilitarian" meets the "Evolver"', *European Journal of the History of Economic Thought*, **17**, 405–37.

Fay, C.R. (1908), *Cooperation at Home and Abroad*, London: King.

Groenewegen, P.D. (1988), 'Alfred Marshall and the establishment of the Cambridge Economic Tripos', *History of Political Economy*, **20**, 627–67.

Groenewegen, P.D. (1995a), *A Soaring Eagle: Alfred Marshall 1842–1924*, Aldershot, UK and Brookfield, US: Edward Elgar.

Groenewegen, P.D. (1995b), 'Keynes and Marshall: Methodology, society, and politics', *History of Political Economy*, **27**, 129–55.

Groenewegen, P.D. (2005), 'A book that never was: Marshall's final volume on progress and his system of ethical and political beliefs', *History of Economics Review*, 42, 29–44.

Groenewegen, P.D. (2007), 'Walter Layton on *The Relations of Capital and Labour* (1914): A Marshallian text *pur sang*?', *History of Economics Review*, 46, 19–31.

Hart, N. (2003), 'From the representative to the equilibrium firm: Why Marshall was not a Marshallian', in R. Arena and M. Quéré (eds), *The Economics of Alfred Marshall*, Basingstoke: Palgrave, pp. 158–81.

Jha, N. (1973), *The Age of Marshall: Aspects of British Economic Thought 1890–1915*, London: Frank Cass.

Kahn, R.F. (1983), *L'economia del breve periodo*, Torino: Boringhieri.

Keynes, J.M. (1913), *Indian Currency and Finance*, London: Macmillan & Co.

Keynes, J.M. (1926), *The End of Laissez-Faire*, London: The Hogarth Press.

Keynes, J.M. ([1938] 1972), 'My early beliefs', in *Essays in Biography. The Collected Writings of John Maynard Keynes*, vol. 10, edited by D.E. Moggridge, London: Macmillan and Cambridge: Cambridge University Press, pp. 433–50.

Langlois, R.N. (2006), 'Industrial economics', in Raffaelli, Becattini and Dardi (2006), pp. 658–63.

Lavington, F. (1927), 'Technical influences on vertical integration', *Economica*, **7**, 27–36.

Layton, W.T. (1912), *An Introduction to the Study of Prices*, London: Macmillan.

Layton, W.T. (1914), *The Relations of Capital and Labour*, London and Glasgow: Collins.

Leijonhufvud, A. (1999), 'Mr. Keynes and the moderns', in L. Pasinetti and B. Schefold (eds), *The Impact of Keynes on Economics in the 20th Century*, Cheltenham, UK and Northampton, MA, USA: Edward Elgar, pp. 16–35.

Loasby, B.J. (1978), 'Whatever happened to Marshall's theory of value?', *Scottish Journal of Political Economy*, **25**, 1–12.

Macgregor, D.H. ([1906] 1938), *Industrial Combination*, Series of Reprints of Scarce Works on Political Economy, No. 1, London: London School of Economics and Political Science.

Marchionatti, R. (1995), 'Keynes and the collapse of the British industry in the 1920s: A microeconomic case against laissez-faire', *Journal of Post Keynesian Economics*, **17**, 427–44.

Marchionatti, R. (2001), 'Sraffa and the criticism of Marshall during the 1920s', in T. Cozzi and R. Marchionatti (eds), *Piero Sraffa's Political Economy. A Centenary Estimate*, London: Routledge, pp. 43–80.

Marcuzzo, M.C., N. Naldi and E. Sanfilippo (2008), 'Cambridge as a *Place* in economics', *History of Political Economy*, **40**, 569–93.

Marshall, A. (1898), 'Distribution and exchange', *Economic Journal*, **8**, 37–59.

Marshall, A. ([1919] 1927), *Industry and Trade*, 3rd edn, London: Macmillan.

Marshall, A. (1920), *Principles of Economics*, 8th edn, London: Macmillan & Co.

Marshall, A. (1923), *Money, Credit and Commerce*, London: Macmillan.

Medema, S.G. (2006), 'Welfare economics: Marshallian welfare economics and the economic welfare of Marshall', in Raffaelli, Becattini and Dardi (2006), pp. 634–47.

Metcalfe, J.S. (2006), 'Evolutionary economics', in Raffaelli, Becattini and Dardi (2006), pp. 651–7.

Moggridge, D.E. (1992), *Maynard Keynes. An Economist Biography*, London: Routledge.

Moss, S. (1984), 'The history of the theory of the firm from Marshall to Robinson and Chamberlin: The source of positivism in economics', *Economica*, **51**, 307–18.

O'Donnell, R.M. (1989), *Keynes: Philosophy, Economics and Politics*, London: Macmillan.

Pethick-Lawrence, F.W. (1899), *Local Variation in Wages*, London and New York: Longmans, Green & Co.

Pigou, A.C. (1905), *Principles and Methods of Industrial Peace*, London: Macmillan.

Pigou, A.C. (1912), *Wealth and Welfare*, London: Macmillan.

Pigou, A.C. (1920), *The Economics of Welfare*, London: Macmillan.

Pigou, A.C. (ed.) (1925), *Memorials of Alfred Marshall*, London: Macmillan.

Pigou, A.C. (1951), 'Some aspects of welfare economics', *American Economic Review*, **41** (3), 287–302.

Prendergast, R. (1992), 'Increasing returns and competitive equilibrium: The content and development of Marshall's theory', *Cambridge Journal of Economics*, **16**, 447–62.

Raffaelli, T. (1998), 'L'economia come "scienza morale" nella concezione della scuola di Cambridge', in P. Barrotta and T. Raffaelli, *Epistemologia ed economia. Il ruolo della filosofia nella storia del pensiero economico*, Torino: UTET, pp. 124–77.

Raffaelli, T. (2000), 'Keynes's apprenticeship with Marshall in 1905', *History of Economic Ideas*, **8**, 121–52.

Raffaelli, T. (2001) 'On Marshall's representative firm: A comment on Marchionatti', in T. Cozzi and R. Marchionatti (eds), *Piero Sraffa's Political Economy. A Centenary Estimate*, London: Routledge, pp. 123–7.

Raffaelli, T. (2003), *Marshall's Evolutionary Economics*, London and New York: Routledge.

Raffaelli, T. (2004), 'Whatever happened to Marshall's industrial economics?', *European Journal of the History of Economic Thought*, **11**, 209–29.

Raffaelli, T. (2006), 'Keynes and philosophers', in R. Backhouse and B. Bateman (eds), *The Cambridge Companion to Keynes*, Cambridge and New York: Cambridge University Press, pp. 160–79.

Raffaelli, T., G. Becattini and M. Dardi (eds) (2006), *The Elgar Companion to Alfred Marshall*, Cheltenham, UK and Northampton, MA, USA: Edward Elgar.

Robbins, L. (1928), 'The representative firm', *Economic Journal*, **38**, 387–404.

Robertson, D.H. (1915), *A Study of Industrial Fluctuations. An Enquiry into the Character and Causes of the so-called Cyclical Movements of Trade*, London: P.S. King & Son, Ltd.

Robertson, D.H. (1924), 'Those empty boxes', *Economic Journal*, **34**, 16–21.

Robertson, D.H. (1928), *The Control of Industry*, Cambridge: Cambridge University Press.

Robinson, E.A.G. ([1931] 1935), *The Structure of Competitive Industry*, London: Nisbet & Co., Cambridge: Cambridge University Press.

Robinson, E.A.G. (1934), 'The problem of management and the size of firms', *Economic Journal*, **44**, 242–57.

Robinson, E.A.G. (1972), 'John Maynard Keynes: Economist, author, statesman', *Economic Journal*, **82**, 531–46.

Robinson, E.A.G. (1990), 'Cambridge economics in the post-Marshallian period', in R. McWilliams Tullberg (ed.), *Alfred Marshall in Retrospect*, Aldershot, UK and Brookfield, US: Edward Elgar, pp. 1–7.

Robinson, J. ([1933] 1965), *The Economics of Imperfect Competition*, London: Macmillan.

Samuelson, P. (1967), 'The monopolistic competition revolution', in R.E. Kuenne (ed.), *Monopolistic Competition Theory, Studies in Impact. Essays in Honor of Edward H. Chamberlin*, New York: John Wiley, pp. 105–38.

Sanger, C.P. (1895), 'The fair number of apprentices in a trade', *Economic Journal*, **5**, 616–36.

Sargant Florence, P. (1933), *The Logic of Industrial Organization*, London: Kegan Paul.

Sargant Florence, P. (1934), 'The problem of management and the size of firms', *Economic Journal*, **44**, 723–9.

Schumpeter, J.A. (1928), 'The instability of capitalism', *Economic Journal*, **38**, 361–86.

Schumpeter, J.A. (1954), *History of Economic Analysis*, London: Allen & Unwin.

Shackle, G.L.S. (1967), *The Years of High Theory. Invention and Tradition in Economic Thought*, Cambridge: Cambridge University Press.

Shove, G.F. (1930), 'The representative firm and increasing returns', *Economic Journal*, **40**, 94–116.

Skidelsky, R. (1983), *John Maynard Keynes. Hopes Betrayed 1883–1920*, London: Macmillan.

Sraffa, P. (1925), 'Sulle relazioni fra costo e quantità prodotta', *Annali di economia*, **2**, 15–65.

Sraffa, P. (1926), 'The laws of returns under competitive conditions', *Economic Journal*, **36**, 535–50.

Whitaker, J.K. (1990), 'What happened to the second volume of the *Principles*? The thorny path to Marshall's last books', in J.K. Whitaker (ed.), *Centenary Essays on Alfred Marshall*, Cambridge: Cambridge University Press, pp. 193–222.

Whitaker, J.K. (ed.) (1996), *The Correspondence of Alfred Marshall, Economist*, 3 vols, Cambridge: Cambridge University Press.

Young, A.A. (1913), 'Pigou's Wealth and Welfare', *Quarterly Journal of Economics*, **27**, 672–86.

Young, A.A. (1928), 'Increasing returns and economic progress', *Economic Journal*, **38**, 527–42.

4. Marshall and Marshallian economics in Britain

Keith Tribe

In late 1884 Henry Fawcett died and was succeeded as professor of Political Economy at the University of Cambridge by Alfred Marshall. Within a few years he had turned Cambridge into the leading British centre for research and teaching in economics. In time, this primacy was challenged by the expansion of the London School of Economics (LSE) in the 1920s, and the re-emergence in the 1930s of Oxford as a major centre. For Oxford had previously been at the heart of British economics in the 1880s; William Ashley, Edwin Cannan, Langford Price, E.C.K. Gonner and W.A.S. Hewins were all 'Oxford men', and the Oxford extension movement played an important part in introducing the principles of political economy to classes up and down the country. Marshall had moved to Oxford from Bristol in 1883 as successor to Arnold Toynbee at Balliol College, pre-positioning himself as the next Oxford candidate for the Drummond Chair of Political Economy, then held by Bonamy Price, aged 76. But Bonamy Price lived on in post until 1888; and to everyone's surprise, he was predeceased by Henry Fawcett, who died suddenly of pneumonia aged 51. And so Alfred Marshall ended up professor of Political Economy in Cambridge, not Oxford; and it was Cambridge, not Oxford, that became the platform for his plan to transform economics into a university discipline. Marshall's attempt to persuade his former pupil, John Neville Keynes, to replace him at Balliol and therefore secure both centres for Marshallianism quickly foundered upon Keynes's reluctance to play a leading role on Marshall's ambitions (Deane 2001, pp. 125–6).

The teaching of political economy in British universities and colleges was in the 1880s a minor part of a broader curriculum. The University of London BA, the most generally accessible qualification, included political economy as a minor optional subject – this was what had supported William Stanley Jevons's classes in Manchester in the 1860s and at University College, London in the 1870s. Likewise the Indian Civil Service examinations included some elements of political economy, which sustained some of the college teaching in Oxford, for example. Shortly after 1900 a variable amount of economics was being taught in the faculties of Commerce in Liverpool, Birmingham and Manchester. At Oxford and Cambridge political economy was included within Greats and History degrees, and the Moral Sciences and History, respectively. An independent degree in Philosophy, Politics and Economics was not initiated in Oxford until 1920. The foundation of the Cambridge Economics Tripos in 1903 represented therefore the first three-year undergraduate degree course in Britain (Tribe 2008), or in the world for that matter. The design of economics curricula around the world was consequently oriented to this original Cambridge model, which represented the culmination of Marshall's efforts on behalf of his subject.

There is of course more to a university discipline than teaching a subject to young men and women. Marshall clearly 'had a plan' which is evidenced by his move first to Oxford, and then by his quick departure to Cambridge. Marshall had taken up an interest in political economy in the later 1860s, and in 1868 he had been appointed to a St John's College lectureship in the Moral Sciences. A number of his pupils went on to make their mark in economics during the following years, among them H.S. Foxwell, William Cunningham, John Neville Keynes, J. Shield Nicholson and Henry Cunynghame; but this first generation of students remained wedded to an older economics if they did not, like Neville Keynes, abandon the field entirely. The one exception was Mary Paley, whom he met while lecturing to young women who sat, unofficially, for the Moral Sciences Tripos examinations. She took the examination in 1874, returned home to Stamford where she began lecturing on her own account, returning in 1875 to study in Cambridge and collaborate with Marshall on a textbook for University Extension lectures. They married in 1877, and in 1879 *The Economics of Industry* appeared under their joint names, the first English introduction to economics explicitly written for use as a textbook in teaching. During the 1880s this was regularly cited as the main text for Extension courses in Political Economy and for those linked to the University of London BA degree. Two elements of the 'plan' had fused here: the creation of a cohort of young people trained in modern economic principles, and the provision of a textbook that could facilitate such training.

On his marriage Marshall had to surrender the St John's fellowship, and in 1877 he became principal of University College, Bristol, with responsibility for teaching political economy. The latter post was surrendered to Mary after a year, and then in 1881 he resigned from the post of principal, departing for the continent with Mary for a long convalescence. During this period he worked on drafts of the *Principles*, for as yet there was no English text capable of guiding students beyond the elementary outline provided in *The Economics of Industry*. As the *Principles* developed, however, he grew increasingly dissatisfied with the book he had written with Mary, and went on to form the curious opinion that women were unsuited to the study of economics, a prejudice that Mary

Paley bore with fortitude. Women's education, which had been the motivating force for adult and extension teaching in Britain since the 1860s, no longer held its appeal for Marshall. The kind of institutional basis he required for the teaching he considered necessary for a thorough training in economics could, he now thought, be found only in the Oxford and Cambridge Chairs of Political Economy.

While he abandoned his early engagement on behalf of women's education, this in no respect implied a general retreat from teaching into writing and research as the true vocation of the university economist. As soon as he had arrived in Cambridge he let it be known that he would be available at his home Friday afternoons and Saturday mornings 'to give advice and informal instruction: he particularly desires to see those students of the subject who are [not] intending to take it up for examination' (*Cambridge University Reporter*, n. 566, 13 January 1885, p. 321; n. 568, 20 January 1885, p. 365). As a university professor, Marshall was not permitted to give formal supervision to students, his duty was only to lecture; his open invitation to students to visit him at home for informal discussion and borrow his books became a fixed, and very idiosyncratic, part of Marshall's presence in Cambridge, regularly advertised in the *Reporter*.

Although Marshall now had a permanent professorial post and £700 a year, he wanted for students – in contrast to the situation he had left behind in Oxford. He therefore sought to attract the attention of students to the study of economics. In 1886 he established an annual 'Political Economy Prize' to be administered through the Moral Sciences Board. In his letter on 15 March 1886 to the Vice Chancellor he explained his intention as follows:

> The events of our own age are leading all thoughtful men constantly to read and talk on economic problems, especially if they intend to become ministers of religion or are looking forward to a political career. Thus Economics holds a singular position. It is, I think, the only subject of which the unsystematic study in the University exceeds the systematic: the only one which finds a great portion of its ablest and most diligent students among those who are preparing for, or have graduated in, Triposes in which it is not represented. I want to supply an Examination which, by offering public recognition of thorough work, will help to steady and systematise this unsystematic study. (Whitaker 1996, I, p. 204)

This Marshall Prize (later with altered conditions the Adam Smith Prize) was a further brick in his efforts to raise the profile of the subject among 'thoughtful men' – among the prizewinners the most notable was A.W. Flux in 1889, who had been bracketed Senior Wrangler in 1887 (that is, shared the first place among those graduating in the Mathematics Tripos); Flux went on to lay the foundations for the teaching of economics in Manchester before moving to McGill, returning in 1908 to the Board of Trade where he presided over the Census of Production and made a substantial contribution during the interwar period to the organisation of national economic statistics. Importantly, he also wrote the first 'Marshallian' textbook, as we shall see.

Many of the notable students that came to Marshall's attention during this period were, like Flux and the other three winners of the Marshall Prize, not Moral Sciences students. And there were few enough of them in any case – in 1891 ten candidates were classed in Part I and four in Part II of the Moral Sciences Tripos, only a minority of whom read for the paper in Political Economy. The numbers taking the papers in Political Economy for the ordinary degree were likewise very modest, and while Marshall did during the 1890s manage to recruit some enthusiastic students to the study of economics – among them Sydney Chapman (founder of the Manchester Faculty of Commerce), John Clapham (Professor of Economics at Leeds, later of Economic History in Cambridge), and D.H. Macgregor (successor to Clapham at Leeds, later Drummond Professor at Oxford as successor to Edgeworth) – there was a want of strong and steady demand for tuition in economics at Cambridge. Marshall would continue his efforts in this direction, but in the meantime he was able to divert his energies into more immediately productive developments: the publication in 1890 of his *Principles of Economics*, together with its subsequent editions, and the formation of the British Economic Association (BEA), chartered in 1902 as the Royal Economic Society.

In the early 1880s Foxwell had sketched a plan for the establishment of a national economic association, but he lacked the institutional leverage to translate the plan into reality. In 1890–91 Marshall was President of Section F of the British Association, and he took advantage of the connections this put at his disposal to propose in April 1890 to the Committee that they support the foundation of an association and the creation of an associated journal 'somewhat similar in character to the American Quarterly'. But the *Quarterly Journal of Economics* (1887–) was linked to Harvard, and the *Journal of Political Economy* (1892–) would be linked to Chicago. Marshall argued against such affiliation and for a national journal open to all schools of thought, arguing that a national association was required to support such a journal. A large public meeting bringing together civil servants, City men, bankers, teachers and the still small number of 'economists' was held in London in November 1890, and a committee elected to run the journal, with Edgeworth as editor. An 11 member executive committee was also formed, composed, unlike the membership, overwhelmingly of 'economists', one of whom was Marshall (Tribe 2001).

The *Economic Journal* first appeared in March 1891 and duly represented in its articles, notes, comments, reports from foreign correspondents and book reviews the contemporary international condition of economic science. Today the Royal Economic Society holds an annual conference and engages in a number of initiatives to further the cause of economics, operating as something approaching a professional association. These are later developments: there was no national conference of economists in Britain until the Association of University Economists began annual meetings in the mid-1920s, and the diversity of the BEA's membership militated against the adoption of any particular position. But this was its purpose – not to take a position, but to secure the functioning of the *Economic Journal* as a periodical open to all reasonable argument in the field of economics. This of course presupposed that one knew reasonable from unreasonable argument, which in turn assumed some systematic knowledge of economic principles.

The publication of Marshall's *Principles* in 1890 provided a modern foundation for such systematic knowledge, and the *Economic Journal* consequently became a vehicle for the propagation of Marshallian economics, in the absence of any coherent alternative. The pages of the *Journal* were open to dissenters – chief among them being William Cunningham, a former student of Marshall's who had indeed read Moral Sciences, graduating joint Senior with Maitland in 1872. From 1891 to 1897 Cunningham was Tooke Professor of Political Economy at King's College London, but the duties involved here were occasional. In Cambridge he was Vicar of Great St Mary's from 1887 to 1908, an advocate of a historical economics and agitator against the creation of the undergraduate programme of economics that Marshall sought to develop. Marshall argued against Cunningham in the pages of the *Economic Journal*, and in the various Cambridge committees related to teaching and examination. Cunningham's open opposition to, and incomprehension of, the principles of the new economics developing internationally during the 1890s was widely aired. It is sometimes suggested that it was here that a fracture developed between a formal Marshallian economics on the one hand, and a new economic history on the other. Certainly William Ashley shared many of Cunningham's reservations, while in the 1920s John Clapham's own firm move into economic history would appear to support this. But this would be to misread the stakes, and misunderstand just what kind of economics Marshall was promoting before the Great War.

Marshall had plenty of time for economic history, and in the first edition of the *Principles* Book I presented a historical survey of the development of economies and of the means to understand them. Economic history, as then understood, came to a halt in the early nineteenth century, a position on which Marshall was in agreement with Cunningham. Economic organisation and institutions structured and moulded economic activity; but to understand economic activity in the present one needed an understanding of modern economic organisation, not of economic history. Marshall and Cunningham agreed on the former but disagreed on the latter. Marshall maintained that the place of economic history was in deepening understanding of the manifold ways in which economic activity could be so moulded; but it provided no key to an understanding of contemporary economic activity. The key to this lay in modern economic analysis. But unlike his continental counterparts, notably

Böhm-Bawerk and von Wieser, Marshall sought to emphasise the continuities between his analytical framework and that of his predecessors, especially Mill and Ricardo. It was for this reason that Thorstein Veblen coined the term 'neoclassical' to describe the tenor of Marshall's work, despite its intrinsic agreement with the work of the Austrians (Veblen 1900, p. 261).

Hence the importance of a modern treatise elaborating the principles of economics which could be placed at the core of an education in modern economic analysis. Two thousand copies of the *Principles* were printed, and sold out within a year of its publication in July 1890 (Groenewegen 1995, p. 435). New editions and reprintings followed until the final eighth edition in 1920, by which time it had long been established as the standard exposition of modern economics. The publishing history itself is very complex, since Marshall altered the text for reprintings between formal new editions, the text being substantially reordered and revised (Whitaker 1988, pp. 60–64). But two general observations can be made about the work. Firstly, what appeared in 1890 was Volume 1 of a two-part work, covering broadly what would today be treated as microeconomics – demand (Book III); production (Book IV); equilibrium conditions of supply and demand, including a treatment of monopoly (Book V); cost of production (Book VI); and distribution and exchange (Book VII). Despite Marshall's early study of Cournot the treatment of monopoly is contrasted simply to competition. Marshall never succeeded in working up the second volume dealing with industry, foreign trade and banking: these were published as *Industry and Trade* (1919) and *Money, Credit and Commerce* (1923).

Secondly, the treatment of these topics, especially in the later two volumes, is discursive, the underlying mathematical framework being placed in an appendix to the *Principles* that could be studied on its own. Not until the later 1950s was this approach decisively abandoned with Loudon Ryan's *Price Theory* (1958). The more concise presentations of economic principles that appeared from mid-century owed more to Marshall's own *Elements of the Economics of Industry* (1892), a work that followed the same plan as the *Principles* but which was just over half as long and in a smaller format. This work was intended to entirely displace the earlier *The Economics of Industry* as a student textbook, and it quickly found a place at the head of university and college reading lists as a more accessible version of the larger *Principles*. As noted above, Marshall's student A.W. Flux is credited with writing the first explicitly Marshallian textbook (Flux 1904). While this first edition appears to have made little impact and is today very rare in university libraries, there was a revised second edition and it is this version that is most commonly found today. Two other influential early textbooks were produced by former students: Shield Nicholson's *Elements of Political Economy* in 1903, which was if anything a more 'Millian' version of Marshall; and Sydney Chapman's *Outlines of Political Economy* of 1911, which recapitulated the structure of

Principles and then moved on to deal with international trade, money and public economics, pulling together a treatment of Marshallian principles which Marshall was no longer capable of producing. Through these and many other publications the arguments advanced in Marshall's *Principles*, together with its logical architecture, were represented to future generations of British students as the basic elements of economic reasoning.

Which brings us back to Marshall's dissatisfaction with the teaching of economics in Cambridge. The doggedness with which Marshall furthered his wish that economics be granted a separate three-year course of honours study – be made a Tripos – alienated many of his colleagues, especially since there was no sign of any strong student demand for such a course of study. Eventually he got his way, on condition that economics be struck out of the syllabuses of History and Moral Sciences. The new Tripos began work in 1903, at that time the two-year Part I examination being held at the end of the second year. As usual with Cambridge teaching, there was no specified syllabus, nor did lectures define the course; instead the intentions of the Tripos's teachers have to be inferred from readings lists and examination papers. Part I was clearly introductory, and included only one specifically economics paper in the examination out of four, including an essay on a set subject. Part II, which could be taken without having completed Part I, had nine papers, with four compulsory papers directed to economics and a minimum of two other papers, among which were two 'law and economics' papers. The balance was modified in 1910, but it is plain that the Tripos presented students with quite the most thorough training in economics then available (Tribe 2000). Very few students were exposed to this, however: the first examination in 1905 had ten successful candidates, falling back to four, eight and eight in the three succeeding years. Only in the 1920s did numbers pick up and consistently exceed 30 candidates each year in Part I; and equally important was the smaller subset who, having completed a Part I in economics, went on to complete the more demanding Part II. For many years the best Part II results were gained by students who had not done Part I, which indicates that the Tripos was far from an unalloyed success in its early years. All told, up until mid-century the history of the Economics Tripos was a very mixed story, with 60 per cent of Part I students receiving third class degrees in the 1930s, and the number of first and upper seconds in the later 1940s more or less equalling the number of eminent economists employed in Cambridge by faculty or college.

The prime function of the Tripos from the 1920s to the 1940s was to generate employment for Cambridge economists, although this was clearly not the intention. Elsewhere, at LSE, Oxford, Manchester, Glasgow or Edinburgh, the occasional nature of teaching in economics made it difficult to recruit specialised teachers of economics. During the interwar years economics was widely taught, but outside LSE, Cambridge and Oxford as part of a broadly

commercial curriculum. At Oxford of course economics was a variable
component of a tripartite degree; and at LSE the BSc (Econ.) was in effect a
social science degree with variable economic content. Only Cambridge had
a dedicated three-year degree in Economics and while student numbers for this
degree were modest, graduates could at least plausibly claim to have had the
kind of grounding in economic analysis that Marshall saw as the *sine qua non*
of a 'trained economist'. Marshall's own students, and graduates of the Tripos,
headed many of the new departments of economics and commerce. Macgregor
graduated in Moral Sciences in 1901; he was Professor in Leeds (1908–19), in
Manchester (1919–21); and Drummond Professor (1921–45). Sargant Florence
gained a first in Part II in 1914 and was Professor of Commerce in Birmingham
from 1929 to 1955. Alexander Henderson, graduating with a first in Part II in
1936, was Professor of Economic Theory in Manchester by 1949. H.O. Meredith
graduated from History in Cambridge in 1901, but clearly knew sufficient
economics to be appointed first lecturer in Economic History and Commerce
in Manchester (1905–08), then Girdler's lecturer in Cambridge in succession
to Pigou (1908–11), and then professor of Economics at Queen's Belfast from
1911 to 1945. There were also those Tripos graduates who, once they had arrived
in Cambridge, hardly ever left it again: the Robinsons Austin and Joan, Gerald
Shove and Dennis Robertson among many others. And of course not least John
Maynard Keynes, graduating as twelfth Wrangler in 1905 and taking supervision
from Marshall that year, became lecturer in Economics in Cambridge in 1908,
and later as a fellow of King's College naturally the most famous pupil that
Marshall ever had.

Marshall saw the Tripos through its first full cycle and then resigned in the
course of the second, in 1908. He was succeeded, among much controversy,
by his star pupil, Arthur Pigou. It is widely acknowledged that Pigou was
spiritually destroyed by his experiences in ambulance units in Italy and France
during the Great War, so that he subsequently played a very minor role in the
work of the Faculty right up to his retirement in 1944. But his published work
had an immediate resonance, even if in the *General Theory* he is caricatured as
a representative of a classical economics. Pigou's early articles in the *Economic
Journal* shine out: they are all around ten pages (unlike Edgeworth's multipart
pieces), and deal succinctly and formally with a specific problem. In this he
prefigured the standard for contributions to economic periodicals that became
the custom decades later. Secondly, he not only invented welfare economics
in 1912 with the publication of *Wealth and Welfare*, but in its revised 1920
version, re-emphasised a specifically Marshallian theme:

> The complicated analyses which economists endeavour to carry through are not
> mere gymnastic. They are instruments for the bettering of human life. The misery
> and squalor that surrounds us, the dying fire of hope in many millions of European
> homes, the injurious luxury of some wealthy families, the terrible uncertainty

overshadowing many families of the poor – these evils are too plain to be ignored. By the knowledge that our science seeks it is possible that they may be restrained. Out of the darkness light! To search for it is the task, to find it, perhaps, the prize, which the 'dismal science of Political Economy' offers to those who face its discipline. (Pigou 1920, p. vi)

This sentiment runs straight back to Marshall's Inaugural of February 1885, which closes with the following peroration:

It will be my most cherished ambition, my highest endeavour to do what with my poor ability and my limited strength I may, to raise the numbers of those, whom Cambridge, the great mother of strong men, sends out into the world with cool heads but warm hearts, willing to give some at least of their best powers to grappling with the social suffering around them; resolved not to rest content till they have done what in them lies to discover how far it is possible to open up to all the material means of a refined and noble life. (Marshall 1885, p. 57)

This specifically Marshallian sentiment has of course long since disappeared from modern economics. When during the 1990s I conducted a series of interviews with senior economists, many of whom had begun their careers in the 1930s, and some of them in Cambridge, I asked as a matter of routine why they had taken an interest in such a new subject as economics. The response was uniform: because the unemployment and depression of the 1930s had wrought such misery and hardship, and the study of economics seemed a constructive step to take towards the amelioration of want. Maynard Keynes shared this concern, as he makes clear in 'Economic possibilities for our grandchildren' (1972).

But this aspect of Marshall's legacy was broadly forgotten by the 1930s among faculty and college staff. However frequently younger Cambridge economists of the 1930s and after invoked the mantle of Marshall, and laid claim to be his heirs in the application of his *organon*, the box of instruments for the analysis of economic problems, the point of so doing was lost on them. Harry Johnson's withering critique of postwar Cambridge economics (E.S. Johnson and H.G. Johnson 1978), to the effect that collegiate life and the individual supervision of very large numbers of Part I students with little interest in economics cultivated an adversarial style of argument and an insularity born of an assumption that Cambridge was the centre of Marshall's heritage – this is certainly a hypothesis which finds support in the somewhat dismal record of the first 50 years of the Tripos results.

REFERENCES

Chapman, S. (1911), *Outlines of Political Economy*, London: Longmans, Green & Co.

Deane, P. (2001), *The Life and Times of J. Neville Keynes. A Beacon in the Tempest*, Cheltenham, UK and Northampton, MA, USA: Edward Elgar.

Flux, A.W. (1904), *Economic Principles: An Introductory Study*, London: Methuen.

Groenewegen, P.D. (1995), *A Soaring Eagle: Alfred Marshall 1842–1924*, Aldershot, UK and Brookfield, US: Edward Elgar.

Johnson, E.S. and H.G. Johnson (1978), *The Shadow of Keynes. Understanding Keynes, Cambridge and Keynesian Economics*, Oxford: Basil Blackwell.

Keynes, J.M. (1972), 'Economic possibilities for our grandchildren', in *Essays in Persuasion, Collected Writings of John Maynard Keynes*, vol. 9, London: Macmillan, pp. 321–32.

Marshall, A. (1885), *The Present Position of Economics. An Inaugural Lecture*, London: Macmillan.

Marshall, A. (1892), *Elements of the Economics of Industry, being the first volume of Elements of Economics*, London: Macmillan.

Marshall, A. (1919), *Industry and Trade*, 3rd edn, London: Macmillan.

Marshall, A. (1920), *Principles of Economics*, 8th edn, London: Macmillan.

Marshall, A. (1923), *Money, Credit and Commerce*, London: Macmillan.

Nicholson, J.S. (1903), *Elements of Political Economy*, London: Adam & Charles Black.

Pigou, A.C. (1920), *The Economics of Welfare*, London: Macmillan.

Ryan, W.J.L. (1958), *Price Theory*, London: Macmillan.

Tribe, K. (2000), 'The Cambridge Economics Tripos 1903–55 and the training of economists', *Manchester School*, **68**, 222–48.

Tribe, K. (2001), 'Economic societies in Great Britain and Ireland', in M. Augello and M. Guidi (eds), *The Spread of Political Economy and the Professionalisation of Economists*, London: Routledge, pp. 32–52.

Tribe, K. (2008), 'Britain, economics in the 20th century', in S.N. Durlauf and L.E. Blume (eds), *The New Palgrave Dictionary of Economics*, 2nd edn, Basingstoke: Palgrave Macmillan, vol. 1, pp. 552–62. Online: http://www.dictionaryofeconomics.com/article?id=pde2008_B00032.

Veblen, T. (1900), 'The preconceptions of economic science. III', *Quarterly Journal of Economics*, **14**, 240–69.

Whitaker, J.K. (1988), 'Editing Alfred Marshall', in D.E. Moggridge (ed.), *Editing Modern Economists*, New York: AMS Press, pp. 43–65.

Whitaker, J.K. (ed.) (1996), *The Correspondence of Alfred Marshall, Economist*, vol. 1: *Climbing, 1863–1890*, Cambridge: Cambridge University Press.

PART III

Marshall in English-speaking countries

5.   Marshall in Canada

Robert W. Dimand and Robin Neill

According to John Maynard Keynes (1956), Marshall's important publications came long after his influence was established in an oral tradition: *Principles of Economics* in 1890 (8th edn in 1920), *Industry and Trade* in 1919, and *Money, Credit and Commerce* in 1923. This view has merit, but needs qualification. *The Economics of Industry (*1879), written jointly with his wife Mary Paley Marshall, came almost as soon as Marshall's interest turned from mathematics to political economy, and it was an introductory text used by many. *The Pure Theory of Trade and the Pure Theory of Domestic Values*, the substance of which was revised and merged into later works, were printed for private circulation in 1879. So publication came early in Marshall's career. Further, *Industry and Trade*, though published in 1919, treated the complex historical conditions of economic activity on which Marshall's much earlier published advice to governments was based. In the *Principles*, these considerations were suppressed in favour of theory, but they were already an element in Marshall's contribution to economics in the last two decades of the nineteenth century. *Money, Credit and Commerce* (1923), coming long after he had retired and based in part on manuscripts drafted in the 1870s, added little to his lectures (before his 1908 retirement from the Cambridge Chair) or to his testimony before official enquiries. It is a nice question, then, whether Marshall's principal publications or his broader, largely oral, contribution was the more important channel of his influence. In short, when accounting for Marshall's influence anywhere, and certainly in Canada, it is necessary to make a distinction between the economics of Marshall, as taught in his lectures, and Marshallian economics as derived from his later publications.

In Canada the sources of Marshall's doctrine, the channels through which his contributions to the discipline were received, were even more diffuse. Most Canadian economists of the first three decades of the twentieth century earned their postgraduate degrees in the United States. The list of Canadian economists who belonged to the American Economic Association between 1914 and 1928 (there was no Canadian association to which they might have belonged, see Neill 1991, pp. 125–8) indicates that Harvard and Chicago were the schools of choice for (English-speaking) Canadians. The two accounted for 18 Canadian graduates living and teaching in Canada. Cambridge (UK) accounted for three: C.R. Fay, G.E. Jackson and G.I.H. Lloyd, all at the University of Toronto. Scottish universities accounted for four. While the handful of Cambridge graduates was directly influenced by Marshall's writings and the Cambridge oral tradition, the Harvard graduates were exposed to an indirect Marshallian influence through the textbook of Frank Taussig. The most prominent of the Cambridge graduates teaching economics in Canada in the 1920s was Charles Ryle Fay, Professor of Economic History at the University of Toronto from 1921 until he returned to Cambridge as Reader in Economic History in 1930. Fay's historical writings included many admiring citations of Marshall (for example, Fay [1928] 1950, pp. 150–51, 212, 244 n., 391). The first edition of his *Great Britain from Adam Smith to the Present Day* appeared in 1928 while he was teaching in Toronto. It contained only a single mention of Marshall's Cambridge rival, the economic historian Archdeacon William Cunningham (but that mention was also positive).

During the first two decades of the twentieth century, when economics became a subject taught in Canadian universities, basic economics in United States universities was taught from John Bates Clark's *Essentials of Economic Theory* (1907) or Frank W. Taussig's *Principles of Economics* (1911). Clark claimed to have elaborated much of marginal utility theory independently of Marshall, and he made no reference to Marshall in his own text. On the other hand, Marshall's work was cited at every point in Taussig's *Principles of Economics*. These textbooks were also influential in English-speaking Canada, but French-speaking students in Québec learned economics from the principles text of Charles Gide, the teacher of Edouard Montpetit. Montpetit, a Sciences-Po graduate, directed the School of Social, Economic and Political Science at the Université de Montréal in the 1920s (Neill 1991, p. 155).

Marshall's influence in Canada was the influence of Marshallian economics, rather than the influence of Marshall himself. It has to be measured by the extent to which his and similar contributions by other European economists (Schumpeter 1954, p. 839) were taken up in Canada as a result of Marshall's doctrine arriving through whatever channel. It has to be measured by the extent to which Canadian economists accepted certain 'principles' that can be attributed to Marshall. According to J.M. Keynes, these principles would be: (1) the determination and definition of value as a product of supply and demand, that is, as relative scarcity; (2) the determination of total value and price by adjustments at the margin; (3) the importance of structuring time into economics, the concepts of the market period, the short, the long and the very long runs, and the concept of quasi-rent; (4) the concept of consumer surplus; (5) the notions of external and internal economies; and (6) the formal definition of elasticity (Keynes 1956, pp. 76–9).

The index in Neill's history of economics in Canada has only two entries for Marshall. One notes the nature of economics in Canada before Marshall.

The other notes that Marshall did not take the macroeconomic approach that was necessary to envisage the problems of the 1930s. Of course, John Maynard Keynes, a member of the 'Marshall school' (Schumpeter 1954, p. 833), did take a macroeconomic approach, so Keynes's considerable influence in Canada (for example, through his students A.F.W. Plumptre and Robert Bryce) might be categorised as a Marshallian influence, but by the 1930s Keynes regarded himself as in revolt against the 'classical' economics of Marshall and Pigou. Over all, however, Neill's account simply leaves a large gap where the influence of Mashallian economics could have been entered.

There are two principal places in which to look for the influence of Marshallian economics in Canada: the scholarly publications of Canadian economists, and what was taught in the classrooms of Canadian universities. There is little to be found in the first of these places. All who were in fact the founders of economics in Canada during Marshall's most influential period (1890–1930), were historians under the influence of the historical economics of the period and of American institutionalism.

Adam Shortt, W.A. Mackintosh and H.A. Innis can be listed as the founders of economics in Canada. All were economic historians. Shortt was simply a good historian. As Sir John A. Macdonald, Professor at Queen's University in Kingston, Ontario, from 1891 to 1908, Shortt 'continued to use the writings of Smith, Malthus and Mill to provide training in theory' although also making some reference to Bagehot, Brentano, Cairnes, List, Marshall and Marx (Goodwin 1961, p. 162). Mackintosh, the Macdonald Professor of Political and Economic Science at Queen's from 1924, in his later years was not ready to depreciate neoclassical theory (Mackintosh, 1965), but when engaged in government work during World War I he wrote of the principles of economics, '[A]s guides to government policy they are as useless as a yardstick in measuring the cross-section of a hair' (Mackintosh 1918–19, p. 4). Subsequently Mackintosh, like Innis, pioneered the staples approach to the economic history of Canada. O.D. Skelton, who was in some sense the dean of Canadian economists until Innis came into his own in the 1930s, was primarily an economic historian. He allowed that a textbook written by D.A. McGibbon had risen 'above the level of dry bones and dogmatic formulas of past controversies' but he questioned the wisdom of presenting young students with simplified versions of such 'highly controverted material' (Skelton 1925). Innis, who produced nothing but history or such theory as an historian would admit (Fay 1934–37), deplored the 'price approach' in economics. In his view it was ill suited to the conditions of new and developing countries (Neill 1972, pp. 36–7).

The likely place of Marshallian influence, then, was the classroom; Canadian economists, without a formal acceptance of the body of thought and without direct reference to Marshall's publications, were aware of useful elements in then current neoclassical theory.

At the University of Chicago Innis came under the influence of a group of economists who believed that 'the usefulness in an introductory course of building the presentation about the abstract type of value and distribution … has been repeatedly questioned by experienced teachers in economics' (L.C. Marshall 1923, pp. v–vi). The group at Chicago, L.C. Marshall, Chester Wright and James Field, wrote texts based on case studies of economic activity. They were used in place of 'authoritative statements based on abstract laws'. Innis's first two books, *The Fur Trade of Canada* and the two volume *Select Documents in Canadian Economic History* that he composed with the historian Arthur Lower, were virtual additions to the series *Materials for the Study of Elementary Economics* produced by the Chicago group (Neill 1972, pp. 27–8).

W.A. Mackintosh, who studied at Harvard and depreciated Chicago as a 'place for economics', asserted that most United States economists had studied in Germany under the German historical school of economics. 'Comparatively few went to Cambridge which was also much more difficult for Canadians than Oxford'. In the United States 'Taussig was the senior of the economists who had done his training wholly in the US. Yet his masters were really Marshall and the Austrians whose theories he considered he had harmonised in his *Principles* published in 1911 or 1912'. In the personal note from which these citations are drawn Mackintosh wrote:

> It has occurred to me that you might pursue your quest a bit further sometime by looking up the use of textbooks in Canadian Universities. It would show a great preponderance of U.S. texts almost throughout the period and a predominance of Taussig's *Principles* to about the middle of the twenties. (Mackintosh 1965)

There was, then, a Marshallian influence, primarily through Taussig's textbook, but also in the person of one undeniable Marshallian who taught in Canada in the first decade of the twentieth century. Alfred W. Flux, a product of Cambridge and influenced by Marshall directly, wrote the 'first post-Marshallian British textbook' (Eatwell, Milgate and Newman 1987, II, p. 395) while teaching as the inaugural Dow Professor of Political Economy at McGill in Montreal between 1901 and 1908. Flux had studied at Marshall's own college, St John's, and was elected a fellow there in 1889, two years after being bracketed first (that is, tied for Senior Wrangler) on the Mathematical Tripos (on which Marshall had been Second Wrangler two decades before). In his textbook, Flux described Marshall as 'the teacher to whom he [Flux] owes his chief guidance in economic study' (quoted by Goodwin 1961, p. 184). On leaving McGill he returned to Britain to spend the rest of his career as a statistician at the Board of Trade. According to Craufurd Goodwin (1961, p. 184), 'Canadians were neither a stimulating nor receptive audience for an economic theorist, and Flux made little impact either upon McGill or upon the country's economics'. His successor as Dow professor, the noted Canadian humorist Stephen Leacock, was trained as a political scientist, not an economist.

William Ashley, founding Head of the Department of Political Economy at the University of Toronto from 1888 to 1892, was an English historical economist who insisted in his inaugural lecture that classical economic theories had only 'a relative truth' and that laissez-faire was no longer acceptable as a general principle. Had he felt otherwise, he would not have been appointed as professor, because the provincial government feared that a classical or neoclassical economic theorist would use the professorship to preach free trade (Drummond 1983, p. 21). James Mavor, Ashley's successor, was a product of the University of Glasgow and primarily an economic historian. He contributed a text, *Applied Economics*, which, according to one reviewer (Philips 1914) was a melange of theory and history not in the Marshallian mould. Mavor's memoirs (1923, II, p. 230) contain one passing mention of 'my dear friend of many years, Professor Alfred Marshall, the doyen of the economic world', but Marshall had little if any influence on Mavor as an economist. Ian Drummond (1983, p. 35) reports that Mavor's lectures in 1892–93 on value, rent and interest 'revealed that he had read Jevons and the Austrians, although it is far from clear that he had read Marshall'. One might have expected to find more Marshallian influence in the works of Vincent Bladen, who taught economics at Toronto for more than half a century from 1921. Bladen, as an historian of economic thought, discussed Marshall's contribution incisively and at length (Bladen 1941, 1974, pp. 358–404), but his *Introduction to Political Economy* (3rd ed., 1956) was a descriptive work about the Canadian economy, displaying no resemblance to Marshall's *Principles*.

Textbooks were written by Canadians for Canadian schools. S.A. Cudmore's *Economics for Canadian Students* (1912) was a lesson book for Shaw's correspondence courses. Ralph E. Freeman in his *Economics for Canadians* (1928) made some use of neoclassical theory, including diagrams to explain the principles of economics and equilibrium prices. D.A. MacGibbon (1924), the only United States-trained Canadian economist to produce a textbook before World War II, accomplished his task without using the word 'utility'.

It is easy to conclude that on the whole the influence of even Marshallian economics was diffuse and weak in Canada before Keynesian Marshallian economics appeared on the scene. The six 'principles' that Keynes found to be original in Marshall's conceptualisation of economics could be found scattered throughout, but they do not appear in the forefront of economics in Canada between 1890 and 1930.

REFERENCES

Bladen, V.W. (1941), 'Mill to Marshall: The conversion of the economists', in *The Tasks of Economic History, Journal of Economic History, Supplement* to vol. **1**, 17–29.

Bladen, V.W. (1956), *An Introduction to Political Economy*, 3rd edn, Toronto: University of Toronto Press.

Bladen, V.W. (1974), *From Adam Smith to Maynard Keynes: The Heritage of Political Economy*, Toronto: University of Toronto Press.

Clark, J.B. ([1907] 1968), *Essentials of Economic Theory*, New York: Augustus M. Kelley.

Cudmore, S.A. (1912), *Economics for Canadian Students*, Toronto: Shaw Correspondence School.

Drummond, I.M. (1983), *Political Economy at the University of Toronto: A History of the Department, 1888–1982*, Toronto: University of Toronto Press.

Eatwell, J., M. Milgate and P. Newman (eds) (1987), *The New Palgrave: A Dictionary of Economics*, London: Macmillan.

Fay, C.R. ([1928] 1950), *Great Britain from Adam Smith to the Present Day: An Economic and Social Survey*, 5th edn, London: Longmans.

Fay, C.R. (1934–37), 'The Toronto school of economics', *Economic History*, **3**, 168–71.

Freeman, R.E. (1928), *Economics for Canadians*, Toronto: Pitman.

Goodwin, Craufurd D.W. (1961), *Canadian Economic Thought: The Political Economy of a Developing Nation, 1814–1914*, Durham, NC: Duke University Press.

Keynes, J.M. (1956), *Essays and Sketches in Biography*, New York: Meridian.

MacGibbon, D.A. (1924), *An Introduction to Economics for Canadian Readers*, Toronto: Macmillan.

Mackintosh, W.A. (1918–19), 'Economics, prices, and the war', *Bulletin of the Departments of History and of Political and Economic Science in Queen's University*, 30, 1–15, Kingston: Queen's University.

Mackintosh, W.A. (1965), *Personal Correspondence with Robin Neill*, Kingston: Queen's University.

Marshall, A. ([1879] 1974), *The Pure Theory of Foreign Trade [and] the Pure Theory of Domestic Values*, Clifton: Augustus M. Kelley.

Marshall, A. ([1890] 1964), *Principles of Economics* (8th edn, 1920), London: Macmillan.

Marshall, A. ([1919] 1970), *Industry and Trade*, 4th edn, New York: Augustus M. Kelley.

Marshall, A. ([1923] 1965), *Money, Credit and Commerce*, New York: Augustus M. Kelley.

Marshall, A. and M. Paley Marshall (1879), *The Economics of Industry*, London: Macmillan.

Marshall, L.C. (1923), *Our Economic Organization*, New York: Macmillan.

Mavor, J. (1923), *My Windows on the Street of the World*, 2 vols, Toronto and London: Dent.

Neill, R. (1972), *A New Theory of Value: The Canadian Economics of Harold Adams Innis*, Toronto: University of Toronto Press.

Neill, R. (1991), *A History of Canadian Economic Thought*, London and New York: Routledge.

Philips, K. (1914), 'Review of J. Mavor, *Applied Economics*', *University Magazine*, **13**, 460–70.

Schumpeter J.A. (1954), *History of Economic Analysis*, Oxford and New York: Oxford University Press.

Skelton, O.D. (1925), 'Review of *An Introduction to Economics for Canadian Readers*', *Canadian Historical Review*, **6**, 87.

Taussig, F.W. ([1911] 1939), *Principles of Economics*, 4th edn, New York: Macmillan.

6. The reception of Marshall in the United States

Roger E. Backhouse, Bradley W. Bateman and Steven G. Medema

INTRODUCTION

In analysing the spread of Marshallian economics, the United States represents a unique case. It was an English-speaking country with a substantial economics profession, but without colonial ties to Britain. It also was free of the influence of Marshall's Cambridge position and the dominance that he exerted over economics in England. John Stuart Mill's *Principles* (1848) had been widely used and, as much if not more than in Britain, was becoming dated. Furthermore, Marshall himself had extensive contacts with American economics. In the summer of 1875, using a legacy from an uncle, he spent four months touring the United States, meeting with American economists and observing American industry, as described by Groenewegen (1995, pp. 193–203; see also Whitaker 1975, sections III.4 and V.3). He stayed at Harvard and had a weekend in Yale, meeting with David Wells, William Graham Sumner and Francis Amasa Walker, as well as with Henry Carey, by then very much a member of an older generation. Moreover, what he learned about American politics and industry on this visit was important to his intellectual development. It strengthened his belief in free trade, convincing him of the importance of what would now be considered public-choice arguments against protection and reinforced his belief in individualism and the importance of human character (Groenewegen 1995, pp. 202–3). These were attitudes that should have resonated with the concerns of the well-established academic American economists in 1875, for they were virtually all advocates of free trade and took an individualistic approach to economics. For the younger generation of economists just beginning to return from their graduate training in Germany, however, Marshall's policy concerns might not have resonated so well, for they were more interested in the possibilities of State intervention in the economy and much less taken with individualism.

This was, however, only the starting point in Marshall's American contacts, and it turns out that he was well respected by both camps of American economists.

In the 1880s he engaged in correspondence with Walker, John Bates Clark and Richard T. Ely. (This information is based on the letters in Whitaker 1996. There may of course be others whose correspondence has not survived.) This list broadened in the 1890s to include Frank Taussig, his most frequent correspondent, Edwin Seligman and Simon Newcomb, whilst in the twentieth century he also had exchanges with Arthur Hadley, Jacob Hollander, Irving Fisher and H.L. Moore. Thus, Marshall had contact with economists of all stripes. This wide appeal may reflect Marshall's care in his *Principles* to include historical and evolutionary analysis alongside the marginalist analysis, which would have appealed to those trained in Germany.

Dorothy Ross (1990, p. 174)) has argued that the success of Marshall's *Principles* was determined by the fact that it presented a unified 'neoclassical paradigm, a perfection and completion of the classical model of political economy, rather than an abrogation of it'. While it is true that Marshall's claim that his work represented a continuity with classical economics made it easier for the older American economists to embrace his work, since it helped them to save face, Ross's argument about its 'neoclassical' form misses the mark for at least three reasons. First, it fails to adequately explain the enthusiasm for Marshall and his *Principles* among the younger, German trained economists, as well as among members of the laissez-faire old guard. Ross (1990, p. 173) argues that 'neoclassicism' was eventually able to 'co-opt' the new liberalism of the younger American economists. Whether or not this is true, it ignores the historical basis of the younger economists' interest in marginalism, which is explained below. Second, it is hard to reconcile this account with the fact that many of the younger, progressive economists greatly admired the *Principles* and some, like John R. Commons, even used it for their advanced teaching. Finally, it ignores the enormous variety of marginalist theories, both in the generation of Marshall and J.B. Clark and in the more formal neoclassical theories that emerged in the 1930s (Parts III and IV below draw a sharp contrast between Harvard and Chicago).

Despite Ross's attempt to identify Marshall with the laissez-faire economists because of his status as a leading marginalist, it was, paradoxically, Marshall's place in the first rank of 'marginalists' that caused him to be popular with both the younger, German trained economists and the older laissez-faire economists; for marginalism was, contrary to a popular caricature, something that both schools valued. For the older school of laissez-faire economists, marginalism represented the new theoretical frontier that might allow American economics to escape from its awkward relationship with Ricardian economics. Despite fealty to the pre-eminence of Ricardian analysis since the 1820s, the scarcity of land had never been a compelling analytical concept for American economists and often left them feeling that their efforts at adapting Ricardian analysis were, likewise, not very compelling. There was certainly nothing very original about the American adaptations of Ricardo. Thus, the conservative members of the old school saw in marginalism a framework that might be more amenable to their ambitions to make original theoretical contributions within a new analytical framework. He also supported free trade, which was a central value for the older academic economists.

For many in the younger generation of German trained economists, Marshall's marginalism was perfectly consonant with what they had learned while they had been abroad. Despite our awareness of their deep interest in historical analysis, cultivated studying under the giants of the German historical school, we now know that they were also exposed to marginalist ideas by those same German historical economists. As Erich Streissler (1990) and John Chipman (2005) have recently made clear, Germany's leading economists in the nineteenth century had a long and intimate connection with marginalist thinking. Joseph Dorfman (1955) somewhat cryptically referred to the marginalist influence that the younger generation brought home as the 'Austrian' influence, perhaps because the German mentor of John Bates Clark, Richard T. Ely, and E.R.A. Seligman, their Heidelberg professor Karl Knies, was also a mentor to the great Austrians Eugen von Böhm-Bawerk and Friedrich von Wieser. Thus, like the older generation, this younger generation of American economists would have also been attracted to Marshall because of his status as a leading marginalist (Bateman 2008). From his earliest textbooks in the 1880s, Ely had included simple forms of marginal utility analysis in his work, and the use of marginal analysis was common amongst almost all of Karl Knies's former American students. Granted, most did not make marginalism the centre piece of their analysis, and J.B Clark was unique in making it the *ethical* centrepiece of his work; but the fact remains that the younger generation of economists returned from Germany conversant in marginal utility analysis and understood it as an important frontier in economic analysis.

Marshall's appeal to members of both these groups is evident in the fact that he sent copies of the fifth edition of the *Principles* (1907) to many American economists of both stripes; those whose letters thanking him for this including Charles Bullock, Frank Haigh Dixon, Langworthy Taylor, Jeremiah Jenks and J. Lawrence Laughlin (Chicago). Dixon (Dartmouth College) wrote that economists in the US had long realised 'the indispensable character of this work' for study and teaching (Whitaker 1996, III, p. 173). Bullock (Harvard) wrote that Marshall's statement of the theory of production and distribution was 'not likely to be superseded speedily'. Jenks (Cornell) simply expressed interest in the change in the plan of the work in the new edition (ibid., p. 177). Seligman (Columbia) was cautious, praising some 'excellent qualities' though observing that it was more likely to be used as secondary reading not as a main text, in part due to '[s]pecial reference to American conditions' (ibid., pp. 184–5). In the second of these quotations, Seligman is quoting Marshall. It would appear that the reason this rendered the book unsuitable as a textbook was that it said very little about American conditions. Laughlin (Chicago) did not comment on the book, though presumably his reaction was positive, for he wrote that Marshall's account of the two volumes on which he was still working tempted him to try again to bring him to Chicago, with an offer of $1200 dollars to conduct a six-week seminar course over the summer.

MARSHALL'S *PRINCIPLES*

The first public American reaction to the *Principles* came quickly, in 1890 when Franklin H. Giddings, then a political scientist at Bryn Mawr College (though later to become a sociologist at Columbia) who had, two years earlier, written a book together with J.B. Clark (Clark and Giddings 1888), reviewed it in the *Annals of the American Academy of Political Science* (see Tanaka 2000 for information on the correspondence between Clark and Giddings). His enthusiasm for it can be captured only by quoting the opening sentences in full:

> The publication of this book is a scientific event of the first magnitude. Announcement was made some time ago that Professor Marshall was preparing an extensive treatise on the Principles of Economics, and students were prepared to find it a well-thought-out and scholarly work. But it is safe to say that very few anticipated a work of such scope, of such fresh interest, of such exhaustive information, of such breadth and thoroughness of method as this proves to be in fact. To call it the greatest systematic work since Mill is to speak far within the truth, for the only other book to which it can be compared is 'The Wealth of Nations'. It does for political economy in the last decade of the nineteenth century what Smith did in the last quarter of the eighteenth, and what Mill did after the discussion of two generations had apparently fixed the fundamental lines. It so marks the close of one scientific period and the beginning of another that in future advanced discussion must start from Marshall as hitherto from Mill. (Giddings 1890, p. 332)

This was followed, the next year, by a review by John Bates Clark, the leading American economist of his generation. He was ecstatic in his praise, saying it surpassed expectations and justified the 'eulogistic reviews' it had received (G.B. Clark 1891, p. 126). However, he went on to offer an appraisal of the book's significance that related to the situation of American economics as he saw it. Economics was going through a time of change, which meant that it was not possible to unify the subject in the way Mill's *Principles* had done a generation earlier. Furthermore, it meant that it would not be desirable for any one book to dominate the subject for 40 years, as Mill's *Principles* had done. The result was that though Clark found much to agree with in Marshall's *Principles* he disagreed with it on important points. However, and this was the key point, even where he disagreed with the book, his admiration for it was not diminished (ibid., p. 132). Clark disagreed with Marshall's view of distribution, but found his treatment full of insights, with the result that it provided a foundation for developing a more satisfactory theory. The reason why the book could do this was that Marshall had a very flexible interpretation of Ricardo that allowed him to claim continuity with the past, without playing down the significance of more modern work. Clark's assessment marks his emerging difference from the other German trained economists. Most of those who had studied in Germany believed that while marginal analysis was important, it did not solve all the problems that the discipline was trying to address; Clark, however, wanted to push even further with marginal analysis and extend its reach.

The *Quarterly Journal of Economics* commissioned a review by a leading economist, Adolphe Wagner (1893), from the University of Berlin. Like Clark, he attached significance to the book's being a statement of the continuity of modern theorising with Ricardo. The younger generation of American economists would have respected Wagner's opinion as a leading German economist and probably would have taken the reference to the continuity of Marshall's analysis with Ricardo's to refer to Marshall's advocacy of free trade.

Wagner's review thus serves to illustrate the comment made by Taussig, an economist of the older generation who was more interested in Marshall's defence of free trade than he was in Marshall's methods (Taussig 1893, p. 95), that 'the general trend and character of the book', together with its statements on policy, had received more attention than the theory of value and distribution. The latter, Taussig argued, was problematic, the principle of substitution being less useful than Marshall's extensive use of it would imply. Here Taussig would seem to have been revealing his own relative lack of familiarity with marginal principles. The result was that, though American economists of all stripes were looking for a book that would become the standard account of the subject, 'it remains a question whether it will attain the authoritative place which, in its day and generation, was achieved by John Stuart Mill's recasting the then accepted doctrines of Political Economy' (ibid., p. 100). Given his earlier enthusiasm for the *Principles*, it is significant that Giddings, in commenting on Taussig's paper, concluded: 'I doubt if we have as yet got very far beyond that restatement of leading principles of political economy that was made by Professor Cairnes' (ibid., p. 101). What American economists found in the *Principles* seems to have been determined by what they were looking for. American pioneers in marginalism, such as J.B. Clark and Jacob Viner (who was Taussig's student), were drawn most to Marshall's cutting-edge methods; the laissez-faire economists like Taussig understood Marshall's status as a theorist, but were more prone to focus on his policy prescriptions.

The extent to which economists from different schools could endorse Marshall's *Principles* is shown by the case of Thorstein Veblen, who acquired a reputation of a critic of orthodox economics. Though Veblen did apply the charge of being 'taxonomic' to Marshall's work, and though he did not deny Marshall's affinity with the classical economists against whom his great rhetorical powers were directed, he admired him, as is shown by his remark that

Professor Marshall's work in economics is not unlike that of Asa Gray in botany, who, while working in great part within the lines of 'systematic botany' and adhering to its terminology, and on the whole also to its point of view, very materially furthered the advance of the science outside the scope of taxonomy. (Veblen 1900, p. 265)

Marshall, in Veblen's view, aspired to treat economic life as in a process of development, and his theory appeared to exhibit evolutionary features, although these were superficial. There was no real analysis of the processes of change. But this was not to disparage Marshall's work; rather it was to point to the direction in which economics needed to be developed. Though criticising Marshall from a different perspective, this was not far from the Clark's attitude to Marshall.

Sales of the *Principles*, which appear to have begun only with the second edition in 1891 (see Table 6.1) ran at around 300 a year till the end of the century, after which they fell to between 150 and 200 a year for the next two decades. The book then took off in the inter-war period, sales averaging around 800 copies a year, far above pre-war levels. What is remarkable is not that they became so high relative to Britain, but that they were so low given the relative size of the two countries' education systems. To place its sales in perspective, the market leading text, by Ely and various co-authors, sold around 14 500 copies per year from the Great Depression to 1953. These figures are all taken from Dorfman (1955, IV, p. 664 and V, p. 211. It is assumed that 'from the Great Depression' means from 1929 but if later, the annual figures would be higher.). They probably overstate the difference with Marshall's book because the rise in sales after 1945 is likely to outweigh any decline during the Second World War. In the same period, Fairchild, Furniss and Buck (1926) sold around 12 500 copies a year, and Bye (1924) and Taussig (1911) around 7200 copies a year. The explanation is that, whereas in Britain the *Principles* was used by

Table 6.1   Sales of Marshall's Principles *in the United States, 1890–1940*

	Total US sales	Percentage of total sales
1890–1900	2554	34
1900–1910	1627	21
1910–1920	2195	24
1920–1930	8440	38
1930–1940	7793	48

Source: Macmillan (1942, pp. 292–3). Macmillan's figures suggest that sales in the US started only with the second edition, in 1891–92. If UK sales of the first edition are excluded, the percentage for the first row should read 84 per cent.

undergraduates, there being no formal graduate programmes, in the US the *Principles* was used as an advanced or graduate textbook. Interestingly, this was true for Richard T. Ely's former student John R. Commons, who used the *Principles* at Oberlin College in the early 1890s as a text for his advanced undergraduate seminar, as well as for Henry Garver who brought 'orthodoxy' back to the University of Minnesota three decades later using Marshall's text for his graduate seminar (Dorfman 1955, V, pp. 487–8).

At Chicago, Viner used it as a graduate textbook.

Marshall became a theoretical reference point for diverse schools of American economic thought. Paul Homan (1928, pp. 268–9) summarised the position by saying '[t]he exposition of economic theory in the United States is at present too diverse to permit any precise generalising [concerning Marshall's influence]'. 'The *Principles* is still current coin to some, debased currency to others, and a museum exhibit to others' (ibid., p. 268). In the United States, Marshall's theoretical work had been 'assailed along its entire front' by critics ranging from utility theorists influenced by the Austrians or John Bates Clark to critics of all systems, such as Veblen. And yet he still felt able to echo Taussig's remark that Marshall held a position of 'practically undisputed pre-eminence. So far as there is today any generally accepted body of economic doctrines, it is largely what Marshall made it. Even for dissenters and nonconformists, Marshall has been very generally the point of departure' (ibid., p. 195).

Americans had developed their own undergraduate textbook industry beginning in the late 1880s with Ely's earliest efforts, and they did not waver far from the mould set then until the rise of neoclassicism in the 1930s. The treatment of marginalism developed through these decades, but it was never as advanced as in the *Principles*. Instead, it was largely limited to basic explanations of marginal utility and the downward sloping demand curve and simple explanations of marginal productivity theory. But these chapters in the leading textbooks were few in comparison with those that gave information about the institutions of American capitalism and the economic history of America. Marshall always represented a more theoretically sophisticated approach to economics, with its ability to use marginalism as an engine of discovery. That increased sales of Marshall's *Principles* in the inter-war period may reflect increased interest in Marshall and is consistent with the rise in the frequency with which Alfred Marshall was cited in the three leading American journals shown in Figure 6.1. The increased interest in Marshall's work coincided very closely with the rise of a more clearly articulated and aggressive neoclassicism in the late 1920s and 1930s. As institutionalism emerged to challenge marginalism, the marginalists like Frank Knight and Jacob Viner began to pull away from their old détente with the historical school and began to develop a tighter and more extensive form of marginal analysis, much more like Marshall's famed 'engine of analysis'.

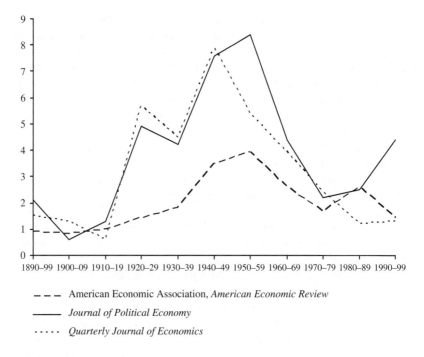

- - - American Economic Association, *American Economic Review*

———— *Journal of Political Economy*

· · · · · *Quarterly Journal of Economics*

Source: Percentage of articles containing 'Alfred Marshall' according to JSTOR (excluding Notes on new books). Denominator is number of articles containing 'economic' or 'economics' or 'price' or 'money'.

Figure 6.1   References to Alfred Marshall in the main American journals

FROM MARSHALL TO MARKET STRUCTURE – HARVARD

For the first three decades of the twentieth century, a key figure at Harvard was Frank Taussig, who, as well as teaching courses in introductory economics and several applied fields, taught a course in advanced theory in most years up to 1917, and then continuously from 1920 to 1935 (see Schumpeter, Cole and Mason 1941, p. 13 for a list of the many courses he taught). Described in his obituary as 'the American Marshall' on account of the parallels between his work and Marshall's, Taussig's economics was, like Marshall's, formed from reading John Stuart Mill and he always considered Ricardo, along with Böhm-Bawerk, the greatest economist of all time (Schumpeter, Cole and Mason 1941, p. 10. It is worth noting that Taussig first taught economics at Harvard in 1882–83, three years before Marshall's appointment as professor at Cambridge.) Though he praised Marshall, a long-standing friend with whom he had extensive correspondence, as the most distinguished economist of his generation (Taussig 1924, p. 1), and though Marshall teaching was 'one of the main sources of his classroom work' (Schumpeter, Cole and Mason 1941, p. 10), he was critical of the *Principles*. Soon after its publication, Taussig (1893, pp. 96, 98–9) praised Marshall for unifying the theory of distribution and exchange yet criticised him for ignoring the problem of explaining the general level of wages. Over 30 years later, in his obituary he praised the book Marshall had written with his wife (Marshall and Paley Marshall 1879), a book still organised on classical lines, in relation to both the *Principles* and *Elements of the Economics of Industry* (Marshall 1892). Taussig's own *Principles of Economics* retained, right up to the fourth edition in 1939, many classical features, opening with chapters on wealth, labour, the division of labour and production, only then turning to problems of exchange.

In 1921, Taussig was joined at Harvard by Allyn Young, a student of R.T. Ely at Wisconsin. He had come, via Cornell, from Stanford where, from 1906, he had taught a Principles course using the third edition of Marshall's *Principles* as the textbook. Two years later he had become a co-author of the revised edition of Ely's *Outlines of Economics* (Ely et al. 1908), basing the eleven theoretical chapters for which he was responsible on Marshall (Blitch 1995, pp. 28–9). Young arranged to send Marshall a copy of the book, and when writing to Marshall provided an assessment of the position of Marshallian ideas in the United States (Whitaker 1996, III, pp. 218–19). The pendulum was swinging away from excessive use of marginal utility analysis towards 'careful analysis of the forces of demand and supply', best presented in Marshall's work. He wanted Marshall to know that there was 'growing appreciation of the fact that the *Principles of Economics* represents the highest achievement in economic analysis up to the present, and that it points the way to the most valuable lines for future work' (ibid.; Blitch 1995, p. 28 quotes much of this letter but leaves out this very important last sentence.) This playing down of marginal analysis in favour of supply and demand, rehabilitating the English classics, was something of which Taussig would have approved.

The last sentence in Young's letter makes clear the role that he saw for Marshall's *Principles*: the reason why it was suitable for advanced students was that it laid down lines along which he thought future work should proceed. A student who took his 'Modern schools of economic thought' course remembered that Young took Marshall's ideas in the direction that Edward Chamberlin was to bring to a wider audience under the label 'monopolistic competition'.

One thing that my notes taken in 1924–26 conclusively showed was that every worthwhile idea in E.H. Chamberlin's subsequent work on imperfect competition had clearly been expounded by Allyn Young in class long before Chamberlin put pen to paper. Curiously, Young credited Cournot for most of what he said! (Quoted in Blitch 1995, pp. 118–19.)

The ideas Young was expounding included, according to another student, product differentiation, selling expenses and the need to focus on the firm rather than the industry, ideas that also appeared in the chapters Young contributed to *Outlines of Economics* (ibid.). In reviewing a book by A.L. Bowley (Young 1925), he put forward a theory of duopoly later taken up by Chamberlin.

Like Taussig, in seeing Marshall's significance as leading back from utility theory to supply and demand, Young focused on the structure of costs and their implication for supply. This is apparent not only in *Outlines of Economics* but also in the few academic articles he published. His best known article, 'Increasing returns and economic progress' (1928b) was clearly a direct development of ideas from Marshall. The Marshallian character of Young's work is perhaps best shown in the inaugural lecture he delivered at the London School of Economics (LSE), shortly after he left Harvard. Not only did he defend 'English political economy' as 'a practical subject', based on a variety of methods, against romantic, positivist, historical and mathematical criticisms but he went on to argue against overemphasising 'strict reasoning' and 'rigid logic' as requirements of economics (Young 1928a, pp. 3, 7). The contrast between pure and applied economics, which might justify the search for logical rigour in the former, was, Young claimed, largely artificial (ibid., p. 5). He urged economists to use a combination of theory, statistics and history that was thoroughly Marshallian. Any doubt that Young was, at least in his work on value, following a Marshallian programme is removed by Nicholas Kaldor's notes on his LSE lectures, in 1927–29 (Mehrling and Sandilands 1990, Chapter 44).

The conscious use of Marshall by Young's most distinguished doctoral student, Chamberlin, is also clear. His work originated in the Pigou–Taussig controversy over railroad pricing, which hinged on the structure of costs. What Chamberlin added to ideas Young was expounding in the early 1920s was a systematic analysis of market structures intermediate between perfect competition and monopoly. In so far as Marshall, despite seeing many features of monopolistic competition, analysed only the cases of competition and monopoly, without the need to postulate an intermediate case, Chamberlin *was* moving away from Marshall (Chamberlin 1962, pp. 316–18). However, whilst he may have wanted to move beyond Marshall, his work was emphatically *not* part of the attack on Marshall that led to Joan Robinson's *Economics of Imperfect Competition* (1933). It was instead an attack on the theory of perfect competition, based on the argument that monopoly (a consequence of advertising and product differentiation) was inherent in the competitive process itself. Though Chamberlin's claims about what he was doing in the 1920s and 1930s seem well justified it is natural to ask whether his stress on this point reflects reading Arrow (1959). Chamberlin recognised that it was wrong to attribute to Marshall 'theories more precise than they really were, or than he ever intended them to be', reminding his readers of Marshall's views on the limitations of mathematics in economics.

Marshall often 'theorised' about situations merely by telling what businessmen did in real life. A fine distinction between 'theory' and 'real life' in Marshall's economics is impossible to draw because Marshall himself did not draw it, and never tired of warning others against drawing it (Chamberlin 1962, p. 317).

Chamberlin was continuing the Marshallian tradition in a way that his British counterparts were not. This was at the same time that his Harvard colleague Talcott Parsons (1931, 1932), who subsequently became the university's most eminent sociologist, was exploring the evolutionary dimension of Marshall's thought, stressing the interaction of wants and activities. In Marshall's hands, Parsons (1932, p. 346) argued, 'the field of economics [showed a] tendency to expand into a general sociology', a tendency he claimed should be resisted.

From the 1930s until well into the postwar era, Chamberlin and Edward Mason, a fellow graduate student of the early 1920s, dominated Harvard industrial economics along with their students, such as Joe Bain. The framework for their work was the notion of industrial structure as pioneered in Chamberlin's *Economics of Monopolistic Competition*. This theoretical framework and the empirical methods they used distanced them from Marshall, though their work still exhibited Marshallian characteristics.

But alongside them were newcomers who were by no stretch of the imagination Marshallian. Wassily Leontief arrived at Harvard in 1931, working on input–output analysis. His drew not on Marshall but on Léon Walras. In two volumes of essays, the only reference to Marshall bracketed him with Edgeworth and Pareto as the source of indifference curve analysis. Joseph Schumpter, who came to Harvard a year later, praised Marshall, focusing in particular on the very useful aggregative concepts he had created. Though he saw their work as substantially the same, his allegiance was to Walras, not Marshall. When he praised Marshall in the 1940s, it was as a way of criticising Keynes and other younger members of the Cambridge school. By the 1940s, Harvard economists had largely moved beyond Marshall (Backhouse 2008 discusses Schumpeter's attitude to Marshall in detail).

APPLYING THE THEORY OF COMPETITIVE MARKETS – CHICAGO

The influence of Taussig's Marshallianism extended well beyond Harvard and was perhaps nowhere more pronounced and enduring than at the University of Chicago. From its origins in the price theory courses taught by Frank Knight and Jacob Viner in the 1920s, Chicago price theory was overtly Marshallian – that is, it is rooted in the economics of Marshall's *Principles*, which has been on the reading list for the basic PhD course in Price Theory at Chicago (Econ. 301) since the 1920s and remains there to this day. The Marshallian tradition at Chicago is rooted in the price theory courses taught by Jacob Viner, a student of Taussig, from the 1920s through the mid-1940s, when he departed for Princeton. Taussig's influence on Viner was sufficiently strong that Viner could say on the occasion of the semi-centennial of the publication of Marshall's *Principles* that 'so much of what knowledge I may have about Marshall has been gained through the years from the late Dr. Taussig's writings, teaching, and conversation that I can no longer separate what I have learned myself from what I have derived from him' (Viner 1941, p. 22). Student notes from Viner's price theory course demonstrate the centrality of Marshall to the early Chicago price theory tradition: Viner's lectures were a virtual walking tour through Marshall's *Principles*, and Viner's refusal to depart from Marshall's real cost approach at a time when the Austrian opportunity cost approach was gaining favour played an important role in the subsequent development of cost theory.

As Viner's students at Chicago included Milton Friedman, Aaron Director, George Stigler and Alan Wallis, all of whom picked up on his Marshallian approach in various ways, Viner's teaching laid the foundation for the Marshallianism that came to be so closely associated with the larger Chicago tradition. Indeed, with the exception of Knight, each of the key figures in the Chicago price theory tradition overtly grounded his work in Marshall and claimed Marshallian heritage for it and for Chicago price theory in general. It is worth noting that the role of Marshall in teaching at Chicago extends beyond the standard Chicago price theory luminaries. For example, Paul Samuelson has remarked that he was steeped in Marshall by Paul Douglas, an institutionalist, before taking Viner's graduate price theory course during his senior year as a Chicago undergraduate. And as noted above, Laughlin had tried to lure Marshall to Chicago to lecture during the summer in the 1890s. Friedman, who occupied centre stage from the mid-1940s until the early 1960s, repeatedly referred to the Marshallian nature of his approach and vociferously defended both the Marshallian system in general and his own interpretation of Marshall in particular – the latter even against his good friend Stigler, whose take on Marshall fell more in line with the dominant professional view than with Friedman's interpretation. The Chicago price theory texts, too, reflect the Marshallian emphasis: Marshall receives significantly more cites than any other individual in the Friedman and Stigler texts, and Marshall is among the most cited by Becker (Friedman, Stigler and Hicks are also heavily cited by Becker).

But in what respects does Chicago price theory reflect Marshall and his system? At the most general level, two significant points of intersection can be identified. First, the Chicago tradition employs partial equilibrium rather than general equilibrium analysis. That is, Chicago price theory is Marshallian as opposed to Walrasian, and it remained steadfastly (and distinctively) wedded to a form of Marshallianism through a long period during which the rest of the profession was immersed in Walrasian analysis, at least in respect to price theory and microeconomics (the last two decades of Chicago macroeconomics evidence a significant Walrasian component). It also bears noting that Chicago price theory has resisted the game-theoretic turn of economics, which explains why Nobel Laureate Roger Myerson is a University of Chicago microeconomist but not one who is identified with the Chicago tradition in price theory or affiliated with the Becker Center on Chicago Price Theory.

A second point of intersection between Marshall and Chicago is that the Chicago approach follows Marshall in the melding of theoretical and empirical work, and, like Marshall, considers both to be necessary for doing good economics and each as incomplete absent the other. Both of these points, and the ability to link them to Marshall, were important for the solidification and defence of the Chicago approach to price theory: the empirical strand solidified the Marshallian tendencies of Chicago as against the Walrasian approach, and the theoretical strand was a Marshallian counterpart to the perceived atheoretical empirical work of the institutional tradition in the first half of the twentieth century.

While Marshall was being criticised by the two Cambridges for neglecting to place sufficient emphasis on firm-level analysis, his focus on analysis at the market level resonated at Chicago, which conceptualised economics around Knight's (1933) definition of economics as the study of the social organisation of economic activity, mainly through markets. This perspective is reflected in Friedman's criticism of monopolistic competition theory on the grounds that it 'furnishes no tools for the analysis of industry', and thus leaves one with 'no stopping place between the firm at one extreme and general equilibrium at the other' (Friedman 1941, p. 390). For Friedman, monopolistic competition contributed little beyond Marshall's analysis of monopoly, and its firm-specific nature meant that it offered little to 'the most important problems of the real world', which he believed related to industries (ibid.). This, Friedman argued, meant that economists 'must continue to employ the Marshallian tools, until better ones are invented' (ibid.).

This view of the primacy of market-level analysis in Marshall extended to the demand side, where Marshall's emphasis was on demand at the market, rather than individual level, an attitude that we see reflected in Chicago price theory until the 1960s. Two aspects of this are of particular import for present purposes. First, until the 1960s, Chicago price theory followed Marshall in resisting the idea of grounding demand theory in a theory of individual behaviour. It was not until Stigler and Becker moved rational choice rather than demand theory to the centre of economic analysis that individual behaviour became central.

Second, Friedman devoted a tremendous amount of effort to challenging the dominant professional view of Marshallian demand. The standard interpretation of Marshall was, and continues to be, that nominal income is held constant (and real income varies) along the Marshallian demand curve, with the Hicksian variant assuming real income to be constant. Against this, Friedman (1949) argued that Marshall's analysis held both nominal income *and* purchasing power constant along a given demand curve. The import of this is that a movement along the Marshallian demand curve has a substitution effect only, and there is no change in consumer's surplus as one moves along the demand curve. Friedman agued that this conception of demand resonates with Marshall's emphasis on constructing a system for the analysis of concrete economic problems, in that it is much more useful toward that end. The standard interpretation of Marshall, while consistent with general equilibrium concerns, falls short on the operational front.

Marshall's influence at Chicago did not end at the doors of the Economics Department or of the Graduate School of Business, where Stigler had his appointment. The appointments of Aaron Director and Ronald Coase in the Law School brought Marshallian analysis to the intersection of law and economics and to the study of the regulatory environment of business. Director had been a student of Viner, while Coase had been steeped in Marshall through his studies under Arnold Plant at LSE. One can question the extent to which the economic analysis of law that emerged out of this – in the hands of Becker, Richard Posner, and William Landes – is consistent with Marshall. Indeed, this question applies to economics imperialism generally. Marshall's sense that calculation does not govern all areas of life, or even particular areas in all circumstances, made him something less than fully confident in the conclusions drawn from economic theorising. Economic theories, for Marshall, were tendency statements, and the further we move away from economic affairs proper within the social realm, the weaker he thought those tendencies became (Marshall [1890] 1920, p. 27). There is, he said, 'a continuous gradation from social laws concerned almost exclusively with motives that can be measured by price, to social laws in which such motives have little place'.

MOVING BEYOND MARSHALL – COLUMBIA, CORNELL AND PRINCETON

There were at other universities economists who were either more critical of Marshall or who sought to develop his thought in directions very different from those pursued at Harvard or Chicago. Wesley Mitchell (simultaneously at the National Bureau of Economic Research) was at Columbia from 1919 until his death in 1946 and had as colleagues Henry Ludwell Moore (1902–29) and John Maurice Clark (1926–53). They and economists such as Herbert Davenport (Cornell 1916–29) and Frank Fetter (Cornell 1901–11 and Princeton 1911–33) illustrate clearly the way in which economists often started from his work, even though they could not be described as Marshallians. (This list clearly picks out no more than a few of those who could be discussed. John Bates Clark was discussed above. Irving Fisher, like Clark, belongs to a generation that learned economics before Marshall's *Principles* – his doctoral thesis was published in 1891.)

For Moore, Marshall was but one exponent of a body of ideas found in a wide range of economists, of whom the others he cited most were Cournot, Walras and Pareto. Thus, when discussing perfect competition, it is Marshall's definition of the term competition that he cites; he also cites Marshall as demonstrating the important point that the static method was of limited use when it came to increasing returns to scale (Moore 1906, pp. 212, 226). Moore also chose Marshall as his starting point in the theory of wages, subsequently citing him for points of theory and statements of fact (Moore 1911, pp. 71, 86, 148–9). Similarly, in analysing the law of demand, Moore (1914, p. 63) took Marshall's statement as the basis for his own arguments. Marshall's name was bracketed together with Pareto and Cournot (Moore 1911, p. 179; 1914, p. 63).

Yet though he treated Marshall as an authority, he made it clear that a new theory was needed. Marshall's theory of wages was abstract, based on hypothetical assumptions, and needed to be replaced with one rooted in concrete facts (Moore 1911, p. 73). Marshall's negatively-sloped demand curve could be found in some markets, but it was not the only type of demand curve (Moore 1914, pp. 110–16). He could cite Marshall as having made arguments that led in the statistical direction along which he wanted to move (Moore 1908, pp. 8 n. 1, 24) but this was not Marshall's own approach to economics: Marshall wrote to Moore that he believed that 'it proceeds on lines which I deliberately decided not to follow' (Whitaker 1996, III, pp. 296–7). Marshall explained in detail why he took this view. He also said he was glad Moore and others were doing such work because, whilst it would not produce results in Marshall's lifetime, it might do so after that. Moore's reply (ibid., pp. 297–8) expresses great appreciation for the frankness of Marshall's letter.

Mitchell's attitude towards Marshall was similar. In his lectures given at Columbia from 1913 to 1937 (published as Mitchell 1969), he paid close attention to Marshall. He praised Marshall for making economics a study of human behaviour and for integrating topics that had for most of the nineteenth century been considered separately (ibid., II, pp. 163–6). Yet he clearly wanted to go beyond Marshall, for Marshall confined his attention to conscious motives. This was consistent with the most prominent statement of his views, in his Presidential Address to the American Economic Association, in 1924, which opened with Marshall's remark that 'qualitative analysis has done the greater part of its work' and that the 'higher and more difficult task [quantitative work] must wait on the slow growth of thorough realistic studies' (Mitchell 1925, p. 1). Marshall was 'the great teacher' on whose work it was necessary to build something new. This comes across clearly when he describes Marshall as having abandoned Jevons's hedonism. That was progress, but it did not go far enough, for the next step was to abandon the analysis of human motives, even by reducing them to money, altogether: quantitative analysis would cause people to lose interest in the analysis of motives and choices (ibid., p. 5). Where Marshall had predicted that quantitative work would progress slowly, Mitchell expressed optimism that economists only just entering the profession would 'make obsolete not only the qualitative work of Dr. Marshall and others, but also the crude beginnings of quantitative work which their elders are now producing' (ibid., p. 12).

Much the same could also be said of J.M. Clark. He cited Marshall less frequently than Moore, and discussed his work much less thoroughly than Mitchell, but his few remarks clearly indicate his position. The first reference to Marshall in Clark's *The Economics of Overhead Costs* (1923), written whilst Clark was at Chicago (he acknowledges debts to Viner and Knight), occurs in a discussion of overhead costs in industries other than railroads. This was a topic on which Marshall had corresponded with Arthur Hadley, and was the topic that had prompted Chamberlin to work on what became monopolistic competition. The discussion suggests that, for Clark, Marshall's *Principles* was simply part of the much broader literature on which he was drawing. More significantly, though he cites Marshall with approval, it is on a point that runs against what might be considered the paradigmatic Marshallian theory, namely normal value. It was that in the presence of large fixed costs and the use of rate wars on railroads, 'cut-throat competition' was seen by businessmen as normal, prompting them to adopt protective measures such as 'combinations, pools, gentleman's agreements, or a mere sentiment against "spoiling the market"' (J.M. Clark 1923, p. 11, citing the 6th edition of the *Principles*, 1910, p. 375). This led to the conclusion that prices would *not* yield normal returns on capital. Similarly, two pages later, Clark (ibid., p. 13) cites approvingly Marshall's use of the concept of the representative firm, but after a single sentence on Marshall, he turned immediately to a longer discussion of J.B. Clark's ideas on competition.

Fetter, at Princeton, was more critical of Marshall. He referred to 'his remarkable talent for eclecticism' but immediately observed that this 'probably embodies and exemplifies better than any one else the more generally prevailing *uncritical* opinion among English and American economists' (Fetter 1920, p. 720, emphasis added). Fetter's concern was the contrast between 'price economics', according to which economics centred on price, as in the classical economics of Ricardo and Mill, and 'welfare economics' concerned with problems of welfare. Marshall, Fetter claimed, was ambiguous, in that he was concerned with welfare, even making some remarks that came close to echoing Ruskin, yet in the interests of science he sought to reduce economics to price. The latter was an aspect of Marshall that Mitchell (1916) endorsed but of which Fetter was sceptical. If adopting price economics really did make it possible to analyse economics mathematically, that would be one thing, but it did not, for there was no way in which economic motives could be measured. The result was that Marshall espoused two notions of economics that could not be reconciled. Fetter favoured a subjective (Austrian) view in which costs were subjective and in which price economics was more clearly subservient to welfare.

Davenport, at Cornell, was a lifelong critic of Marshall, his most substantial work being a posthumously published book, *The Economics of Alfred Marshall* (1935), in which he carefully dissected the *Principles*. He saw Marshall as representing classical economics, sharing the classical economists' 'real cost' theory of value, of which he was highly critical, on Austrian grounds. This continued the argument of a much earlier book, *Value and Distribution* (1908) in which he sought to rid the subject of such notions.

SAMUELSON AND THE DEMISE OF MARSHALLIAN ECONOMICS

In the 1930s and 1940s, Marshall continued to be cited and discussed (see Figure 6.1) but his work was increasingly seen to be of no more than historical interest. Economists made extensive use of Marshallian concepts and their theories used equations that could be found in the Mathematical Appendix to the *Principles* or diagrams that had roots in its footnotes, but they did so in a theoretical framework that was distinctly un-Marshallian. Theorists increasingly found inspiration in Pareto or Walras rather than Marshall. For example, Henry Schultz (1938) at Chicago was inspired primarily by Walras (on the significance of Schultz, see Hands and Mirowski 1998). As the pluralist economics of the 1930s, in which Marshall's ideas had been taken up and his *Principles* had been used as a textbook by a wide range of economists, evolved into a narrower neoclassicism, Marshall's wide-ranging and realistic analysis of economic processes ceased to be a strength and became a weakness.

Nowhere was this clearer than in Paul Samuelson's highly influential *Foundations of Economic Analysis* (1947). His introduction amounted to a declaration of war on precepts central to Marshall's thinking:

> I have come to feel that Marshall's dictum that 'it seems doubtful whether any one spends his time well in reading lengthy translations of economic doctrines into mathematics that have not been made by himself' should be exactly reversed. The laborious working over of essentially simple mathematical concepts such as is characteristic of much of modern economic theory is not only unrewarding from the standpoint of advancing the science, but involves as well mental gymnastics of a peculiarly depraved type. (Ibid., p. 6)

Twenty years later, he appraised Marshall's legacy under the heading 'Exorcizing the Marshallian incubus'. His claim was that, though 'Marshall was a great economist', his ambiguities 'paralysed the best brains in the Anglo-Saxon branch of our profession for three decades' (Samuelson 1967, p. 109). Marshall obscured the theories of monopoly, perfect and imperfect competition through treating 'at the same time cases of less-than-perfect and perfect competition', trying to achieve 'a spurious verisimilitude by talking about vague biological dynamics, and by failing to distinguish between reversible and irreversible developments. Marshall was so afraid of being unrealistic that he merely ends up being fuzzy and confusing – and confused' (ibid., p. 111).

Aside from his great influence on postwar economics, Samuelson's denunciation of Marshall is of interest because it illustrates what happened to Marshallian ideas as economics became more technical (see Solow 1997). Discussing Chamberlin, Samuelson concedes that he may have reached his conclusions before Sraffa's article, published only four months before his thesis came out, but argues that his readers would have read it in the light of the cost controversy. Ideas have a fate independent of their authors which justifies 'emancipating [the terms monopolistic competition and imperfect competition] from their first associations with different conceptions and using them as convenient names for the best current models of price theory' (Samuelson 1967, p. 108). This is precisely what happened to Marshall.

Chamberlin's monopolistic competition was, as Samuelson explained, e-quated with Robinson's imperfect competition. Economists stopped seeing the geometry as a device for clarifying the analysis of a theory that had to be expressed in words: for postwar economists the mathematics was the theory. The same happened to Marshallian economics, where the elements that survived were what remained after translation into mathematics. There might be debate over the relevance of market structure and whether intervention was needed to curb monopoly power (the ongoing conflict between Harvard and Chicago over competition policy) but there was no need to go back to Marshall.

Against this background, even if textbooks paid homage to Marshall as the developer of partial equilibrium analysis or of the theory of the firm, there was no need to read the *Principles*, for there were better, clearer, more rigorous expositions, shorn of the confusing logical contradictions identified by Samuelson. Why read Marshall's *Principles* when one could study one of the many editions of Samuelson's *Economics*? The unsuitability of Marshall's *Principles* as a textbook was exacerbated by the changing style in which text-books were written. Not only did diagrams of a type Marshall would have recognised move out of his footnotes into the text and appear in larger numbers (one of the first textbooks to have a large number of diagrams was Boulding 1941) but they were used in new ways (Giraud 2010), making even textbooks of the 1930s seem dry and dated. The slow but inexorable spread of mathematics in economics meant that more advanced courses increasingly trained economists to use mathematical tools, for which Marshall's text was, *a fortiori*, unsuitable.

It would seem likely that the Keynesian revolution also played a part. This clearly shifted the discipline away from subjects on which Marshall could provide guidance: not only had the subject moved on enormously, but *Money, Credit and Commerce* (1923) had become dated even by the time it was published. The Keynesian revolution also came to be intertwined with the movement towards a more technical economics, thereby contributing to the demise of institutionalism and, more significantly, to the demise of 'casual empiricism'. Keynes's theoretical constructs in his *General Theory* so closely matched the emerging categories of national income analysis that exact econometric measurement of macroeconomic relationships became possible almost immediately. Marshall would no doubt have revelled in the possibilities provided by so much economic data, but the appearance of the data together with econometric models undoubtedly made Marshall's own work seem vague and imprecise in an unflattering way.

CONCLUSIONS

The key to understanding the influence of Marshall's *Principles* in the United States is that, paradoxically, it represented orthodoxy and yet there was never any Marshallian school. This was due, in part, to the fact that in the first two decades after the *Principles* was published, Marshall was embraced by different schools of thought within American economics, who despite their high respect for his marginalism, initially took quite different things from his book. His closest followers in the next generation were arguably Young, Chamberlin and Viner. However, they did not form, by any stretch of the imagination, a Marshallian school. Young propagated Marshall's ideas both in the chapters he contributed to Ely's textbook and through his teaching, at Stanford and Harvard. As demonstrated by his collaboration with Ely, this placed him at the heart of the historical wing of American economics. Chamberlin and Viner both followed Marshall but they took his ideas forward, in directions that were to confront each other directly in the disagreements between the Harvard and Chicago schools of industrial economics. At the same time, Marshall was respected by institutionalists such as Mitchell who sought a different type of economics.

How was this possible? The *Principles* was clearly an important theoretical work. Of that, no one was in any doubt, even Veblen. But more than that, Marshall's attempt to synthesise the classical economics of Ricardo and Mill with newer work based on marginal utility, his endorsement of historical and theoretical methods, and his emphasis on scientific economics, whilst not abandoning laissez-faire all resonated with the broad concerns of a profession that, a generation earlier, had been thoroughly divided. Perhaps the fact that, as an outsider who, though strongly influenced by his experience of the United States, did not take a stance on the concerns that had come to dominate American economists – notably the problems of trusts and big business dissected so vividly by Veblen – the way was left open for economists to draw on his work without having to choose between accepting or rejecting it *in toto*. Even economists inspired by the Austrians, such as Fetter and Davenport, though they saw Marshall as not having escaped classical errors, could see elements of their own ideas in his work. At the same time, these non-classical ideas were not sufficiently strong to deter those such as Taussig, who kept even closer to the classics than he did.

That Marshall's *Principles* could play this role reflects the state of American economics in the first half of the twentieth century. It echoed the position held by John Bates Clark, at the same time a thoroughly marginalist economist generally regarded as even more a utility theorist than Marshall and someone to whom Veblen and the institutionalists could trace their intellectual ancestry. The decades after the first appearance of the *Principles* were also a time when professional education in economics was being established, with the creation of graduate schools following the example of Johns Hopkins in 1876. The Marshallian perspective, exuding scientific rigour yet not abandoning broader concerns, filled a need, if not as a textbook, as a source on which teachers and writers of textbooks could draw.

It was a period when American economists were rapidly developing new theories and approaches to economics, from the quantitative economics of Moore and Mitchell to the theories of Chamberlin. It was clearly necessary to go beyond the *Principles* but as late as the 1930s (remarkable for a book the essentials of which dated back to the 1880s) Marshall still provided a theoretical framework that had to be taken seriously. The rise in the frequency of references to Marshall in the 1920s and 1930s shown in Figure 6.1, though it might reflect changing citation practices, could be the result of the rise of more rigorous theorising: only when economists started to go beyond Marshall, finding technical faults in his analysis, did it became necessary to focus in detail on his work, paying closer attention to the diagrams and algebra that earlier generations, with their generally verbal analysis, had been able to read less closely.

However, as economics became more technical, two things happened. Theories developed in ways that meant that, with one exception, Marshall no longer provided a suitable foundation. His ambiguities and inconsistencies became a serious problem, rendering his theories increasingly of no more than historical interest. At the same time, his work was littered with technical terms, from elasticity to consumer's surplus, that proved invaluable in expounding the new theories. Invocations of his name rose sharply just as economists were moving firmly away from anything that could be called Marshallian economics. The exception to this generalisation was the University of Chicago where Friedman and Stigler, sceptical about the abstraction of postwar Walrasianism and about Harvard's approach to market structure, continued to uphold a Marshallian approach, Friedman even using the *Principles* as his textbook.

REFERENCES

Arrow, K.J. (1959), 'Towards a theory of price adjustment', in A. Abramovitz (ed.), *The Allocation of Economic Resources*, Stanford: University of California Press, pp. 41–51.
Backhouse, R.E. (2008), 'Schumpeter on Marshall: A reconsideration', in T. Nishizawa and Y. Shionoya (eds), *Marshall and Schumpeter on Evolution: Economic Sociology of Capitalist Development*, Cheltenham, UK and Northampton, MA, USA: Edward Elgar, pp. 48–61.
Bateman, B.W. (2008), 'Economics in the United States, 1885–1945', in S.N. Durlauf and L.E. Blume (eds), *The New Palgrave Dictionary of Economics*, 2nd edn, London: Palgrave Macmillan, vol. VIII, pp. 513–22. Online at http://www.dictionaryofeconomics.com.
Blitch, C. (1995), *Allyn Young: The Peripatetic Economist*, London: Macmillan.
Boulding, K.E. (1941), *Economic Analysis*, New York: Harper.
Bye, R.T. (1924), *Principles of Economics*, New York: Alfred A. Knopf.

Chamberlin, E.H. (1962), *Economics of Monopolistic Competition*, 8th edn, Cambridge, MA: Harvard University Press.

Chipman, J.S. (2005) 'Contributions of the older German schools to the development of utility theory', in C. Scheer (ed.), *Studien zur Entwicklung der oekonomischen Theorie*, vol. 20: *Die aeletere historische Schule: Wirtschaftstheoretische Beitraege und wirtschaftpolitische Vorstellungen*, Berlin: Duncker & Humbolt.

Clark, J.B. (1891), 'Marshall's *Principles of Economics*', *Political Science Quarterly*, **6** (1), 126–51.

Clark, J.B. and F.H. Giddings (1888), *The Modern Distributive Process*, Boston: Ginn.

Clark, J.M. (1923), *The Economics of Overhead Costs*, Chicago: University of Chicago Press.

Davenport, H.J. (1908), *Value and Distribution*, Chicago: University of Chicago Press.

Davenport, H.J. (1935), *The Economics of Alfred Marshall*, Ithaca: Cornell University Press.

Dorfman, J. (1955), *The Economic Mind in American Civilization*, 5 vols, New York: Viking.

Ely, R.T., T.S. Adams, M.O. Lorenz and A.A. Young (1908), *Outlines of Economics*, 2nd edn, New York: Macmillan.

Fairchild, F.R., E.S. Furniss and N.S. Buck (1926), *Elementary Economics*, New York: Macmillan.

Fetter, F.W. (1920), 'Price economics versus welfare economics: contemporary opinion', *American Economic Review*, **10** (4), 719–37.

Friedman, M. (1941), 'Review [of R. Triffin, *Monopolistic Competition and General Equilibrium Theory*]', *Journal of Farm Economics*, **23** (1), 389–91.

Friedman, M. (1949), 'The Marshallian demand curve', *Journal of Political Economy*, **57** (6), 463–95.

Giddings, F.H. (1890), 'Review of Marshall's *Principles*', *Annals of the American Academy of Political and Social Science*, **1**, 332–7.

Giraud, Y. (2010), 'The changing place of visual representation in economics: Paul Samuelson between principle and strategy, 1941–1955', *Journal of the History of Economic Thought*, **32** (1), 175–97.

Groenewegen, P.D. (1995), *A Soaring Eagle: Alfred Marshall 1842–1924*, Aldershot, UK and Brookfield, US: Edward Elgar.

Hands, D.W. and P. Mirowski (1998), 'A paradox of budgets: The postwar stabilization of American neoclassical demand theory', in M.S. Morgan and M. Rutherford (eds), *From Interwar Pluralism to Postwar Neoclassicism*, Durham, NC: Duke University Press. *History of Political Economy, Annual supplement* to vol. **30**, 260–92.

Homan, P.T. (1928), *Contemporary Economic Thought*, New York: Harper.

Knight, F.H. (1933), *The Economic Organization*, Chicago: University of Chicago Press.

Macmillan, D. (1942), 'The *Principles of Economics*: A bibliographical note', *Economic Journal*, **52**, 290–93.

Marshall, A. (1890), *Principles of Economics*, London: Macmillan, 6th edn 1910; 8th edn 1920.

Marshall, A. (1892), *Elements of the Economics of Industry*, London: Macmillan.

Marshall, A. (1923), *Money, Credit and Commerce*, London: Macmillan.

Marshall, A. and M. Paley Marshall (1879), *The Economics of Industry*, London: Macmillan.

Mehrling, P.G. and R. Sandilands (1990), *Money and Growth: Selected Papers of Allyn Abbott Young*, London: Routledge.

Mill, J.S. (1848), *Principles of Political Economy and Their Application to Social Philosophy*, London: J.W. Parker.

Mitchell, W.C. (1916), 'The role of money in economic theory', *American Economic Review*, **6** (1), 140–61.

Mitchell, W.C. (1925), 'Quantitative analysis in economic theory', *American Economic Review*, **15** (1), 1–12.

Mitchell, W.C. (1969), *Types of Economic Theory: From Mercantilism to Institutionalism*, 2 vols, New York: A.M. Kelley.

Moore, H.L. (1906), 'Paradoxes of competition', *Quarterly Journal of Economics*, **20**, 211–30.

Moore, H.L. (1908), 'The statistical complement of pure economics', *Quarterly Journal of Economics*, **23** (1), 1–33.

Moore, H.L. (1911), *The Law of Wages: A Statistical Analysis*, New York: Macmillan.

Moore, H.L. (1914), *Economic Cycles: Their Law and their Cause*, New York: Macmillan.

Parsons, T. (1931), 'Wants and activities in Marshall', *Quarterly Journal of Economics*, **46** (1), 101–40.

Parsons, T. (1932), 'Economics and sociology: Marshall in relation to the thought of his time', *Quarterly Journal of Economics*, **46** (2), 316–47.

Robinson, J.V. (1933), *The Economics of Imperfect Competition*, London: Macmillan.

Ross, D. (1990), *The Origins of American Social Science*, Cambridge: Cambridge University Press.

Samuelson, P.A. (1947), *Foundations of Economic Analysis*, Cambridge, MA: Harvard University Press.

Samuelson, P.A. (1967), 'The monopolistic competition revolution', in R.E. Kuenne (ed.), *Monopolistic Competition Theory: Studies in Impact*, New York: John Wiley, pp. 105–38.

Schultz, H. (1938), *The Theory and Measurement of Demand*, Chicago: Chicago University Press.

Schumpeter, J.A., A.H. Cole and E.S. Mason (1941), 'Frank William Taussig', *Quarterly Journal of Economics*, **55** (3), 337–63.

Solow, R.M. (1997), 'How did economics get that way, and what way did it get?', *Daedalus*, **126**, 39–58.

Streissler, E.W. (1990), 'The influence of German economics on the work of Menger and Marshall', *History of Political Economy*, *Annual supplement* to vol. **22**, 31–68.

Tanaka, T. (2000), 'Introductory essay to the correspondence: The development of John Bates Clark's economic thought and Franklin Henry Giddings', *Research in the History of Economic Thought and Methodology*, **18**, 7–31.

Taussig, F. (1893), 'Value and distribution as treated by Professor Marshall', *Publications of the American Economic Association*, **8**, 95–101.

Taussig, F. (1911), *Principles of Economics*, New York: Macmillan.

Taussig, F. (1924), 'Alfred Marshall', *Quarterly Journal of Economics*, **39** (1), 1–14.

Veblen, T. (1900), 'The preconceptions of economic science', *Quarterly Journal of Economics*, **14** (2), 240–69.

Viner, J. (1941), 'Marshall's economics in relation to the man and his times', *American Economic Review*, **31** (3), 22–35.

Wagner, A. (1893), Marshall's *Principles of Economics*', *Quarterly Journal of Economics*, **5** (3), 319–38.

Whitaker, J.K. (ed.) (1975), *The Early Economic Writings of Alfred Marshall, 1867–1890*, London: Macmillan.

Whitaker, J.K. (ed.) (1996), *The Correspondence of Alfred Marshall, Economist*, 3 vols, Cambridge: Cambridge University Press.

Young, A.A. (1925), 'Review of A.L. Bowley, *The Mathematical Groundwork of Economics*', *Journal of the American Statistical Association*, **20** (149), 133–5.

Young, A.A. (1928a), 'English political economy', *Economica*, **22**, 1–15.

Young, A.A. (1928b), 'Increasing returns and economic progress', *Economic Journal*, **38**, 527–42.

7. Marshall and Australia

Peter D. Groenewegen

Australia featured indirectly in Marshall's early life as student and graduate. His uncle Charles had made his fortune there during the time of the 1850 gold rushes, and from his accumulated wealth 'financed' two important events in Marshall's early life. He lent Marshall the money he needed to study mathematics at Cambridge in the early 1860s; on his death, a legacy from his will enabled Marshall to travel to the United States in 1875, a segment of his education from which he benefited greatly and the lessons from which trip Marshall claimed to have never forgotten.

Australia also featured in Marshall's economic writings, even if only in a limited way. Australian minimum wage legislation as a unique phenomenon was mentioned by Alfred Marshall before the Labour Commission (Groenewegen 1996, p. 85), as was also done in his *Principles of Economics* (Marshall [1890] 1920, p. 715). In fact, the index of the *Principles* includes a number of references to Australia. These relate to Australia's birth and death rates, particularly its rapidly declining birth rate (ibid., p. 192); Australian wool and mutton were used as a key example in its treatment of the economics of joint products (ibid., p. 389); Australia's introduction of the eight-hour working day and its association with Australia's vast mineral wealth is drawn to the attention of the reader (ibid., p. 701), as are aspects of Australian economic progress (favourably compared to that in the United States) and its 'substantial borrowing power' (ibid., p. 752). Marshall also praised Australia as a place for 'bold ventures' in social improvements for the working class, something in which its borrowing power was also said to play a substantial role (ibid., p. 45). *Industry and Trade* contains fewer references to Australia. A note (Marshall 1919, p. 24 n.) draws attention to the large reduction in recorded Australian foreign trade when its six colonies federated in 1901. Australia's social experiments with respect to the improvement of labour are mentioned in somewhat more detail than in the *Principles* (ibid., pp. 160–61), and its experiments in monopoly control legislation (Australian Interstate Commission, *Industries Preservation Act 1906–10*) are noted (ibid., pp. 522–3 n. 2). No references to Australia are recorded in the index of *Money, Credit and Commerce* (1923).

Likewise, several Australian economic writers were noticed by Marshall in his economic publications. The most important was W.E. Hearn, the author of *Plutology* (1864), a book which Marshall had studied early in his life as an economist. Another was David Syme, a Melbourne writer on industrial economics (Syme 1876) and a protectionist (see Groenewegen 1988, for a detailed analysis). Moreover, Marshall's library contained a copy of Timothy Coghlan's *Statistics of the Seven Colonies of Australia*, published in two volumes in 1900, but this work is not listed in the index of any of Marshall's books. Nevertheless, it was almost certainly the major source of Marshall's statistical knowledge of the Australian economy of the late nineteenth century.

THE IMPACT AND USE OF MARSHALL'S ECONOMIC WRITINGS ON AUSTRALIAN ECONOMICS EDUCATION

By 1890, the publication year of Marshall's *Principles of Economics*, Australia had three universities: the University of Sydney founded in 1850, the University of Melbourne founded in 1856, and the University of Adelaide founded in 1876. The foundation of the University of Tasmania in 1892 coincided with the publication of the *Elements of the Economics of Industry*, Marshall's abridgement of the *Principles*, and a text frequently used in Australian economics education, as shown below. Two more universities were established in the early twentieth century: the University of Queensland in 1910 and the University of Western Australia in 1912. It should be noted that with the exception of the University of Melbourne, economics was not part of the early curriculum of these universities. Melbourne was the exception because its foundation professors included W.E. Hearn appointed to exercise responsibilities for the teaching of Modern History, Modern Literature, Law and Political Economy.

At Australia's first university, the University of Sydney, economics teaching did not begin formally until 1906 with the establishment of a Department of Commerce under R.F. Irvine. Irvine also became the first professor of Economics at the University on his appointment to that position in 1912. His courses were part of the Bachelor of Arts syllabus, until the formation of the Faculty of Economics in 1920, when they became part of the B.Ec. degree. In Economics I, as taught by Irvine, Marshall's economics was part of the syllabus, including the use of his *Principles of Economics* as a text, for which the easier *Elements of the Economics of Industry* could be substituted. When R.C. Mills succeeded Irvine in 1922, the Economics sequence of courses offered by the new Faculty of Economics continued with Marshall's economics as part of the syllabus, and sections from his *Principles of Economics* and from his *Industry and Trade* featured on students' reading lists. These books survived in that capacity up to the end of the 1950s, though at that stage their importance was reduced to small segments of these works. By way of illustration, these segments included the material on consumer surplus and, more generally, on the demand curve. They also included material on business organisation from Book II of *Industry and Trade*, and on monopolistic tendencies from its Book III. *Money, Credit and Commerce* was rarely used as a text at Sydney given the availability of local textbooks on money and banking written by Mills and his colleagues, and from its lack of Australian illustrations, previously mentioned. However, by the late 1950s it was still used as a reference for Economics III in the term's work devoted to money, largely because of its simple and concise explanation of the Cambridge cash-balance equation of the demand for money.

Before the formal introduction of economics as part of the University of Sydney's course offerings, some economics training was provided externally in courses for the general public given under the auspices of the university and taught by its staff. One such course, presented in conjunction with the Institute of Bankers of New South Wales, provided lectures specifically aimed at bank employees and used Marshall's 1892 *Elements of the Economics of Industry* as one of its prescribed texts. From 1891, the Professor of Logic and Philosophy, Francis Anderson, a strong advocate of university teaching of the social sciences, included a political economy segments in his Philosophy courses for the MA. Marshall's economics tended to feature explicitly in this postgraduate course, and his *Elements of Economics of Industry* was part of the suggested reading for students. The Professor of History, Arnold Wood, did likewise in the history syllabus for the MA. This contained lectures on Political Economy based on a number of classical texts including Marshall's economics. Once again, it was Marshall's *Elements of the Economics of Industry* rather than his *Principles of Economics* to which Wood referred his students.

Economics education started early at the University of Melbourne given Hearn's appointment among its foundation professors but at this time (the late 1850s and 1860s), Marshall's economic writings could not appear on the book lists issued for the Political Economy course. Hearn's successors, Charles Pearson, followed by J.S. Elkington, failed to advance the teaching of economics at Melbourne and in fact appear to have brought the subject into disrepute. This generated a situation where university commerce and economics teaching was for some time unsupported by government funding. Only with the appointment of Douglas Copland as professor of Commerce was satisfactory economics instruction restored to Melbourne University. As a consequence Marshall's major texts became part of the syllabus as set reading, a situation which lasted until well after the end of World War II. Marshall's *Principles of Economics* was used over these years as a basic text for the second year course, Economics II, devoted to price theory and other issues of micro-economics.

At the University of Adelaide, economics was taught off and on from its inception in 1871. By the end of the 1890s, when William Mitchell taught courses in Political Economy, Marshall's *Elements of the Economics of Industry* became the text for pass students. During the early decades of the twentieth century, after the appointment of Herbert Heaton in 1917, and Leslie Melville in 1929, Marshall's two major books (*Principles of Economics* and *Industry and Trade*) were firmly placed on the economics reading lists as important aids to study. These books were to remain on the economics reading lists at the University of Adelaide until well after the end of World War II.

For the University of Tasmania, the last of the Australian universities established in the nineteenth century, Marshall's *Principles of Economics* was a prescribed text for economics honours students in the BA degree and this practice was continued when Herbert Heaton was Chief Lecturer in Economics (from 1914 to 1916), when Douglas Copland became Foundation Professor in Economics (from 1917 to 1924), and when he in turn was succeeded by Brigden and Hytten. As was the case with the other Australian universities, Marshall's economics books stayed on the reading lists of University of Tasmania economics courses until the end of the 1950s.

This leaves the two Australian universities established in the early twentieth century. The University of Queensland commenced teaching economics in 1910, with Edward Shann as Foundation Lecturer in Economics until 1912. Shann's courses used Marshall's *Elements of the Economics of Industry* as a basic text. Shann was succeeded by a series of teachers, all of whom kept Marshall's book as a major text, until the appointment of John Gifford, first as lecturer and then as professor of Commerce. By 1920, Marshall's *Elements* was abandoned as a text, but his *Principles of Economics* and *Industry and Trade* featured on the reading lists of economic students for the remainder of the inter-World War period, first for the honours syllabus established in 1925, and then for the more general economics courses which came with the establishment of a Faculty of Commerce in 1926. They stayed there, though in a diminishing degree, until the end of the 1950s.

At the University of Western Australia, established in 1912, Edward Shann taught Economics and History from the beginning. In the two Economics courses taught by him, the first, on industrial systems and value theory, used Marshall's *Elements of the Economics of Industry* as one of three textbooks. A third Economics course, added in 1920, covered recent developments in economics including trusts, combines and modern credit systems and used Marshall's *Industry and Trade* as part of the recommended reading for students. These books retained their place in this capacity until the 1950s, with the *Principles of Economics* replacing its abbreviation, *Elements of the Economics of Industry*, by the late 1920s, as in fact was the case with most Australian universities.

CONCLUSION

In short, Marshall's *Principles of Economics* and his *Industry and Trade* played significant roles in Australian university economics education from the 1920s until the end of the 1950s, an experience which it seems to have shared with economics education in most of the English-speaking world. Interestingly, during the 1890s and the early decades of the twentieth century, Marshall's *Elements of the Economics of Industry* was the preferred text, presumably because its greater simplicity and brevity made it more suitable for student use. The continued emphasis on Marshall's work was undoubtedly assisted by the strong Cambridge orientation of much of the Australian academic community in economics during the first half of the twentieth century.

At the University of Sydney, Marshall's *Principles of Economics* returned for some time to the honours economics and postgraduate syllabus, when Peter Groenewegen included this book as one of the texts for intensive study in his Economic Classics course. This course was first presented in 1965, and continued intermittently until his retirement in 2002. By then, of course, Marshall's views on economics had become a subject for treatment as part of the history of economic thought, even if many of the students who took this course viewed its insights and its method as somewhat superior in treatment as compared with the micro-economics of prices and markets offered in more contemporary texts.

REFERENCES

Coghlan, T.A. (1900), *Statistics of the Seven Colonies of Australia*, 2 vols, Sydney: William Applegate Gullick, Government Printer.
Groenewegen, P.D. (1988), 'Alfred Marshall and Australian Economics', *HETSA Newsletter*, 9, Winter, 1–15.
Groenewegen, P.D. (ed.) (1996), *Official Papers of Alfred Marshall: A Supplement*, Cambridge: Cambridge University Press.
Hearn, W.E. (1864), *Plutology*, London: Macmillan.
Marshall, A. (1890), *Principles of Economics*, 1st edn, London: Macmillan.
Marshall, A. ([1890] 1920), *Principles of Economics*, 8th edn, London: Macmillan.
Marshall, A. (1892), *Elements of the Economics of Industry*, London: Macmillan.
Marshall, A. (1919), *Industry and Trade*, London: Macmillan.
Marshall, A. (1923), *Money, Credit and Commerce*, London: Macmillan.
Syme, D. (1876), *Outlines of an Industrial Science*, London: Henry S. King and Company.

8. Marshallian economics in New Zealand, c. 1890–1940

Anthony M. Endres

In the last decade of the nineteenth century and up to about 1940 the influence of Alfred Marshall on economics instruction and economic research in New Zealand was diffuse and indirect. The intellectual atmosphere in this relatively young country had an intensely practical orientation so that only certain aspects of Marshall's brand of economics were found to be agreeable. Economists who became active practitioners of the subject in early twentieth-century New Zealand were especially involved in public policy formation and in this role they drew on some fundamental Marshallian insights. They followed somewhat superficially and often in an *ad hoc* manner, certain currents of Marshallian thought transmitted from abroad. Indeed, consistent with Marshall's views on the use of economics in general, economics in New Zealand in these early years became a servant of practice; it was, to paraphrase Marshall's words, an engine of analysis to be used for the clarification of concrete economic issues. In the first instance Marshall's ideas were inculcated through a strong Cambridge bias in the University of New Zealand's economics curriculum. Therefore we shall begin with a survey of distinctive Marshallian features and influences evident in economics instruction from the 1890s.

The University of New Zealand was made up of several geographically dispersed colleges; it had both examining and degree awarding functions. Examinations and curricula were set for the most part in Great Britain. While Marshall was not directly involved in setting the economics curriculum and in examining students, many of his followers are listed as official examiners. These examiners had been taught by Marshall in either the Moral Sciences Tripos or the Economics Tripos; by their activity in the curriculum establishment and examining process they left an indelible mark on graduating students. Furthermore these examiners aligned themselves to some extent with Marshall's conception of the scope, method and purpose of economics. The following list contains all the relevant University of New Zealand examiners (the full list from 1880 – when political economy was first established in the University of New Zealand curriculum – is contained in Blyth 2007):

- 1894–98: H.S. Foxwell;
- 1899–1903: J.N. Keynes;
- 1904–08: J.S. Nicholson (1907–08 in conjunction with A.L. Bowley);
- 1914–18: S.J. Chapman;
- 1919: J.M. Keynes;
- 1920–24: J.S. Nicholson;
- 1930–34: D.H. Macgregor.

All of those listed above figure in what Giacomo Becattini (2006) has called the 'Marshallian school of economics'; they were also collectively responsible for creating a 'profession' of economics and economists in Great Britain in the period 1890–1930 (Maloney 1991). Naturally, they also had a similar effect in New Zealand.

The examination questions were diverse, incorporating classical economics, neoclassical theory exhibiting Marshall's innovations, economic history, economic statistics and applied questions relating to institutional conditions in New Zealand. In the 1902 examination for instance, J.N. Keynes set the following question (amongst others): 'The Law of Supply and Demand is controlled but not set aside by the law of the cost of production. Examine carefully the two laws here referred to'. Here candidates are required to reconcile Marshall's treatment with the older classical approach. In another question Keynes expected candidates to evaluate as 'incomplete or imperfect' J.S. Mill's theory of value. Such a question would not have been handled very well without some familiarity with Marshall's *Principles*. After World War I, J.M. Keynes's remarkable examination for New Zealand students (discussed at length in Blyth 2007) required candidates to 'Discuss carefully the part played by demand and cost of production respectively in the determination of prices' (question 1 paper A, examination for Honours and MA, 1919); in several other questions with Marshallian overtones Keynes asks: 'What do you understand by Quasi-rent?' (question 2 paper A); 'What are the chief economies of large scale production? Why do they not lead in practice to the concentration of each principal industry in the hands of a single firm?' (question 7 paper A); 'What is meant by speculation? What are its chief economic advantages?' (question 8 paper A).

Some outstanding New Zealand graduates of these Cambridge-inspired examinations during the 1890–1940 period were to make significant contributions not only to economics in New Zealand and Australia; they also contributed to applied economics on the international scene. Douglas Copland, John Condliffe and Horace Belshaw deserve special mention in this connection. Copland was appointed to the prestigious Chair of Commerce in the University of Melbourne (1924); Condliffe was appointed to the inaugural Chair of Economics at Canterbury College in Christchurch, New Zealand (1921), and Belshaw to the inaugural Chair of Economics in the University of Auckland (1926). These economists were initially taught from key Marshall texts: the latest edition of the *Principles* and *Elements of the Economics of Industry*. Nicholson's *Principles* (in three volumes, 1902–08) was also relied upon. Nicholson paid more attention than did Marshall to classical economics; more importantly for New Zealand students his text had a more practical orientation. These texts were supplemented by other texts including Sidgwick and J.N. Keynes on method; Clapham on economic history and Jevons and Bowley on statistics (Endres 1991, p. 174).

The work and career of J.B. Condliffe (1891–1981) warrants attention as a representative of the early cohort of New Zealand economists evincing Marshall's influence. After initially occupying the Chair of Economics at Canterbury, Condliffe later held a position in the Secretariat of the League of Nations; he moved to a chair at the London School of Economics (LSE) in the late 1930s and later to the University of California, Berkeley (Lloyd 2007). Condliffe began studying economics 'in an old tin shed in a small remote college' in the South Island of New Zealand in 1911. He remembers getting his 'teeth into Marshall's *Principles*' in 1913–14. Along with his fellow students Condliffe completed his graduate studies 'as a master of the essential core of our subject as it was then taught by the followers of Marshall so that we could move easily into the Cambridge atmosphere as many of us did' (Condliffe 1950b, p. 23). He spent a year in Cambridge in 1919 under the guidance of Pigou, but this guidance he found unedifying. Instead he preferred to use the basic tools of Marshallian economics to study practical problems, policy questions and a range of episodes in economic history. Therefore it is scarcely surprising that he spent most of the Cambridge sojourn attending Clapham's lectures as well as those of J.M. Keynes. Condliffe's subsequent Doctoral thesis at the University of Canterbury on economic development problems in East Asia was examined by Clapham, one of Marshall's 'more promising students' (Koot 2006, p. 179). In his magnum opus *The Commerce of Nations*, Condliffe (1950a, p. 111 n. 3) cited Marshall's supreme influence on his early training, especially in forming fundamental beliefs about the scope and purpose of economics as an applied discipline. Increasingly during the formative stages of his career as an economist Condliffe

> was led to believe that economic questions are always inseparable from the particular social environment in which they arise, that this is greatly influenced by historical tradition and inertia, and that individuals can often exercise considerable influence. It is also true that the statistical data available to economists is crude and imperfect so that it will seldom bear precise and refined analysis. The imponderables that must be excluded by such an analysis are often more important than the application of theory to such crude material. (Unpublished autobiography, cited in Endres 1991, p. 177)

There were certainly exciting potentialities in New Zealand for economists trained in the Marshallian tradition. The *Cambridge History of the British Empire* reported that New Zealand was a 'comparatively simple society' free from class conflicts; therefore 'economists should be interested in New Zealand, not only because of its "experimental" economic legislation, but also because it is more possible there to measure the real effects of introducing some piece of economic machinery, some new institution' (Hight 1933, pp. 3–4). Imbued with this outlook the first 'Marshallian' trained cohort of economists launched themselves into serious applied research. They were not unlike J.M. Keynes (1924, p. 223) who came away from Marshall's lectures seeing 'endless possibilities [for economic research] not out of reach'. There are too many examples of research in the 1920–40 period to cite here though Condliffe (1924) is exemplary; with copious New Zealand evidence it attempts directly to confirm Marshall's hypothesis in the third edition of *Industry and Trade* (1919) that a higher volume of international trade per capita was neither proof of higher levels of income per capita nor of internationally efficient export industries.

It was probably the equal pungency of Marshall's 'liberalism and historical empiricism' (as Koot 2006, p. 180 calls it) that had a profound effect on the training and subsequent research interests of New Zealand economists before 1930. They all possessed a pragmatic, yet liberal attitude to trade policy; public finance; the management of economic fluctuations; labour relations and the economic role of government. They held to a broad view that government had a limited but important role in the process of economic development. Condliffe's 'liberalism and historical empiricism' is clearly evident in his inaugural lecture delivered at the LSE in 1937 (Condliffe 1938).

The indirect influence of Marshall definitely contributed to the 'professionalisation' of economics in New Zealand up to 1940. Apart from developing an applied economic research culture in New Zealand universities, the expanding group of academic economists led by Douglas Copland established an Antipodean journal, *The Economic Record*, in 1925. Maloney's estimation of the impact of Marshall on the professionalisation of economics in Great Britain is completely consistent with parallel events in New Zealand. The new journal had to be filled with something other than journalism; the academics were expected to do original research and report their results and thereby develop professional awareness. Moreover, New Zealand academic economists were training students who by the 1920s could utilise their specialised body of knowledge in business and public policy analysis.

In terms of direct influence on a specific branch of New Zealand economics there is only one important instance where Marshall's impact led to some original, internationally-recognised work up to 1940. Ralph Souter (1897–1946), Professor of Economics at the University of Otago, whose entire career and contributions to economics are discussed in Donoghue (2007), tried to extend and elaborate on Marshall's (1898, p. 43) dictum that economic biology was the 'Mecca of economic science'. In his postgraduate training in the early 1920s Souter was exposed to Marshall's *Principles* and was encouraged by the evolutionary message contained in Book IV. According to Souter's elaborations,

Marshall transcended the static aspects of supply and demand that he formulated in earlier sections of the *Principles*. Souter (1933a) demonstrates that he was one of the few Marshall followers before 1940 to attempt, in a rather turgid style, to explain and extend the organic, developmental approach that Marshall was groping towards. Souter tried to recast the theory of value into a 'theory of relativity'. In this view, 'Marshallian demand and supply curves are [transformed into] theoretical instruments for the analysis of an economic price-quantity-time continuum' (Souter 1933b, p. 395). This position was advanced explicitly against Robbins's contemporary conception of economic science as a 'static formalist' discipline (ibid., p. 382). Robbins is said to have created an excessively narrow definition of economics in which decision makers are conceived as mechanical agents who allocate given, unchangeable scarce means among unchangeable ends. Souter's work drew the attention of Frank Knight (1934). Knight (ibid., p. 226) accused Souter of offering an 'apologetic' for Marshall's confusing and incomplete reasoning on evolutionary subjects. Moreover according to Knight, Souter's 'organic' theorising was founded uncritically on worshipping Marshall as some 'kind of hero-saint' (ibid., p. 225–6).

On the New Zealand scene Souter's philosophical approach extended to the theory of economic policy. Importantly, as far as Marshall's philosophy of economics is concerned, Souter (1939) perceived a place for promoting Marshall's idea of 'economic chivalry'. The idea is applied in a debate among New Zealand economists over the ongoing insulation of the local economy from international market forces. He argued that as a 'vigorous infant nation' New Zealand would not be served well by 'an all-embracing State Socialism' (ibid., p. 16). In a similar vein to Marshall (1907) Souter warned of the menaces associated with collectivism and he maintained that creating 'economic chivalry' would lead neither to a crass 'materialism nor to totalitarianism' (ibid., p. 13). He implored economists to entertain the larger questions of economic and social philosophy; this meant retaining in view Marshall's comprehensive (and more precise) conception of 'maximum net advantage' as part of a systematic approach to economic and social policy and as a means ultimately to realising the possibilities inherent in 'economic chivalry'. It was, in this view, entirely inappropriate for economists to consider the economic role of government in isolation. The government's responsibilities in economic and social reform must be considered as a whole; these must mature to the point of advancing beyond a mere 'purely manipulative or compensatory mechanistic approach' turning on the technical methods for controlling trade cycles such as interest rate manipulation, countercyclical public works expenditure or designing complex regulations for controlling imports or setting tariffs (ibid., p. 14). For Souter 'economic chivalry' implied the creation of a decent society in which the role of the State was to encourage an organic process that he called the 'diffused moralisation of the economy' in harmony with the economy understood as a progressively evolving organism (ibid.). A truly 'socialised individualism' would be the happy outcome. Souter brought Marshall's idea to the attention of local economists; he offered an elaboration of Marshall (1907) in a concrete case and it was strikingly consistent with modern interpretations of Marshall's agenda for creating a fair and noble society (for example, Gerbier 2006).

New Zealand economists tended to react opportunistically and with a certain native wisdom when offered a menu of Marshallian tools and concepts for application as the case or problem demanded. Doubtless their early training, which exhibited a heavy Marshallian emphasis, encouraged this pragmatic approach. Of course they could not lay claim to having contributed significantly to the international advancement of Marshallian economics. However, they were quick to recognise the applicability of Marshallian refinements in neoclassical economics to problems in the local economy. Notwithstanding the indirect influence of Marshall on New Zealand economics in the 1890–1940 period, New Zealand's geographical isolation was not a barrier to the transmission of Marshallian economic thought in the early twentieth century.

REFERENCES

Becattini, G. (2006), 'The Marshallian school of economics', in Raffaelli, Becattini and Dardi (2006), pp. 609–16.

Blyth, C.A. (2007), 'Maynard Keynes: External examiner for the University of New Zealand, 1919', *History of Economics Review*, **46**, 151–61.

Condliffe, J.B. (1924), 'Changing price levels: Their effects on the economic development of New Zealand', *Accountants Journal*, **2** (December), 139–46.

Condliffe, J.B. (1938), 'The value of international trade', *Economica*, **5**, 123–37.

Condliffe, J.B. (1950a), *The Commerce of Nations*, New York: Norton.

Condliffe, J.B. (1950b), 'The teacher and his influence', in R.S. Allan (ed.), *Liberty and Learning: Essays in Honour of Sir James Hight*, Christchurch: Whitcombe and Tombs Ltd, pp. 19–30.

Donoghue, M. (2007), 'Ralph William Souter (1897–1946)', in J.E. King (ed.), *A Biographical Dictionary of Australian and New Zealand Economists*, Cheltenham, UK and Northampton, MA, USA: Edward Elgar, pp. 261–4.

Endres, A.M. (1991), 'J.B. Condliffe and the early Canterbury tradition in economics', *New Zealand Economic Papers*, **25** (2), 171–97.

Gerbier, B. (2006), 'Economic chivalry', in Raffaelli, Becattini and Dardi (2006), pp. 532–5.

Hight, J. (1933), 'Introduction', in J.H. Rose et al. (eds), *Cambridge History of the British Empire*, vol. 7, Part II, Cambridge: Cambridge University Press, pp. 3–7.

Keynes, J.M. (1924), 'Alfred Marshall, 1842–1924', *Economic Journal*, **34**, 311–72.

Knight, F.H. (1934), 'The nature of economic science in some recent discussion', *American Economic Review*, **24** (2), 225–38.

Koot, G.M. (2006), 'Economics and economic history', in Raffaelli, Becattini and Dardi (2006), pp. 172–81.

Lloyd, P.J. (2007), 'John Bell Condliffe (1891–1981)', in J.E. King (ed.), *A Biographical Dictionary of Australian and New Zealand Economists*, Cheltenham, UK and Northampton, MA, USA: Edward Elgar, pp. 62–5.

Maloney, J. (1991), *The Professionalisation of Economics: Alfred Marshall and the Dominance of Orthodoxy*, London: Transaction Publishers.

Marshall, A. (1898), 'Distribution and exchange', *Economic Journal*, **8**, 37–59.
Marshall, A. (1907), 'The social possibilities of economic chivalry', *Economic Journal*, **17**, 7–29.
Marshall, A. (1919), *Industry and Trade*, London: Macmillan.
Raffaelli, T., G. Becattini and M. Dardi (eds) (2006), *The Elgar Companion to Alfred Marshall*, Cheltenham, UK and Northampton, MA, USA: Edward Elgar.
Souter, R.W. (1933a), *Prolegomena to a Relativity Economics: An Elementary Study in the Mechanics and Organics of an Expanding Economic Universe*, New York: Columbia University Press.
Souter, R.W. (1933b), 'The nature and significance of economic science in recent discussion', *Quarterly Journal of Economics*, **47** (3), 377–413.
Souter, R.W. (1939), 'How do we want the New Zealand economy to behave?', *The Economic Record*, **15** (October), 7–16.

PART IV

Marshall in Continental Europe

9. Marshall's influence on Swedish economic thought

Bo Sandelin*

At the end of the nineteenth and beginning of the twentieth centuries, science and culture in Sweden were most dependent on the German-language countries. From the 1880s through the 1910s, half of the foreign economics books bought by Swedish university libraries were published in Germany, while only a fourth were published in Britain or the US. Doctoral theses in economics were written in Swedish or German; the first in English was in 1929. Thus, although Alfred Marshall (1842–1924) was by no means ignored, there was hardly a massive and direct early inflow of his thought into Sweden. He had a place among others on reading lists for economics courses at Swedish universities at the beginning of the twentieth century, but none of his books was ever translated into Swedish.

As an individual economist, Marshall played a role, however. He was included in the references or cited in the footnotes in 68 per cent of the Swedish doctoral theses in economics during 1895–1926. Knut Wicksell and Gustav Cassel were mentioned in slightly fewer, though with a larger number of works per thesis. During 1927–49 Marshall was cited in 45 per cent of the economics theses, more than any other foreigner, though surpassed (in order of importance) by the domestic economists Erik Lindahl, Knut Wicksell, Gunnar Myrdal, Gustav Cassel and Bertil Ohlin (Sandelin 2001). In Myrdal's own thesis, *Prisbildningsproblemet och föränderligheten* (1927), Marshall played a more important role than in earlier Swedish theses, which may be indicative of the gradual shift from German and Austrian to Anglo-Saxon influence.

In a small country like Sweden, where there were only two chairs in economics in 1900, and eight in 1940, a few individuals embodied the development of the discipline. Wicksell introduced neoclassical thought to Sweden, followed – in an anti-marginal-utility version – by Cassel. Let us see who influenced them, as well as Eli Heckscher and Gunnar Myrdal, focusing especially on the role of Marshall. We will not scrutinise individual economists after those four, because as Marshall's thought increasingly constituted a large part of mainstream economics, his influence became more indirect, spread by authors who might not even know the original source.

KNUT WICKSELL AND THE FOUNDERS OF NEOCLASSICISM

Wicksell's first book, *Value, Capital and Rent*, whose original German edition was published in 1893, was mainly influenced by Böhm-Bawerk but also by Jevons and Walras, as is evident from the preface and a preparatory work (Wicksell 1892), as well as from the actual analysis in the book. Wicksell seems to have read Marshall's *Principles* (published in 1890) so late that he was not able to let the book play any significant role, though he added a couple of comments on Marshall more or less in passing. Thus he says in a footnote in the introduction that 'Marshall's *Principles of Economics*, which is based throughout on recent investigations, was, when this book was written, not yet published'.

In publications after *Value, Capital and Rent*, Wicksell refers incidentally to Marshall, but does not build his main analysis on him. In *Finanztheoretische Untersuchungen* (1896) he mentions, for instance, that Marshall had treated the principle of marginal-cost pricing, and in *Interest and Prices* ([1898] 1936) he comments on details in Marshall's monetary ideas. Some authors (Boianovsky and Trautwein 2001; Smith 2004) have noticed that Wicksell characterises Marshall's contribution to the English Gold and Silver Commission of 1887–88 as 'the most valuable contribution towards a solution' of the question

> how it was possible at the present stage of economic development for the quantity of the gold in the banks, or anywhere else, to exert an influence on prices; and how, in particular, the surplus of gold possessed at that time by the banks and the prevailing low rates of discount could be compatible in the light of the Quantity Theory with the falling level of prices. (Wicksell [1898] 1936, p. 76)

Yet Wicksell's assessment of Marshall's contribution was only relative for, although 'England's most distinguished monetary theorists and practitioners were summoned before the commission', Wicksell had 'not been able to discover that this fundamental question received any solution worthy of the name'. And he criticises Marshall for laying 'too much emphasis on the *direct* influence that he alleges is exerted by the magnitude of banking reserves on the rate of interest and consequently on prices' (ibid.).

In the first volume of Wicksell's *Lectures on Political Economy*, Marshall continued to play a subordinate role. Wicksell comments on a few details in Marshall's *Principles*, but he gives more credit to the founders of the 'new theory of exchange' (Wicksell [1901] 1934, p. 28), that is, Menger, Jevons and Walras, and – especially concerning capital theory – Böhm-Bawerk. In the second volume, Marshall is not even mentioned, but there is a reference to the English Gold and Silver Commission (Wicksell [1906] 1935, p. 127).

Böhm-Bawerk remained more influential on Wicksell than was Marshall. Wicksell's own writings suggest this, but also in the Wicksell Archive at Lund University Library, 40 letters from Böhm-Bawerk to Wicksell are preserved, whereas only a few from Marshall. Wicksell and Marshall did correspond a bit in 1904–05, elicited by a comment by Cassel about Marshall's view on Böhm-Bawerk's interpretation of Turgot. Wicksell thought that Marshall had misinterpreted Böhm-Bawerk on the increased productivity of lengthening the period of production, though he also thought that Böhm-Bawerk's interpretation of Marshall's theory of waiting was wrong (Groenewegen 1995, pp. 473–5; the letters are printed in Gårdlund 1996).

After giving a lecture at the Royal Economic Society in London in 1906 on 'The influence of the rate of interest on prices' (where Marshall was not present), Wicksell apparently tried to continue correspondence with Marshall, but without much success (noted by Carl G. Uhr in his introduction to the fifth Swedish edition of Wicksell's *Lectures*).

GUSTAV CASSEL

Gustav Cassel was early convinced of his own capability and grandeur, recounting in his memoirs how 'unsatisfactory and almost ridiculous' he found the teaching in Tübingen, Germany, which he attended in the summer of 1898. 'During these weeks, my decision to abolish the whole theory of value and build up an economic theory directly on a study of price formation came to maturity', he concludes (Cassel 1940, p. 15).

His first attempt was his long essay 'Grundriss einer elementaren Preislehre' (Cassel 1899). Although Marshall is mentioned several times, this was not a work in the Marshallian tradition. Instead, it reminds more of Walras's general equilibrium analysis, which Cassel acknowledges in the introduction: 'Among the authors, who in a way should be regarded as my forerunners, I will here only mention Walras' (ibid., p. 396). Nor does Marshall appear prominent in *Das Recht auf den vollen Arbeitsertrag* (1900), which mainly reviews the literature in the field. Similarly, in *The Nature and Necessity of Interest* (1903), the handful of references to Marshall do not indicate more than that Cassel probably preferred Marshall to Böhm-Bawerk.

A concept like marginal utility was important for Marshall, but an abomination to Cassel. In his mature work, *The Theory of Social Economy* ([1918] 1932), Cassel says that, from the beginning of his study of economics, he felt 'that it ought to be possible to do away with the whole of the old theory of value as an independent chapter of economics and build up a science from the beginning on the theory of prices' (ibid., p. vii). Marshall would not play an important role in his approach, as Cassel makes clear in the main text: 'In pursuing our study of pricing, we deviate almost entirely from the path which the customary method takes' (ibid., p. 169). Cassel sees Marshall as the foremost representative of the latter, and thus indicates here the chief difference between his approach and Marshall's.

Cassel comes back to this in his memoirs, where he recounts meeting Marshall in 1901:

> I learnt to hold both him personally and his work in high esteem, and I understood that the economic system I wanted to build first of all must be confronted with the Marshallian system. It was, however, not easy to get any detailed conversations with Marshall. His time was severely occupied, and his health imposed certain restrictions on him. He could at a lunch make an exceptionally fruitful conversation of general character, but it was impossible to go deeper into a topic. He must have complete stillness for his digestion. (Cassel 1940, pp. 39–40)

Marshall seems to have thought that he should have given Cassel more time. On 18 June 1901, he wrote to Cassel:

> Now that I have said adieu, I feel how much more I should have liked to talk to you about, how many questions I should have liked to ask you as to your continental experience. But I am over-driven. During the last three months I have only given five lectures and I had reckoned on having about 50 days *net* for my own work. But interruptions, which are always numerous, have been so heavy, that in three months I have done less of my own work than in an uninterrupted three days. Family affairs have occupied me somewhat; but for the greater part I have busied with the concerns of other students of economics of all ages from 20 to 50; and my own work makes no progress. I feel very guilty towards you; I wish very much I could put myself more at your service and had enjoyed and profited by your delightful and energizing conversation more than I have. Yours very sincerely Alfred Marshall. (Quoted in ibid., p. 40)

ELI HECKSCHER – ECONOMIC HISTORIAN

The bulk of Eli Heckscher's scholarly work was in economic history, though this would not exclude influence from Marshall. Carlson (1994, p. 15) sums up the view of several students of Heckscher: 'The persons usually held to have been specially important for Heckscher's development are his teachers, the historian Harald Hjärne and the economist David Davidson, along with philosophers and economists such as John Stuart Mill, Alfred Marshall, and Knut Wicksell'.

Heckscher set his hope on Marshall in a 1906 article about the general importance of the communication system for economic development. The literature in the field is weak, he complains, and the reason is to a large part 'the well-known difficulty, or rather impossibility, to demonstrate the importance of a single factor in a total development' (Heckscher 1906, p. 293). 'Maybe, one cannot indulge in expectations on a real profound treatment of the subject before Marshall's *Principles* reach the treatment of international trade and the location of industries between the countries' (ibid., p. 294).

In the introduction to his doctoral dissertation about the significance of railways, *Till belysning af järnvägarnas betydelse för Sveriges ekonomiska utveckling*, Heckscher again mentions Marshall, but also William Cunningham.

The question of the effect of one factor in a society is absurd, he says, because 'the real relationship between most social phenomena is not cause and effect, but interaction, *reciprocal* dependence' (Heckscher 1907, p. 1). This is one of Marshall's fundamental ideas in his *Principles*, Heckscher adds in a footnote, but it is difficult to find traces of Marshall in the rest of the text. In fact Olsson (1992, p. 52) argues that there 'are no signs of theory or hints of the *problématique* in the dissertation. Its character is more one of statistical description'.

Much later, in his introduction to the English edition of *Mercantilism* (1935), Heckscher states that Marshall's *Principles* 'was not only the starting-point of my theoretical studies, but also profoundly influenced my approach to economic history'.

These seemingly contradictory observations raise the question of what kind of influence Marshall had on Heckscher. It seems to have been mostly of a general character, for Marshall was one of the foremost suppliers of economic theory when Heckscher was young. Heckscher pondered the relation between economics and history, and pleaded for the use of economic theory to explain economic history. Olsson (1992) points to similarities between Marshall's and Heckscher's views on Ricardo, on the younger historical school and sociology, and to their common lack of interest in scientific-philosophical questions; but those similarities were not reflected in explicit references in Heckscher's work.

GUNNAR MYRDAL

With his doctoral dissertation *Prisbildningsproblemet och föränderligheten* (1927) in mind, Gunnar Myrdal says in his quasi-memoirs *Against the Stream: Critical Essays on Economics* (1973) that his writings until the end of the 1920s 'had been in the great neoclassical tradition of economics'. But it was not primarily Marshall's version that he had adopted. Instead, like Cassel, he had built on Walras, in particular trying to introduce 'anticipations into the Walras model' (ibid., p. 6).

Marshall was one of several economists who played a secondary though not unimportant role in Myrdal's dissertation; Cassel, Clark and Knight were others. Myrdal discusses the relationship between statics and dynamics in Marshall and Cassel (ibid., pp. 25–7); mentions, not uncritically, Marshall's concept of the 'representative firm' (ibid., p. 112); refers, with assent, to Marshall's 'personal risks' and 'trade risks' (ibid., p. 138); argues against Marshall's view on insurance costs (ibid., p. 153); and compares his own view with Marshall's concerning the course of time, the experience of an individual firm and the result of a whole trade (ibid., p. 185). On the whole, Myrdal was knowledgeable about Marshall and other main characters, and made comments on, and comparisons with, their writings when it made sense to do so, while remaining fairly independent.

Marshall played a similar role in Myrdal's very special book on the history of economic thought, *The Political Element in the Development of Economic*

Theory (1930), which contains about a dozen comments on Marshall. In some cases Myrdal just mentions Marshall's attitude, in others it is possible to discern approval, and in still others Myrdal is critical.

For instance, Myrdal says that early economists, because of lack of data and for other reasons, were not much concerned with concrete problems, but from the later years of John Stuart Mill onwards, 'most economists endeavoured to make their theory more concrete. Marshall was the chief proponent of this ambition' (Myrdal [1930] 1953, p. 9).

Myrdal criticises Marshall's interpretation of Ricardo's theory of value, saying that Marshall's 'credulity drove him to new extremes'. He not only 'obscured Ricardo's arguments', but 'interpreted Ricardo and read views into him which Ricardo had never held nor could have held' (ibid., p. 78).

Similarly, Myrdal opines that the 'great treatises on welfare economics by Sidgwick, Marshall, Pigou, and Cannan are largely vain attempts to put into a system arguments which, by their nature, cannot be systematized' (ibid., p. 127).

There are also a few examples where Myrdal gives Marshall credit. Thus, 'the controversy between the subjective theory of cost and the theory of utility can be considered as settled, in principle, by Marshall's dictum about the two blades of a pair of scissors' (ibid., p. 82).

To sum up, Myrdal was well aware of Marshall's positions, but Marshall does not seem to have been an especially important source of inspiration. In Myrdal's later writings, when he considered himself an institutionalist, Marshall meant even less.

MARSHALL IN EARLY SWEDISH TEACHING

Both Wicksell's *Lectures on Political Economy* and Cassel's *The Theory of Social Economy* were textbooks which also contributed to the development of economic theory, which is why they are remembered. In 1911 Sven Brisman published a more elementary textbook, *Nationalekonomi*, in which Marshall was missing in the review of literature; only Swedish books and books translated into Swedish were mentioned. In 1916 Brisman published the first edition of a more extensive book with the same name, in which Marshall is still not mentioned in any of the reviews of international and domestic literature that introduce each chapter, but only in a final section on 'general literature', where Joseph Shield Nicholson's *Principles of Political Economy* is considered the best of the more comprehensive works. Then Brisman declares:

> Beside this one, we notice Marshall's work *Principles of Economics*, which is probably the most famous one among the economic works that deal with the fundamental economic questions, and there is hardly any work of this kind that can compete with this one when it comes to descriptive power and interesting ideas. However, it is mainly restricted to the purely theoretical field, and it suffers from a certain lack of concentration. It is full of

telling and interesting observations, but it investigates hardly any problem thoroughly, and it is therefore not an appropriate basis for individual study. (Brisman 1916, p. 267)

Did students have to read anything by Marshall? Marshall's *Principles of Economics* and *Economics of Industry* (that is, *Elements of Economics of Industry*) appeared on the reading lists for the economics courses at Swedish universities in the early twentieth century. According to the *Studiehandbok* (student's manual) for 1904, the basic course in Lund, where Wicksell was professor, included works by Gide, Wicksell himself, Nasse, Scharling, Goschen, Leffler, Bücher and Herkner. The student should also choose among works by Helfferich, Webb, Marshall and Böhm-Bawerk. However, some of these specific readings could be replaced by 'a more comprehensive textbook', of which Marshall's *Principles* is one option. By 1930 this option remained.

According to the *Studiehandbok* for 1904 in Uppsala, where David Davidson was professor, Marshall played a more prominent role, as his *Economics of Industry* was included in the basic course along with part of Wicksell's *Lectures* and articles by various authors. *Economics of Industry* remained on the list in 1920, when both volumes of Wicksell's *Lectures* were also included in full.

The reading list in Stockholm under Cassel was very flexible. The *Studiehandbok* of 1908 required one work by Sundbärg plus four books chosen in a certain way among more than thirty, including Marshall's *Economics of Industry*. It remained in that position 20 years later.

In Gothenburg, Gustaf Steffen was the first professor of Economics and Sociology from 1903 to 1929. In 1890 he had written an enthusiastic report of Jevons's theory of value, but should himself be regarded as an economist of the historical school. Nevertheless, the reading list he prepared for his students for the basic degree included, among other things, Wicksell's *Lectures*. For the honours degree another 17 books were required, including Marshall's *Principles* and Böhm-Bawerk's *Positive Theorie des Kapitals* (Lönnroth 1998, p. 269).

Thus some economics students during this period, but not all, were probably acquainted with some of Marshall's work.

CONCLUSION

During the decades around 1900, the German-language area had the most important cultural and scientific influence on Sweden. Swedish economists – from Wicksell to the Stockholm school and beyond – also leaned more to macroeconomic questions than did Marshall, who devoted more attention to the theory of the firm, industrial organisation and other microeconomic questions that were not central for the Swedes.

So, although Marshall's *Principles of Economics* and *Economics of Industry* could be found in the large reading lists at the Swedish universities during the first decades of the twentieth century – often as optional books – he played a relatively modest role in this early period of modern economics in Sweden, compared to his ultimate international significance for the discipline.

Wicksell had been impressed especially with Böhm-Bawerk's but also with Jevons's and Walras's thought before he read Marshall's *Principles*, and thus Böhm-Bawerk meant more to Wicksell's theory of value and capital, although Wicksell and Marshall had a 'common language' in their mathematical background, which Böhm-Bawerk did not possess. In a letter to Wicksell (printed in Gårdlund 1996, p. 342), Marshall blamed Böhm-Bawerk for making elementary mathematical mistakes: 'A boy in a village school who made such a blunder in his arithmetic would be punished'. Concerning monetary theory, which was hardly Marshall's main area, Marshall was one among many whom Wicksell noticed.

Nor did the main points in Cassel's thought come from Marshall. Cassel's basic approach was general equilibrium, inspired by Walras, while partial equilibrium meant more to Marshall. Furthermore, Cassel saw no sense in the concept of marginal utility – or utility at all – while it was important in Marshall's analysis.

With the next generation of Swedish economists – Heckscher, then Myrdal and others – the influence from the German-language area was diluted, while Anglo-Saxon influence grew. As time went on, the number of important economists that researchers should be aware of increased, and much of Marshall's thought was also included in Swedish mainstream economics without reference to the original source, although occasional citations of specific points continued.

NOTE

*   I am grateful to Rolf Henriksson, Lars Jonung and Rick Wicks for valuable comments.

REFERENCES

Boianovsky, M. and H.-M. Trautwein (2001), 'An early manuscript by Knut Wicksell on the bank rate of interest', *History of Political Economy*, **33** (3), 485–507.
Brisman, S. (1911), *Nationalekonomi*, Stockholm: P.A. Norstedt & Söner.
Brisman, S. (1916), *Nationalekonomi*, extended edn, Stockholm: P.A. Norstedt & Söner.
Carlson, B. (1994), *The State as a Monster. Gustav Cassel and Eli Heckscher on the Role and Growth of the State*, Lanham: University Press of America.
Cassel, G. (1899), 'Grundriss einer elementaren Preislehre', *Zeitschrift für die gesamte Staatswissenschaft*, **55** (3), 395–458.
Cassel, G. (1900), *Das Recht auf den vollen Arbeitsertrag*, Göttingen: Vandenhoeck & Ruprecht.
Cassel, G. (1903), *The Nature and Necessity of Interest*, London: Macmillan.
Cassel, G. ([1918] 1932), *The Theory of Social Economy*, revised English trans., New York: Harcourt, Brace & Company.
Cassel, G. (1940), *I förnuftets tjänst*, vol. 1, Stockholm: Natur och Kultur.

Gårdlund, T. (1996), *The Life of Knut Wicksell*, Cheltenham, UK and Brookfield, US: Edward Elgar.

Groenewegen, P.D. (1995), *A Soaring Eagle: Alfred Marshall 1842–1924*, Aldershot, UK and Brookfield, US: Edward Elgar.

Heckscher, E.F. (1906), 'Kommunikationsväsendets betydelse i det nittonde århundradets ekonomiska utveckling', *Ekonomisk Tidskrift*, **8**, 293–320.

Heckscher, E.F. (1907), *Till belysning af järnvägarnas betydelse för Sveriges ekonomiska utveckling*, Stockholm: Centraltryckeriet.

Heckscher, E.F. (1935), *Mercantilism*, [S.I.]: Allen and Unwin.

Lönnroth, J. (1998), 'Gustaf Steffen', in W.J. Samuels (ed.), *European Economists of the early 20th Century*, vol. 1: *Studies of Neglected Thinkers of Belgium, France, The Netherlands and Scandinavia*, Cheltenham, UK and Lyme, USA: Edward Elgar, pp. 263–82.

Marshall, A. (1890), *Principles of Economics*, London: Macmillan.

Marshall, A. (1892), *Elements of Economics of Industry*, London: Macmillan & Co.

Myrdal, G. (1927), *Prisbildningsproblemet och föränderligheten*, Uppsala och Stockholm: Almqvist & Wiksells Förlag.

Myrdal, G. ([1930] 1953), *The Political Element in the Development of Economic Theory*, London: Routledge & Kegan Paul.

Myrdal, G. (1973), *Against the Stream: Critical Essays on Economics*, New York: Pantheon Books.

Olsson, C.-A. (1992), 'Eli Heckscher and the problem of synthesis', *Scandinavian Economic History Review*, **11** (3), 29–52.

Sandelin, B. (2001), 'The de-Germanization of Swedish economics', *History of Political Economy*, **33** (3), 517–39.

Smith, M. (2004), 'Thomas Tooke's legacy to monetary economics', in T. Aspromourgos and J. Lodewijks (eds), *History and Political Economy: Essays in Honour of P.D. Groenewegen*, London and New York: Routledge, pp. 57–75.

Studiehandbok för de studerande inom den stats- och rättsvetenskapliga fakulteten vid Stockholms högskola (1908), Uppsala: Almqvist & Wiksells Boktryckeri.

Studiehandbok för de studerande inom den stats- och rättsvetenskapliga fakulteten vid Stockholms högskola (1928), Uppsala: Almqvist & Wiksells Boktryckeri.

Studiehandbok för de studerande inom juridiska fakulteten vid universitetet i Lund (1904), Lund: Berlingska Boktryckeriet.

Studiehandbok för de studerande inom juridiska fakulteten vid universitetet i Lund (1930), Lund: Grahns Boktryckeri.

Studiehandbok för de studerande inom juridiska fakulteten vid universitetet i Uppsala (1904), Uppsala: Almqvist & Wiksells Boktryckeri.

Studiehandbok för de studerande inom juridiska fakulteten vid universitetet i Uppsala (1920), Uppsala: Almqvist & Wiksells Boktryckeri.

Wicksell, K. (1892), 'Kapitalzins und Arbeitslohn', *Jahrbücher für Nationalökonomie und Statistik*, **59**, 852–74.

Wicksell, K. ([1893] 1954), *Value, Capital and Rent*, London: Allen & Unwin.

Wicksell, K. (1896), *Finanztheoretische Untersuchungen nebst Darstellung und Kritik des Steuerwesens Schweden*, Jena: Verlag von Gustav Fischer.

Wicksell, K. ([1898] 1936), *Interest and Prices*, London: Macmillan.

Wicksell, K. ([1901] 1934), *Lectures on Political Economy*, vol. 1, London: George Routledge & Sons.

Wicksell, K. ([1906] 1935), *Lectures on Political Economy*, vol. 2, London: George Routledge & Sons.

10. Marshall in Norway

Tore Jørgen Hanisch and Arild Sæther

Before the first edition of Marshall's *Principles of Economics* was published in 1890, economic thinking in Norway had, for almost fifty years, been dominated by Professor Anton Martin Schweigaard (1808–70). He was mainly in agreement with the liberalistic economic policy recommended by the classical school. However, in several important respects, he distanced himself from this school and was closer to some classical economists on the continent, especially the Germans Friedrich B.W. von Hermann (1795–1868) and Karl Heinrich Rau (1792–1870), two economists held in high esteem by Marshall, who called Hermann 'a brilliant genius'.

TORKEL ASCHEHOUG'S ROLE

In 1870, when Schweigaard died, Professor of Law Torkel H. Aschehoug (1822–1909) was asked to take over his teaching responsibilities in economics and statistics. Aschehoug had been Schweigaard's student and, after completing his degree in Law, he started his career in 1846 as a state research scholar in economics. At this time, he viewed political economics as his primary interest and it is likely that he wanted to become an economist. However, he returned to law a few years later and, in 1862, he was appointed to a chair in Law. Somewhat reluctantly he left this position in 1870 when asked to assume Schweigaard's Chair in Law, Political Economics and Statistics.

By 1877, a chair in 'pure' economics and statistics was already established and Ebbe Hertzberg (1847–1912), also a student of Schweigaard, was elected but was forced to resign in 1886 because of his homosexuality. Aschehoug, who in the 1880s had made economics his primary interest, took over the chair. Until his death in 1909, he was the dominating figure in economics both within the academic world and beyond. In 1883, he took the initiative in establishing an association for Norwegian economists called *Statsøkonomisk forening*. This association soon became a forum for an enlightened elite of bureaucrats, government ministers, parliamentarians and economists. Its aim was to spread knowledge about economic issues by organising public meetings with invited speakers, and by publishing a Norwegian economic journal, *Statsøkonomisk Tidsskrift* from 1887 onwards, the first genuine economic journal in the Nordic countries since the short life of *Danmarks og Norges Oeconomiske Magazin* (1757–64). With his active participation in the association and his numerous contributions to the journal, Aschehoug was a driving force.

As a consequence of Aschehoug's diligent work, an independent study programme in Political Economy was established at the university in 1905. The programme was divided into three parts: theoretical, historical and practical economics. Aschehoug strongly believed that economic theory could be used to solve present-day economic and political problems. However, he had, for several years, been unsatisfied with economics as presented by the classical and, indeed, neoclassical economists. Like Schweigaard, he was particularly dissatisfied with its practical application.

Alfred Marshall was well known in Norway since the publication of his books *The Economics of Industry* (with his wife Mary Paley) and *The Pure Theory of Foreign Trade* in 1879. His attempt, in *Principles of Economics* (1890) 'to present a modern version of old doctrines', was well received. Aschehoug thought that Marshall had succeeded in his attempts and he made the study of Marshall's *Principles* compulsory for his students.

Aschehoug decided, as early as 1886, to give an account of the science of economics in the Norwegian language. The first version of his *Socialøkonomik* (*Economics*) was completed in 1891. In large part, it was an edited version of his lectures in political economy from the 1870s, although he had taken into account developments in the intervening years. The theories of Gustav von Schmoller (1838–1917) and Carl Menger (1840–1921) had a prominent place. However, he was not satisfied with the result. He started from scratch and a new version was finished in 1896. And yet, although he included some of Marshall's work in this version, he was still not satisfied. At the age of 80, he started work on a final version. This resulted in a complete revision, which was published in four volumes in the period 1902–08. Why did Aschehoug have such a problem completing his work? According to Bergh and Hanisch (1984), this stemmed from developments within the theory of value. The works of William S. Jevons (*Theory of Political Economy*, 1871), Menger (*Grundsätze der Volkswirtschaftslehre*, 1871) and Marie Esprit Léon Walras (*Élements d'économie politique pure*, 1874–77), had such an influence on the content and development in economics that it was said that they created 'a scientific revolution'.

The works of these authors, who were writing independently of each other, are similar in content but not in form. This led to a number of speculations. The Austrian influence had, as a consequence, the effect that marginal utility theory in Norway was formulated in verbal and qualitative terms. Mathematics played a minor role in this period among Norwegian economists and was not a widely-used tool among economists before the time of Ragnar Frisch. Aschehoug managed to change the attitude towards mathematics; he pointed again and again to Marshall's graphical presentation.

As Marshall's *Principles of Economics* was a benchmark in the development of the discipline of economics internationally, so too was Aschehoug's four-volume work *Socialøkonomik* in Norway. This work had been published as articles in *Statsøkonomisk Tidsskrift* or as compendiums from the University of Oslo, and was published as a complete work shortly before his death in 1909. It became an important landmark in the development of economics as a theoretical and applied science in Norway. Marshall's influence can be seen in all four volumes. In this work, Aschehoug makes more than 170 references to Marshall's own works. No other author is quoted nearly as many times.

Aschehoug noticed the significance of Marshall's *Principles* for the development and teaching of economics shortly after its first edition in 1890. He made the *Principles* part of his teaching, recommended it to his students and made references to it, or other works by Marshall, in most of his numerous contributions to *Statsøkonomisk Tidsskrift*. With Aschehoug's comprehensive use of Marshall's works, there was a substantial shift from German to English influence.

JÆGER AND ÅRUM

Oskar Jæger (1863–1933) was the central person in the Norwegian profession of economists between Aschehoug and Ragnar Frisch. His contributions span treatises on methodology to thoughts on public finance, and an active, although disputed, participation in economic politics (Jæger 1922). In his historical lectures in political economics, he is greatly occupied with the development of 'modern' analysis from an Austrian point of view. He mentions of course Marshall, but his mainstay is Eugen von Böhm-Bawerk (1851–1914).

Peder Thorvald Årum (1867–1926) graduated from the University of Oslo in 1893 with a degree in Law. Between the years 1899 and 1910 he served as a bureaucrat in the Ministry of Justice. In 1908, he was awarded the degree Doctor of Philosophy on the strength of a thesis on the labour theory of value. He became a scholarship recipient in economics in 1908. In 1913, he was appointed permanent secretary to the Ministry of Social Affairs, and in 1917 he became Professor of Economics at the University of Oslo. His university career was relatively short, but due to his two textbooks in theoretical and practical economics published in 1924 and 1928 respectively, his influence was considerable in the years following his death.

As a university fellow, Årum edited, revised and extended Aschehoug's major work, *Socialøkonomik*. His own research was summarised in his already-mentioned two-volume work, which had circulated among students as compendiums before they were published in 1924 and 1928. Building on Marshall, he noticed the distinction between the short, intermediate and long term, and understood the process that determines price as a result of individual demand and supply functions that merge into a common demand and supply. On the supply side, Årum especially emphasised the different interpretation of the cost of production depending on decreasing, constant and increasing return.

Årum was regarded as 'the modern' among Norwegian economists. He put great emphasis on Marshall in his writings, in his teaching and in his research. As a consequence the more advanced students increasingly read Marshall's *Principles*.

The classical school had claimed that the value of a good, its price, was determined by the labour costs. The Austrian school took the opposite extreme viewpoint and claimed that the value was determined by marginal utility alone; the cost of production had no significance. Årum followed Marshall and claimed that the truth was somewhere in between. The interactions of demand and supply in the market worked like a pair of scissors: neither blade cut without the presence of the other. Demand and supply simultaneously determined price and quantity. Market equilibrium became a key concept. By following Marshall, Årum also introduced the extensive use of diagrammatic exposition in his lectures and books on economics.

RAGNAR FRISCH

In his last years, Årum concentrated his research on the theory of production. In 1925, an assistant, Ragnar Frisch (1895–1973), was attached to this research. Frisch had graduated from the University of Oslo study programme in political economy in 1919. Thereafter he went abroad and studied economics and mathematics. He was awarded the degree Doctor of Philosophy at University of Oslo in 1926 on a mathematical and statistical subject. In 1925, he was appointed assistant professor at the university, where he became Årum's assistant and lectured on the theory of production. In 1928, he was appointed associate professor and, in 1931, professor and director of research at the newly-established Economic Institute. Together with Jan Tinbergen, Frisch was awarded the first Nobel Prize in 1969.

In the years 1933–38, Frisch taught the basic course in economic theory for the students of economics, first for the students in the old programme of political economy, and thereafter for the new honours degree in Economics that was introduced in 1936. He took up the tradition from his predecessors, Aschehoug and Årum, and used Marshall's *Principles of Economics* as his main textbook. In particular, he emphasised Book V, which contains Marshall's theory of value. This part is, according to Frisch, the central part of Marshall's exposition and it gave students a basis in economic theory that could not be neglected 'in our time'.

However, he believed that Marshall's exposition needed supplements in several areas. These supplements were given in the nature of a few independent 'excursuses'. The objective of these 'excursuses' was to give a more systematic exposition of the main points in Marshall's theory of value in particular and the *Principles* in general. They were, together with what Frisch called 'marginal notes' to the *Principles*, published, as a compendium, in 1939 under the title *Notater til Grunnkurs i økonomisk teori* (*Notes on Economic Theory*). Marshall's textbook was used as the main textbook, or one of them, for students of economics until after World War II.

It is clear from the preface to the *Notes on Economic Theory*, that Frisch had a great respect for Marshall. He considered his *Principles* to be the best textbook ever written in economics: 'The most valuable aspect of Marshall's presentation is the richness of his details and his taste for the connection between theory and practice'.

Frisch also expressed his views on Marshall's theory of value in a 30 pages article in the *Quarterly Journal of Economics* in 1950. He starts by pointing out that 'like all human work' his theory 'had its definite shortcomings', but went on to maintain that despite shortcomings 'this theory holds its own'. 'It contains elements about which no economist can afford to be ignorant, however "modern" he claims to be'. In his presentation, Frisch outlines and systematises the reasoning in Marshall's theory and concludes: 'Only the general features [of the theory] have been considered. To appreciate the wealth of detail one must study the book itself. What is most valuable in Marshall's work is the way in which he succeeded in combining the theoretical and the concrete'.

It should also be noted that it was not only Marshall's *Principles* that were known in Norway. Thanks to Århum and Frisch, Marshall's works *Industry and Trade* (1919) and *Money, Credit and Commerce* (1923) were well known among both students and staff at the University of Oslo. The language knowledge among Norwegian students and economists was such that there was not, at any point, an interest in translating Marshall's work into the Norwegian language.

Frisch's compendium *Notes on Economic Theory* was revised and extended by Frisch and his staff, and published again and again. Although they disappeared from curricula in the end of the 1970s, they were used by professors and students of economics at the University of Oslo until the late 1990s. On this evidence, we can safely conclude that Alfred Marshall had a profound influence on the teaching of economics, and thus on Norwegian scholars, for more than a hundred years.

REFERENCES

Årum, T.P. (1924), *Læren om Samfundets Økonomi*, vol 1: *Teoretisk Socialøkonomi*, Kristiania: Olaf Norlie.

Årum, T.P. (1928), *Læren om Samfundets Økonomi*, vol. 2: *Praktisk Socialøkonomi*, Oslo: Olaf Norlie.

Aschehoug, T.H. (1908), *Socialøkonomik*, Kristiania: Aschehoug og Nygaard.

Bergh, T. and T.J. Hanisch (1984), *Vitenskap og politikk. Linjer i norsk sosialøkonomi gjennom 150 år*, Oslo: Aschehoug og Nygaard.

Frisch, R. ([1939] 1947), *Notater til økonomisk teori*, 4th edn, Oslo: Socialøkonomisk Institutt, University of Oslo.

Frisch, R. (1950), 'Alfred Marshall's theory of value', *Quarterly Journal of Economics*, **44** (4), 495–524.

Jæger, O. (1922), *Teoretisk Socialøkonomik*, Kristiania: Centrum Avskrivningsbyraa.

Statsøkonomisk Tidsskrift 1890–1936, Kristiania: Aschehoug og Nygaard.

11. Marshall in Poland

Michal Brzezinski

INTRODUCTION

In 1918, after 123 years of division between Prussia, Russia and Austria, Poland regained its political and cultural independence. Prior to this date, only two Polish universities had taught economics: Jagiellonian University (JU) in Cracow and Lvov University. Traditions of economic research and education had been unusually weak. With a basic lack of theoretical research, economic studies had been either descriptive or devoted to popularisation of basic economic concepts (Kowalik 1992, p. 139). Most economists had practiced one or other – usually unoriginal – product of the historical school of economics. In the interwar period, however, the situation improved. Economics was now taught at the new universities of Lublin, Poznan, Warsaw and Wilno, as well as many higher schools of commerce and technical universities. The theoretical standing of Polish economists advanced, and also became more pluralistic. The approach of the historical school slowly declined, while the views of Austrian and neoclassical economics became more influential.

The impact in the interwar period of neoclassical economics in general, and Alfred Marshall's thought in particular, is especially evident in the works of the members of the so-called 'Cracow school' and 'Poznan school' of economics (Kowalik 1992, pp. 151–66; 2002). In general, these economists shared pro-market attitudes and advocated liberal economic policies. Other significant groups of economists in the period, including agrarians, catholic economists, communists, socialists of the chair, supporters of the historical school and theoreticians of the cooperative movement, also drew inspiration from non-neoclassical as well as anti-neoclassical approaches. However, it must be admitted that the Cracow and Poznan schools of economics did not produce many original theoretical results. Their members engaged rather in presenting Western economic theories, developing case studies, and discussing practical economics in an attempt to provide instant advice to policy-makers.

The only camp that was able to achieve substantial and lasting theoretical results was a socialist one. Oskar Lange (1904–65) and Michal Kalecki (1899–1970) are both famous for their contributions to various parts of economic theory. While it is obvious that Marshall influenced Lange in several respects, the same cannot be said, however, about Kalecki. Kalecki was an autodidact, never systematically educated in neoclassical economics. In the early 1930s, when he turned to professional economics, he became a socialist and was inspired mainly by socialist writers.

It is also important to stress that Polish interwar economic literature was especially focused upon the methodological aspects of economics, and more demanding theoretical issues were rarely pursued (Zawadzki 1927, p. 183). This was probably related to the historical conditions of the development of Polish economic thought – economic backwardness of the country, elimination of the sovereign State of Poland for over a century and so on. The methodological discussions of Polish economists were to a great extent inspired by Marshall's methodological views.

There is little evidence of Marshall's influence on Polish economics after World War II, but even in the interwar period it was rather limited – only a few economists were persuaded or inspired by the author of *Principles of Economics*, and not many of these few were able to creatively develop his thought beyond the field of the methodology of economics.

TRANSLATIONS AND REVIEWS

The only work of Marshall translated into Polish is the seventh edition of *Principles of Economics*, published in two volumes in 1925 and 1928 (Marshall 1925–28). Original editions of Marshall's work were not reviewed in Polish economic journals. The main reason for this was that the most important journals began to be issued regularly only in the interwar period. Edward Taylor, the main supporter of Marshall's economics in Poland, reviewed favourably, and with admiration, the first volume of the Polish edition of the *Principles* (Taylor 1925). Taylor exclaimed with regard to Marshall that 'it is not possible to find another author regarding the depth, thoroughness and comprehension of his thought constructions. Reading his works, and especially this fundamental one is a necessity and duty for every economist who wants to keep up to the standards of contemporary science' (ibid., p. 749). He also explained that 'This work, since its first edition in 1890, occupies a superb position in economic literature as a synthesis and an attempt to reconcile the results of classics and modern psychological and mathematical schools' (ibid., p. 748).

Taylor hoped that the *Principles* would serve as the most advanced textbook of economics in Polish higher education. Until 1925, Marshall's ideas were transmitted only very indirectly within the Polish education system, due to the language barrier and also to the fact that the dominant textbook (a translation of Charles Gide's *Principes d'économie politique*) propagated the perspective of the Austrian school of economics. Marshall's ideas, however, were already explicit in the lectures and seminars of such early advocates of the neoclassical approach as Adam Krzyzanowski (1873–1963), Edward Taylor (1884–1964) and to a lesser extent Wladyslaw Zawadzki (1885–1939).

INFLUENCE ON POLISH ECONOMISTS

In 1900 Marshall was awarded an Honorary Doctorate by the JU (Groenewegen 1995, p. 632). He had been proposed as a candidate by Wlodzimierz Czerkawski (1867–1913), Professor of Political Economy and Statistics at the JU and founder of the 'Cracow school'. The impact of Marshall on Polish economists is most evident in the works of Czerkawski's students – Adam Krzyzanowski, Professor of Political Economy at the JU, and Edward Taylor, Professor of Economics at Poznan University and the founder of the 'Poznan school'. In his *Zalozenia ekonomiki* (*Assumptions of Economics*) Krzyzanowski (1919) presented outlines of the theories of supply, demand, value and price, which are definitely similar to Marshall's respective theories. He referred implicitly to Marshall also when he offered an account of the nature of 'economic laws', claiming that they are not strictly quantitative, and that they are hypothetical tendencies (ibid., p. 79). In addition, in other works Krzyzanowski made use of Marshall's concepts of consumer and producer rent. It should be emphasised that Krzyzanowski did not attempt to advance Marshall's ideas, but rather adopted them uncritically.

The impact of Marshall's economics is also apparent in the works of Krzyzanowski's students: Adam Heydel (1893–1941), Ferdynand Zweig (1896–1988) and also Oskar Lange. Heydel, following Marshall, was interested in, among other things, the problem of measuring elasticity of demand, while Zweig developed theories of value and price which bear a close resemblance to Marshall's theories. Their accomplishments, however, were neither rigorous nor original. Lange, who became acquainted with Marshall's ideas through Krzyzanowski and Heydel, was from the beginning of his career rather a disciple of Walras's general equilibrium theory than Marshall's partial equilibrium framework. In one of his early works (Lange 1932), however, he admitted that Marshall's approach was very useful in studying many economic processes, and he tried to formulate a synthesis of partial equilibrium method and general equilibrium theory. He introduced a notion of partial elasticity of all pairs of economic variables, which allows for the elimination of those variables that change only relatively slightly in response to a particular change in the economic system. Lange concluded that Marshall's method is not only fully compatible with general equilibrium theory, but also presents the only practical way out from the excessive generalisations of the latter.

Edward Taylor, a leading proponent of neoclassical economics in interwar Poland, referred to Marshall's ideas in many of his books and articles. In 1919 Taylor published a book on static versus dynamic approaches to studying the economy (Taylor 1919). Here he applauded Marshall for introducing time into the analysis of market equilibrium, but also argued that in fact Marshall's short and long periods of analysis are nothing more than fictions, since both demand and supply are in reality changing independently in time. Marshall's constructions, Taylor concluded, are therefore not dynamic but – and contrary to Marshall's intentions – essentially static. Taylor's main treatise on the methodology and theory of economics, *Wstep do ekonomiki* (*Introduction to Economics*), was first published in two volumes in 1936 and 1938 (Taylor 1947). The book is an erudite and systematic presentation of neoclassical economics and Marshall is the third most-cited author in it (after Adam Smith and John Stuart Mill). It offers, for example, a strong defence of the method of partial equilibrium, which is based partly on the arguments developed by Lange discussed above.

Finally, some traces of Marshall's influence are to be found in the works of Wladyslaw Zawadzki, the most eminent Polish mathematical economist before Oskar Lange. Zawadzki was Professor of Economics at the University of Wilno from 1919 to 1931, co-founder of the Econometric Society and member of the Council of the Society from 1930 to 1938. In his first and most influential book, *Les mathématiques appliquées à l'économie politique* (1914), which was discussed at length by Francis Y. Edgeworth (1915), he reviewed the achievements of general equilibrium theorists and also some other applications of mathematical economics, including Marshall's method of deriving demand and supply curves in a partial equilibrium framework. In his review of 'Recent contributions to mathematical economics', Edgeworth (1915) touched on several crucial points in Zawadzki's book. He defended Marshall against the Polish economist's claim that the former did not appreciate the interdependence and complexity of economic processes. Although Zawadzki explicitly criticised Marshall for relying on inexact analytical constructions, for not recognising the interdependence of economic variables, and for not acknowledging the usefulness of mathematics in economics, he nevertheless praised the *Principles* as one of the greatest treatises on economics, the merits of which stood beyond question.

CONCLUSIONS

The influence of Marshall in Poland is clearly evident, but limited to the interwar period. Before 1918 Polish economics had been underdeveloped and severely restricted in its capabilities. For the two decades that followed World War I,

economics blossomed in Poland, but its growth was cut short by World War II
and by the subsequent period of intensive Sovietisation (1948–56). In this latter
period, the official position of the State declared 'bourgeois' economics to
be unscientific, with Marxian-Leninist theory the only acceptable economics.
Polish advocates of Western economics, and followers of Marshall in particular,
were persecuted for adhering to ideologically wrong opinions. Taylor and
Krzyzanowski were forced to move to emeritus status (they were reinstated in
1956 and 1957, respectively). Even after the political liberalisation of 1956 it is
very difficult to find any significant evidence of Marshall's influence on Polish
economics. His economics was taught in history of economic thought courses,
but at least until the 1980s the ruling textbooks criticised him from a Marxian
standpoint for his methodological individualism and for his supposedly
'apologetic' attitude towards the beneficial effects of free competition. In 1958
Lange, at the time the most prominent Polish economist and a deputy chairman
of the Council of the Polish People's Republic, suggested in a letter to a leading
State-owned publishing house that it would be valuable to republish Marshall's
Principles, but this proposal was never carried out. Lange himself gave a
fairly accurate account of Marshall's thought in his *magnum opus*, *Political
Economy* (Lange 1959), in which he tried to provide a synthesis of Marxian
political economy and neoclassical economics. This work was planned as three
volumes, of which Lange managed to publish only the first (unfinished parts
of the second volume were published in Polish in 1966). In his book, Lange
criticised the founders of neoclassical economics for providing an inadequate
theory of political economy (treated as a theory of historical development of
'social laws of production'), but admitted that some methodological postulates
of the neoclassical economists, such as the maximisation of utility assumption,
could be very useful in a synthesised political economy.

After the collapse of State socialism in 1989, the attention of Polish economists turned to more recent developments, and they quickly started to adopt
the formalised tools of modern economics. Marshall's ideas are analysed,
often superficially, in history of thought textbooks or monographs devoted to
particular economic ideas, which also trace the evolution of the views of eminent
past economists on the topics under consideration. In 2007 the first Polish book
devoted solely to Marshall was published. Joanna Dzionek-Kozlowska (2007)
produced an extensive historical analysis that aims at assessing the consistency
of Marshall's methodological postulates and also his recommendations and
advice in matters of economic policy.

REFERENCES

Dzionek-Kozlowska, J. (2007), *System ekonomiczno-społeczny Alfreda Marshalla* (*Alfred Marshall's Socio-economic System*), Warszawa: Wydawnictwo Naukowe PWN.
Edgeworth, F.Y. (1915), 'Recent contributions to mathematical economics, I', *Economic Journal*, **25**, 36–63.
Groenewegen, P.D. (1995), *A Soaring Eagle: Alfred Marshall 1842–1924*, Aldershot, UK and Brookfield, US: Edward Elgar.
Kowalik, T. (1992), *Historia ekonomii w Polsce 1864–1950* (*History of Economics in Poland, 1864–1950*), Wroclaw: Ossolineum.
Kowalik, T. (2002), 'Economics – Poland', in M. Kaase and V. Sparschuh (eds), A. Wenninger (co-editor), *Three Social Science Disciplines in Central and Eastern Europe: Handbook on Economics, Political Science and Sociology (1989–2001)*, Berlin and Budapest: Social Science Information Center and Collegium Budapest. Online: http://www.cee-socialscience.net/archive/economics/poland/report1.html.
Krzyzanowski, A. (1919), *Zalozenia ekonomiki* (*Assumptions of Economics*), Krakow: S.A. Krzyzanowski.
Lange, O. (1932), 'Die allgemeine Interdependenz der Wirtschaftsgrössen und die Isolierungsmethode', *Zeitschrift für Nationalökonomie*, **4** (1), 52–78.
Lange, O. (1959), *Ekonomia polityczna* (*Political Economy*), vol. 1, Warsaw: PWN; English edn (1963), *Political Economy, General Problems*, vol. 1, Oxford–Warsaw.
Marshall, A. (1925–28), *Zasady ekonomiki* (*Principles of Economics*), vol. 1, 1925, vol. 2, 1928, Warszawa: Wyd. M. Arcta.
Taylor, E. (1919), *Statyka i dynamika w teorii ekonomii* (*Statics and Dynamics in Economic Theory*), Krakow: Akademia Umiejentności.
Taylor, E. (1925), 'Alfred Marshall, Zasady ekonomiki', *Ruch Prawniczy, Ekonomiczny i Socjologiczny*, **5** (3), 748–9.
Taylor, E. (1947), *Wstep do ekonomiki* (*Introduction to Economics*), 2nd edn, Gdynia: Zeglarz.
Zawadzki, W. (1914), *Les mathématiques appliquées à l'économie politique*, Paris: Riviere; Polish edn, *Zastosowanie matematyki do ekonomii politycznej*, Wilno: Wyd. J. Zawadzkiego, 1914.
Zawadzki, W. (1927), 'Polen', in H. Mayer (ed.), *Die Wirtschaftstheorie der Gegenwart*, vol. 1, Wien: Julius Springer, pp. 182–92.

12. Marshall in Russia

Irina Eliseeva

The backwardness of the Russian economy strongly affected the development of Russian economic thought. However, the period after the abolishment of serfdom in 1861 was marked by a rapid growth of industrial production, railway construction, expansion of Russian markets, and increasing exposure to international trade. The new trends in economic development, quite naturally, had an impact on the evolution of economic theory. Vincent Barnett calls the period between 1890 and 1930 'the golden age' of Russian economics, a reference to both the international stature and the intellectual originality of the thought of these four decades (Barnett 2005, p. 137).

It was in this period that Alfred Marshall's *Principles of Economics* (1890, 1st edn) was published, a book that immediately gained for him, in the West, the reputation of an original theoretician who had discovered new approaches to economic reality by way of a theory of value founded upon the analysis of marginal utilities. However, it took a long time for Marshall's ideas to gain a foothold in Russia, and the road was bumpy and riddled with problematic potholes. As it turned out, those scholars who first understood his ideas and grasped their importance were themselves forgotten. Perhaps the main reason why Marshall's work did not receive widespread attention was the enormous popularity of Marxism in Russia. The only strong rival to Marxism in Russian economic thought at the turn of the nineteenth century was the German historical school, which approached economic problems from a 'nation-State perspective'. An important role was also played by the liberal *Narodnichestvo* – a term that originates from the word *Narodnik* (derived from the Russian expression 'going to the people'), and came to be the generic name for those members of *intelligentsia* who left cities for villages attempting to instigate the peasantry to rebellion. The exponents of *Narodnichestvo* in economics included professors Yuly Yanson, Alexander Chuprov Sr, Alexander Chuprov Jr, and many others. Most scholarly publications, however, were focused on discussion and popularisation of Marxist ideas. The first volume of *Das Kapital*, translated by H. Lopatin, N. Danielson and N. Lyubavin was published in 1872 and immediately won a great popularity among Russian economists (Marx 1872). Not surprisingly most of them did not pay any attention to such new trends in economic thought as marginal utility theory. The very idea of a rational individual who maximises her/his own utility was alien to the Russian mind. A prominent Russian economist and philosopher, Semen Frank, wrote:

> The development of the theory of political economy during the last 20 or 30 years has not left any imprint on us, because it does not fit the accepted dogmas of Marxist theory; the theories of Knies, Menger, Böhm-Bawerk, Jevons, Marshall and many others seem to be 'terra incognita' for a large part of our educated circles. (Frank 1900, p. 111)

The only example of success of the new economic ideas, albeit relative, was the diffusion of works of the Austrian school. At the end of the 1890s, the Austrian school began to take hold in Russia.

Few Russian economists accepted the ideas of Alfred Marshall and the theory of marginalism. The first Russian scholarly publications incorporating marginalist ideas included Mikhail Tugan-Baranovsky's paper 'Uchenie o predel'noy poleznosti khozyaystvennykh blag kak prichine ikh tsennosti' ('On the marginal utility of economic goods as a determinant of their value') (1890). In this paper Tugan-Baranovsky synthesised the marginal utility and labour theories of value; an approach that also underlies his later work (Tugan-Baranovsky 1911). Two monographs were published in the meantime: Vladislav Zalessky's (associate professor at Kazan University) *Uchenie o proiskhozhdenii pribyli na capital* (*On the Origin of Profit on Capital*) (1893) and Roman Orzhentsky's (associate professor at Novorossiysk University in Odessa) *Poleznost i tsena* (*Utility and Price*) (1895). The ideas developed in both works were close to those prevailing in the first stage of the marginal revolution.

A remarkable example of analysis of Marshall's writings was provided by R. Orzhentsky's works. In his book *Uchenie ob economocheskom yavlinii. Vvedenie v teoriju tsennosti* (*Study of the Economic Phenomenon. Introduction to the Theory of Value*) Orzhentsky (1903) discussed Marshall's views on wealth. He noted that Marshall tried to reconcile contradictory definitions of wealth, such as 'simple wealth' (meaning 'individual wealth'), 'national wealth' and 'cosmopolitan wealth'. Here is how Orzhentsky interpreted the relevant terms in Marshall's foundational work, *Principles of Economics* (of which he used the second, 1891, edition: pp. 108–9, 111–13):

> According to Marshall, simple wealth includes: among material things – things which are privately owned and have a monetary value and, thus, can be passed on to others or exchanged (debt obligations, by the way, belong to this category as well); among non-material things – goods that, external to a man, directly help acquire material wealth (including business connections, setting up a business). Wealth, in this sense, encompasses things that undoubtedly come within the scope of economic science. (Orzhentsky 1903, p. 8)

Orzhentsky continued:

[I]n order to compare the economic situation of the nations at different times and places, we need to have a definition of wealth which would apply to society in general ... National wealth is such a definition, and it encompasses the previous, simple elements of wealth plus some material goods, such as publicly owned goods (roads, canals, buildings, etc.) and free goods (rivers), as well as some immaterial goods, such as polity. (Ibid.)

Orzhentsky then noted that cosmopolitan wealth was a similarly constructed concept:

[I]t differs from national wealth much as that differs from individual wealth, and it is composed of public material property of all kinds plus goods that are extended over the whole area of the globe (ocean, science, music, technical innovations, and among literary works, only those that do not lose their merits in translation; others are a national wealth). (Ibid., p. 9)

But Orzhentsky emphasised that Marshall also made a different division within the concept of wealth, between individual and collective wealth, with the latter including goods not privately owned (ibid., p. 9). On the one hand, Orzhentsky obviously approved of Marshall's classification, especially his inclusion of immaterial assets as wealth and the attempt itself to produce an exhaustive definition of wealth. But on the other hand, he criticised this classification – in his opinion, it was a mixture of categories that had nothing in common. From this perspective, Orzhentsky criticised the notions of each of these levels of wealth. Marshall's most essential failing, in Orzhentsky's opinion, was that he included within the notion of wealth only inanimate objects. Orzhentsky, on the contrary, argued that political economy was not a science of inanimate objects. He supported this argument with a reference to John Stuart Mill, who had written that political economy was a moral and social science which studied the economical condition of nations, 'in so far as the causes are moral or psychological, dependent on institutions and social relations, or on the principles of human nature' (quoted from Russian translation of Mill 1874, I, p. 28).

Orzhentsky's criticism, however, had its own flaws: alongside the quote from Mill just given above, he furnished a quote from Marshall to the effect that economic science was not so much concerned with inanimate objects as with human beings. He extracted from the *Principles of Economics* Marshall's idea that political economy is on the one side a study of wealth; and on the other, and more important side, a part of the study of human beings.

Another of Marshall's tenets that attracted Orzhentsky's attention was Marshall's definition of the essence of economic activity as an activity the purpose of which was to satisfy needs and which had a monetary dimension. From this, he concluded, 'monetary measurability is essential for understanding economic phenomena' (Orzhentsky 1903, p. 38). Meanwhile, and in fact in the very next paragraph, he criticised Marshall for not having linked monetary value with other characteristics of economic phenomena. Yet Orzhentsky, once again, contradicted his own argument.

Orzhentsky was sympathetic with a number of Marshall's ideas, such as his claim that economics studies quantity as well as quality. Highlighting the importance of this idea, and with reference to Marshall, Orzhentsky elaborated:

> The specific of economics is that 'the force of a person's motives ... can be approximately measured by the sum of money which he will just give up in order to secure a desired satisfaction; or again by the sum which is just required to induce him to undergo a certain fatigue'. (Marshall 1891, p. 73, quoted from Orzhentsky 1903, p. 74)

According to Orzhentsky, one can agree with Marshall's notion of profit on accumulated capital as the measure of unwillingness to defer satisfaction, that is, to save capital for future use. Economic activity, as Orzhentsky noted in line with Marshall's thinking, can also include numerous altruistic motives, for instance, love for family, philanthropic motives (ibid., p. 74). He remarked that whenever economists ignored these motives, they did so because it was difficult to measure them. Orzhentsky elaborated on Marshall's important idea that in monetary measurements of this kind 'money does not play an important part; money per se is not the main focus of study in political economy; money owes its importance solely to the fact that in our world it is the most fitting instrument for measuring man's motives' (ibid., p. 75). Orzhentsky noted that other economists, such as K. Marx, argued that whenever an object had a monetary value it became an economic phenomenon. But it was Marshall, wrote Orzhentsky, who showed that monetary value was only an external symptom of the economic phenomenon, and not its essence:

> First of all, the matter does not concern monetary measurability, as Marshall is absolutely right to point out, but the accuracy thereof; money, while not being the sole instrument of accurate measurement, is in any case the most convenient among such instruments at our disposal in the present circumstances of our lives. (Ibid., p. 76)

Discussing social relations within the framework of political economy, Orzhentsky pointed to Marshall's remark that 'political economy can study only those relations between people which ensue from their normal or average behaviour and which are thus typical' (ibid., p. 89). Summing up his position concerning an economic phenomenon, Orzhentsky observed that contemporary economic theory defined an economic phenomenon through the notion of value, whose material expression was money. 'The presented concept of the essence of the economic phenomenon is endorsed in the writings of one of the foremost modern theoreticians Karl Menger and the prominent economist Alfred Marshall' (ibid., p. 337).

Our review of the theses set forth in Orzhentsky's main work strongly suggests that he was one of the first Russian scholars who understood the essence of the new era in economics that began with the publications of the Austrian school economists and of Marshall's *Principles*.

It is certainly no overstatement to claim that Orzhentsky did much to introduce Marshall's ideas into Russian economic thought. Apparently influenced by Marshall, Orzhentsky came up with one of the best definitions of value in Russian discourse: 'Value is a sentiment projected onto the object' (ibid., p. 256). A person looks and sees something. He likes or dislikes it, and the intensity of his liking determines the object's value. It may be noted that Orzhentsky's interpretation of Marshall was largely alien to the then prevalent one, which concerned itself mainly with analytical issues. However, ethical and philosophical considerations played an important part in forming Marshall's ideas, and they have gained proper attention in recent times (see for example, Coats and Raffaelli 2006).

Orzhentsky did not win recognition as an economist. His doctoral (*doktorskaya*) dissertation was in statistics – the monograph *Svodnye priznaki* (*Composite indices*). In general, Russian economists of the time did not pay attention to Orzhentsky's works. The discussions of the time were centred on the disagreements between Marxists, Narodniks, legal Marxists and social democrats.

Only a few Russian economists alongside with Orzhentsky took notice of Marshall's ideas. Let us trace the diffusion of these ideas chronologically. Perhaps the first Russian scholar to refer to Marshall's work was Dmitry Ivanovich Pikhno (1853–1913), a graduate of, and later a professor at, Kiev University, and a member of the State Council (supreme consulting body of the Imperial government) since 1907. He belonged to the Kiev school of economists (whose other members included Ivan Vernadsky, Nikolay Bunge, Alexander Bilimovich, Yevgeny Slutsky and Victor Novozhilov), which contributed greatly to the development of Russian economic thought. The scholars of this school opposed Marxism and widely used the contemporary concepts and ideas of Western economists and championed especially the idea of free competitive markets.

Pikhno approached economic analysis within the framework of the theory of value, and thus in the spirit also of Marshall. In this context, two of his works in particular are worth mentioning: *Zakon sprosa i predlozheniya* (*The Rule of Supply and Demand*) (Pikhno 1886) and *Osnovaniya politicheskoi ekonomii* (*The Foundations of Political Economy*) (Pikhno 1899). Pikhno theorised that no product owner was able to know the product's price or to accurately estimate the range of price fluctuations (Pikhno 1886, p. 58). He believed that it was impossible to predict market prices. Marshall, too, while exploring these avenues, concluded that in reality it is possible to determine commodity prices only for wholesale trade. In line with Marshall's theory, Pikhno considered consumption as the main economic category.

After Pikhno, the next scholar to introduce Marshall's ideas to the Russians was Vladimir Yakovlevich Zheleznov (1869–1933), with his book *Ocherki politicheskoi ekonomii* (*Essays on Political Economy*) (1912). He too graduated from Kiev University, and subsequently taught political economy in Moscow. His tract *Glavnye napravlenya v razrabotke teorii zarabotnoi platy* (*The Main Trends in the Evolution of the Theory of Wage*) was published in 1904 in Kiev. In this book, he thoroughly analysed the various theories of wage formation put forward by non-Russian economists of the nineteenth century. The chapter on 'The adaptation of wage theory to the newest theories of value and price' is devoted to the analysis of wage theories of Marshall, J.B. Clark, Davidson and Hobson. Zheleznov examined in detail the theory of wages found in Marshall's *The Economics of Industry* (Marshall and Paley Marshall 1881) and *Principles* (1898, 4th edition), as well as in papers such as 'Wages and profits' (Marshall 1888), and 'Theories and facts about wages' (Marshall 1885).

Zheleznov noted that, after Eugen von Böhm-Bawerk and Frank Taussig came up with their 'paradoxical' constructs, economists resorting to marginal analysis tried to bring the wages theory into line with the new value theory. The chief proponent of this trend was Marshall. Zheleznov named him the 'Nestor' (that is, the grandfather) of contemporary English political economy. According to Marshall, as Zheleznov noted, the normal supply price of 'unskilled labour' is determined by the standard of comfort at a given place and time; and the normal supply of skilled labour is determined by available funds and the desire of parents to groom their children for 'different' occupations. Moreover, Marshall analysed in detail the significance of both trade unions and industrial alliances. Zheleznov wrote: 'In general, Marshall's doctrine is more interesting ... because it identifies the problem rather than because it offers a solution' (Zheleznov 1904, p. 418). According to him, Marshall was a 'modern writer' because he came up with the principle of marginal analysis and substitution. In this respect, he was developing the ideas of W.S. Jevons and the economists of the Austrian school such as von Thünen.

Zheleznov examined in detail the theory of wages set forth by Marshall in *Principles of Economics*. He noted that Marshall accepted Malthus's doctrine concerning the reproduction of population while disagreeing with his views concerning the decline of agricultural production, which indeed had been starkly contradicted by the socio-economic realities of the age. He appreciated Marshall's arguments concerning the influence of 'cultural progress' on wages, which can be summed up as follows: the rise of education and the subsequent relative increases in the skilled workforce, on the one hand, contribute to the growth of the national dividend, and on the other hand, lead to declining wages for some categories of skilled workers because of the erosion of their monopoly.

Another tenet of Marshall's theory that attracted Zheleznov's attention concerned the progressive shortening of working time. He agreed with Marshall's conclusion that the reduction of working hours, while causing insignificant material losses, could create a considerable moral good.

Finally, Zheleznov has given a general overview of Marshall's system:

[I]t is a typical example of what the marginal utility school gives and can give. As an intellectual broker, Marshall judiciously encapsulates the discussion, leaving out the extremes and trying to find an accurate point of equilibrium for all the theories put forward by economists coming from the same strain of thought as he. (Ibid., p. 442)

Zheleznov pointed out that Marshall examined the phenomenon of 'living reality' with a good dose of common sense and in a manner typical of English economists. Marshall's assertions, however, prompted Zheleznov to analyse the psychological aspirations of an individual entrepreneur and an individual worker. He concluded that although Marshall 'gave very fine characterisations of these individual, psychological features ..., he very poorly described, and sometimes left out altogether, all other circumstances influencing wage formation' (ibid., p. 442).

Zheleznov pondered Marshall's ideas concerning the impact of technical progress, such as, for instance, the idea that 'the investment of labour and capital into a given amount of land would sooner or later lead to a situation in which any further investments of labour and capital would generate only a declining marginal product' (Zheleznov 1912, p. 127). He argued that Marshall underestimated the impact of technical progress in general. He relied on Marshall's authority to establish his own idea that factory work was not necessarily associated with either stupidity or moral degeneration. On the contrary, he insisted, corporate culture fostered manual workers' cultural abilities, and the widespread view as to the destructive effect of factory work was absolutely wrong. Zheleznov quoted a passage from Marshall on the advantages of large-scale production resulting from division of labour and use of machinery (ibid., p. 317). Exploring price changes, he agreed with Marshall's ideas concerning the impact of the conditions of production of traded commodities: average production costs can increase, decrease or remain constant as production increases.

Unlike Tugan-Baranovsky, Zheleznov agreed with Marshall's opinion that 'the wages of any worker ... tend to be equal to the net product of his labour' (ibid., p. 538). Relying on Marshall's *Principles*, he emphasised that rent had always been the payment for rare advantages, be they temporary or permanent. He also appreciated highly Marshall's idea of a close correlation between profit and price theory.

Zheleznov agreed with Marshall's thesis that the size of profit on capital depends on supply and demand (ibid., p. 176). He also subscribed to Marshall's position regarding the role of consumer's intertemporal choice and savings, and emphasised the crucial importance of these categories in Marshall's theory. He translated *Principles of Economics*, completing the translation circa 1917 (the year of the Russian revolution). It was not published, and Russian readers had to wait for almost 70 years before a Russian translation of this book was issued (Marshall 1983) – and then it was not Zheleznov's translation (see below).

Marshall's name comes up in the Russian economic literature in different contexts. For example, Alexander Miklashevsky (1909) criticised the term 'economics' as used by Marshall, and proposed to re-introduce the term 'political economy'.

Russian accountant Alexander Pavlovich Rudanovski (1863–1931) offered to introduce Marshall's synthesis of marginal utility and labour value approaches into the accounting system of Moscow's economy (Rudanovski 1912, pp.134–5).

The beginning of the Soviet era in Russian history was marked by relative pluralism in economic thought. Leonid Naumovich Yurovsky's *Ocherki po teorii tseny (Essays on Price Theory)* (1919) was published at this time. The author popularised the ideas of both Léon Walras and Alfred Marshall. In his preface he observed how persuasively and lucidly Marshall had shown how economists working at different time periods had given coherent shape to the price/value (ibid., p. III).

According to Yurovsky, Marshall accurately pinpoints the place of mathematics in economic theory, arguing that economic reasoning does not usually require long deductive chains. He considers particularly important Marshall's remark that 'direct application of mathematics to economic research is rarely useful, except when stochastic averages and probabilities are calculated or correlations between statistical series are sought' (ibid., p. 77).

In a chapter that outlines the theory of microeconomic equilibrium and relies on assumptions of static and dynamic analysis, Yurovsky made ample use of Marshall's ideas. He used Marshall's words as an epigraph to the chapter:

> Again, markets vary with regard to the period of time which is allowed to the forces of demand and supply to bring themselves into equilibrium with one another … For the nature of the equilibrium itself, and that of the causes by which it is determined, depend on the length of the period over which the market is taken to extend. (Marshall 1920, p. 330)

In his analysis of equilibrium theory, Yurovsky noted that if a system of exchange equations, which links all prices and quantities of goods, is set in place, then prices $p_a, p_b, p_c \dots p_n$ are determined by it. If the ratios between these prices are in line with the production cost ratios, and if there are no changes in population, tastes, technologies, organisation and capital, then these prices remain stable and become prices of dynamic equilibrium. If prices do not correlate with production costs, then they 'regroup' into another economic equilibrium featuring different prices, for example $p'_a, p'_b, p'_c \dots p'_n$ (Yurovsky 1919, p. 154). Yurovsky posed a question: 'But what will happen if the equilibrium in the existing stationary economy is disturbed?' According to

Marshall, 'such an equilibrium is stable; that is, the price, if displaced a little from it, will tend to return, as a pendulum oscillates about its lowest point' (Marshall 1920, p. 345). Yurovsky concluded that 'this analogy is inaccurate, to say the least, because we do not deal with a static equilibrium (the pendulum example) but with a dynamic one. But most essentially, even the assertion about the stable character of this equilibrium, strictly speaking, is wrong'. And he went on to expound his argument, which ran like this: the achievement of any sort of equilibrium calls for the fulfilment of certain conditions, which are predicated on certain assumptions, and such an equilibrium itself is too static a concept for the kind of dynamics he, Yurovsky, has in mind. So, Yurovsky, in his work, not only analysed Marshall's ideas, but also criticised them.

It should be noted that Yurovsky was the initiator of the first Soviet financial reform of 1922–24. He became a victim of political purges in 1938, and this prevented his views from gaining a wide recognition during the Soviet era.

Marxism was becoming the dominant ideology in the course of the 1920s, and this impeded the dissemination of Marshall's ideas among Russian economists. Marshall was mentioned in the *Introduction to Political Economy* by Sergey Solntsev (1922), a professor at St. Petersburg University (1872–1936). Solntsev argued that Marshall was one of the economists influenced by the Austrian school of marginal utility analysis (Solntsev [1922] 2007, p. 530). Marshall met with a warm response from the Russian economists because he, like Brentano and Lexis, introduced ethical aspects into economic theory (ibid., p. 519). However, he rarely merited a mention in Russian economic literature. Nevertheless, we do find a passing mention of Marshall in the *Encyclopedic Dictionary Granat* in the article entitled 'Tzennost menovaya' ('Value') by Piotr Maslov (n.d.).

This relative pluralism in Russian economics ended by 1929–30 – the years of the Great Turning Point. Prior to this date, Marshall's name continued to appear occasionally in the economic literature every now and again, albeit mostly in passing and as a casual reference, rather than as the subject of analysis.

From the end of the 1920s Marxism–Leninism had completely replaced liberal attitudes in Soviet economic theory. Marshall's theory was considered an instance of 'vulgar political economy'. In the writings of this period he was treated not as the founder of neoclassical economics, but as a follower of the political economists of the mid-nineteenth century, such as J.S. Mill and J.R. McCulloch. Marshall's work was viewed as an attempt to connect the views of these scholars with the newer marginal utility theory. For example, in his treatise *Sub'ektivnaya shkola v politicheskoi ekonomii* (*Subjective Trends in Political Economy*) (Blyumin 1928), Izrail Grigorijevich Blyumin (1897–1959) named Marshall 'a prolific producer of dogmatic formulas mixing various vulgar theories'. The methodology of Marshall's research – in particular, his failure to start research into functional dependencies – was also criticised.

Blyumin emphasised a lack of continuity between Marshall's ideas and those of the classical school, asserting that Marshall relied only on 'the wrong ideas of Ricardo' (ibid.).

The greatest amount of criticism was aimed at Marshall's theory of supply and demand – 'according to Marshall', so the argument ran, 'cost is a metaphysical category; only prices are real'. Actually, Marshall did not talk of metaphysics, but simply drew a distinction between *real* costs (disutilities and waiting) and *money* costs or *production expenses*. In fact, costs, for Marshall, are real too. Price is a quantitative ratio between the quantity of goods and the quantity of money. So, quantitative proportions of the exchange of goods are real. This definition of price as independent from cost had a wide currency in the earlier Russian economic literature. In Russia the main exponent of this line of thinking was Piotr Berngardovich Struve (1870–1944). In his work *Khozyaistvo i tsena* (*Economy and Price*) (vol. 1, 1913; vol. 2, 1916) he asserted that cost was a metaphysical counterpart of price. Such views contradicted Marx's theory of value and were treated in the Soviet Union as incontestably wrong.

Blyumin's works were re-issued in 1962 in three volumes, under the general title *Kritika burzhuaznoi politicheskoi ekonomii* (*Criticism of Bourgeois Political Economy*) (Blyumin 1962). Professor Blyumin wrote an all-encompassing, detailed, but absolutely biased analysis of Marshall's theory. He said that Marshall was an apologist of capitalism, supported the policy of monopolies and British imperialism, and certainly must be classified as a reactionary economist.

But even behind the 'iron curtain' Marshall's ideas continued to circulate.

In 1950 in Moscow, at the Institute of Economy of the USSR Academy of Sciences, Z.P. Sviridova defended a PhD thesis (*kandidatskaya dissertatsiya*) entitled *Kritika ekonomicheskogo uchenija A. Marshalla* (*Critique of Alfred Marshall's Economic Doctrine*) (Sviridova 1950). This thesis included a thorough analysis and critique of Marshall's main works from the viewpoint of Marxist theory. Sviridova's dissertation, while being a local event, shows that Russian scholars were interested in Marshall during the period of the Cold War.

Despite all the obstacles, Marshall's ideas continued to gain a foothold in Soviet Russia, meeting not only with criticism but sometimes with approval as well. This latter happened thanks to the publication of a series of books entitled 'for Academic Libraries' (this label meant that in order to get an access to the book a scholar had to present a special permission from the authorities; this permission indicated that the person was reliable). In 1968, the publisher of these series printed a Russian translation of Ben B. Seligman's *Main Currents in Modern Economics* (1968). A special section of the book was devoted to Marshall's contribution to economic theory.

Only a few scholars had access to Western economic literature. The group of 'eligible' Soviet economists was concentrated at the Institute of World Economy and International Relations of the Academy of Science of USSR in Moscow. Not accidentally, in the early 1970s the Institute's staff researchers published three books incorporating elements of Marshall's views (Nikitin 1970; *Burzhuaznye ekonomicheskye teorii i ekonomicheskaya politika imperialisticheskih stran 1971 – Bourgeois Economic Theories and Economic Policy of Imperialist Countries*; Kozlova and Entov 1972).

These scholars, while engaging in traditional Soviet-style criticism and lambasting Marshall as an exponent of the vulgar school of political economy, were the first to write with a hint of approval about the most outstanding Western economists (including Marshall). S.M. Nikitin noted that Marshall's contribution to economics should be carefully looked into and emphasised the fact that Marshall was the first to see price as a result of interaction between such complex factors as supply and demand. Nikitin stressed that, with his concept of demand elasticity, Marshall had made an outstanding contribution to the theory of consumption. 1975 saw the publication of a four-volume set *Ekonomicheskaya enciklopediya. Politicheskaya ekonomiya* (*Economic Encyclopaedia. Political Economy*). The encyclopaedia contained an entry on Marshall (Loschinsky 1975), which labelled him a founder of the Cambridge school of 'bourgeois political economy' that related subjective marginal utility to production costs.

At last, the first Russian translation (but not those by Zheleznov) of Marshall's *Principles of Economics* was published in Russia in 1983 with a critical introduction by S.M. Nikitin (Marshall 1983).

In their writings the Soviet economists generally commented on the ideas of Western scholars, including Alfred Marshall, in terms of traditional Soviet critique. In this period, however, a Russian translation of Antonio Pesenti's *Manuale di economia politica* (in two volumes) was also published, with texts from original course books on micro- and macroeconomics included in the appendix to the second volume. These texts were written by two Italian economists: G. La Grassa – 'Microeconomics. The subjective approach in economics' (first part: 'Consumption'; second part: 'Production') and C. Casarosa – 'Macroeconomics' ('Short-term macroeconomic models'; 'Inflation and business cycle'; 'The theory of growth') (Pesenti 1976, II, pp. 337–870). Thus, all the foundational ideas of neoclassical economics, along with references to essential works, including Marshall's *Principles*, were introduced without the slightest disparagement.

After the fall of socialism in 1993 Marshall's *Principles of Economics* became available to wide circles of Russian readers (Marshall 1993). This was a reprint of the already mentioned translation (of the 8th English edition) published in 1983. The 1983 publication contained Nikitin's introduction, in which Marshall was criticised from a Marxist perspective. In the 1993 publication Nikitin's introduction was replaced with a translation of Keynes's obituary essay, 'Alfred Marshall, 1842–1924' (Keynes 1924).

It is interesting to mention the changes in the translation of its title. Russian translations of Marshall's *Principles of Economics* had been given different titles:

• 1983: *Principles of Political Economy*;
• 1993: *Principles of Economic Theory*;
• 2007: *Fundamentals of Economic Theory*.

Marshall believed in Russia:

> Great futures may also await Russia and China. Each is large, continuous and self-contained: each has enormous resources, which could not be developed so long as good access to ocean highways was a necessary condition for great achievement. Their populations differ in temperament; the persistence of the Chinese being complementary to the quick sensibility of the Russian: each has inherited great powers of endurance. (Marshall 1919, p. 162)

The reception of Marshall's ideas in Russia involved initial attempts at discussion, subsequent rejection, and finally recognition. It took time to redress a historical injustice, but now Marshall occupies the place he deserves among the founding fathers of modern economic theory.

REFERENCES

Barnett, V. (2005), *A History of Russian Economic Thought*, London: Routledge.
Blyumin, I.G. (1928), *Sub'ektivnaya shkola v politicheskoi ekonomii*, Moscow: Communisticheskaya Academiya.
Blyumin, I.G. (1962), *Kritika burzhuaznoi politicheskoi ekonomii*, 3 vols, vol. 1: *Sub'ektivnaya shkola v burzhuaznoi politicheskoi ekonomii*, Moscow: Izdadelstvo Academii Nauk SSSR.
Burzhuaznye ekonomicheskye teorii i ekonomicheskaya politika imperialisticheskih stran (1971), edited by A.G. Mileikovsky, Moscow: Mysl.
Coats, B.W. and T. Raffaelli (2006), 'Economics and ethics', in T. Raffaelli, G. Becattini and M. Dardi (eds), *The Elgar Companion to Alfred Marshall*, Cheltenham, UK and Northampton, MA, USA: Edward Elgar, pp. 182–9.
Frank, S. (1900), *Teoriya tsennosti Marxa i eye znachenie*, Saint Petersburg: izdanie M.I. Vodovozovoi.
Keynes, J.M. (1924), 'Alfred Marshall, 1842–1924', *Economic Journal*, 34, 311–72.
Kozlova, K.B. and R.M. Entov (1972), *Teoriya tseny*, Moscow: Misl.
Loschinsky I.T. (1975), 'Marshall Alfred', in A.M. Rumyantsev (ed.), *Economocheskaya Encyklopediya. Politicheskaya Economiya*, vol. 2, Moscow: Sovetskaya Encyklopediya, p. 395.
Marshall, A. (1885), 'Theories and facts about wages', in The Co-operative Wholesale Society Limited, *Annual and Diary for Year 1885*.
Marshall, A. (1888), 'Wages and profits', *Quarterly Journal of Economics*, **2**, 218–23.
Marshall, A. (1891), *Principles of Economics*, 2nd edn, London: Macmillan & Co.
Marshall, A. (1919), *Industry and Trade*, London: Macmillan.
Marshall, A. (1920), *Principles of Economics*, 8th edn, London: Macmillan & Co.
Marshall, A. (1983), *Principy politicheskoi ekonomii*, trans. R.I. Stolper, with an introduction by S.M. Nikitin, Moscow: Progress.
Marshall, A. (1993), *Principy ekonomicheskoi nauki*, 3 vols, Moscow: Progress.

Marshall, A. (2007), *Osnovy economicheskoi nauki*, trans. V.I. Bomkin and others, Moscow: Ecsmo.

Marshall, A. and M. Paley Marshall (1881), *The Economics of Industry*, 2nd edn, London: Macmillan.

Marx, K. (1872), *Kapital*, Russian trans. *Das Kapital*, vol. 1, Saint Petersburg: izdatel N.P. Polyakov.

Maslov, P. (n.d.), 'Tsennost menovaya', in *Encyclopedic Dictionary Granat*, vol. 45, part 3, pp. 292–308.

Miklashevsky, A.N. (1909), *Istoriya politicheskoi economii*, Yur'ev: Tipographiya K. Mattisenko.

Mill, J.S. (1873–74), *Osnovaniya politicheskoi economii* (*Principles of Economics*), 2 vols, Saint Petersburg: Tipographiya M. Stasyulevicha.

Nikitin, S.M. (1970), *Teorii stoimosti i ikh evolyuciya*, Moscow: Misl.

Orzhentsky, R.M. (1895), *Poleznost i tsena*, Odessa: Tipographiya A. Hakalovskogo

Orzhentsky, R.M. (1903), *Uchenie ob economicheskom yavlenii. Vvedenie v teoriju tsennosti*, Odessa: Economicheskaya Tipographiya.

Pesenti, A. (1976), *Ocherki politicheskoi ekonomii kapitalizma*, Russian trans. of A. Pesenti, *Manuale di economia politica*, edited by A.G. Mileikovsky, 2 vols, Moscow: Progress.

Pikhno, D.I. (1886), *Zakon sprosa i predlozheniya*, Kiev: Universitetskaya Tipographiya.

Pikhno, D.I. (1899), *Osnovaniya politicheskoi ekonomii*, Kiev: Tovarischestvo pechatnogo dela i torgovli I.N. Kushnerev i co.

Rudanovski, A.P. (1912), *Obschaya teoriya i otsenka Moskovskogo gorodskogo schetovodstva*, Moscow: Gorodskaya Tipographiya.

Seligman, B.B. (1968), *Osnovnye techeniya sovremennoi ekonomisheskoi mysli*, Russian trans. of B.B. Seligman, *Main Currents in Modern Economic Thought since 1870*, edited by A.M. Rumyantsev, L.B. Alper and A.G. Mileikovsky, Moscow: Progress.

Solntsev, S. ([1922] 2007), 'Vvedenie v politicheskuju economiju', in S. Solntsev, *Obschestvennye klassy*, Moscow: Astrel.

Struve, P. (1913–16), *Khozyaistvo i tsena*, vol. 1, 1913, vol. 2, 1916, Saint Petersburg: Tipographiya Shredera.

Sviridova, Z.P. (1950), *Kritica ekonomicheskogo ucheniya A. Marschalla*, Avtoreferat dissertacii, Moscow: Institute Economiki AN SSSR.

Tugan-Baranovsky, M.I. (1890), 'Uchenie o predel'noy poleznosti khozyaystvennykh blag kak prichine ikh tsennosti', *Juridichesky Vestnik*, 10, 192–230.

Tugan-Baranovsky, M.I. (1911), *Osnovy politicheskoi ekonomii*, 2nd edn, Saint Petersburg: Izdatelstvo Pravo.

Yurovsky, L.N. (1919), *Ocherki po teorii tseny*, Saratov: Soyuz Potrebitelskih Obschestv Saratovskogo Kraya.

Zalessky, V. (1893), *Uchenie o proiskhozhdenii pribyli na capital*, Otdel 1: *Uchenie o Tsennosti. Chast Dogmaticheskaya*, Kazan: Tipographiya Imperatorskogo Universiteta.

Zheleznov, V.Ya. (1904), *Glavnye napravlenya v razrabotke teorii zarabotnoi platy*, Kiev: Tipographiya Tovarischestva I.N. Kushnerev i co.

Zheleznov, V.Ya. (1912), *Ocherki politicheskoi ekonomii*, 7th edn, Moscow: Tovarischestvo I.D. Sytina.

13. Marshall in German-speaking countries

Volker Caspari

While Marshall's economics was well known in the Anglo-American world, the situation in the German language area was different. Most members of the younger historical school ignored his approach, whereas the leaders of the Austrian school criticised it. Particularly the reaction of the younger historical school was a little perplexing because the careful reader of the *Principles* and of *Industry and Trade* will realise that Marshall thought highly of the historical school. However, there was no reciprocity on the side of the historical school.

A first look at the reviews of the *Principles* by German-speaking economists gives an impression of this attitude towards Marshall's economic thinking. Katzenstein presumed in his review (1893) that 'Marshall had written his *Principles* to rescue Ricardo and the whole old-English school from the icon-oclasm of the present time'. Schmoller, one of the leading heads of the younger historical school, characterised Marshall's approach as 'outlived' (1897). However, economics in the German language area in the 1890s was not completely conquered by the younger historical school. Adolph Wagner, a then leading economist did not hold their views. In a review published in English in the *Quarterly Journal of Economics*, Wagner pointed out that not all German economists 'approved of the patronising and pretentious attitude towards the classical school, which was taken by some of the extreme German representatives of the historical school' (Wagner 1891, p. 319). Wagner and other non-Austrian economists like Dietzel welcomed Marshall's approach as an improved and completed version of Ricardo's theory.

In the same year Robert Zuckerkandl reviewed the *Principles* from the Austrian perspective. Starting with a glorification of Marshall which borders on adulation Zuckerkandl exposes Marshall's short- and long-period theory of normal prices and gives a brief though comprehensive account of Marshall's ideas on the theory of distribution. Then he continues, 'if one compares [Marshall's] theory of prices and distribution with what the German literature has to tell about the same subject, some remarkable differences will come across'. Zuckerkandl stresses that in the German literature the formation of prices is explained by tracing them back to their psychological foundations (causal-genetic method) while Marshall emphasises that both cost of production on the supply side and utility on the demand side work together to determine prices.

Besides the reviews of the *Principles* some widely-used textbooks in the German-speaking area between 1890 and 1920 deserve to be examined. In Wagner's *Grundlegung der politischen Oekonomie* (1892–3) 16 references to Marshall can be discovered. One of Wagner's main points is that Marshall holds the same view on the influence of supply and demand on prices as he himself: that to acknowledge the influence of demand, does not entail to abandon the influence of cost of production on value. A very important role in academic teaching after the 'Methodenstreit' can be ascribed to Eugen von Philippovich who held a chair in Vienna. Philippovich's very popular textbook *Grundriß der politischen Oekonomie* was first published in 1893; its last (20th) edition dates from 1923. Philippovich's approach can be characterised as an amalgamation of the historical and the Austrian school. In Philippovich's *Grundriß* one finds references to many at that time well-known European and American economists but none to Marshall, not even in the index. Schmoller made only a few references to Marshall in his textbook *Grundriss der allgemeinen Volkswirtschaftslehre* (1900–04). None of them refers to Marshall's approach to economic theory.

As matters stand, there was a broad spectrum of attitudes towards Marshall's economics ranging from ignorance or even rejection to welcome. Between 1900 and 1915 the situation in academic economics in the German-speaking countries became increasingly complex and therefore difficult to survey. A first indication for this bewildering situation are the debates on the annual conferences of the *Verein für Socialpolitik*, the German economic association. In 1905, 1909 and 1914 the topics were almost exclusively methodological questions (methodology and normative judgements). Passionate and sometimes fierce discussions were noticed in the records of the conference proceedings. Furthermore, an increasing number of articles and books with titles referring to 'crisis' were published. This too indicates that there was an increasing number of economists and social scientists who had become dissatisfied with 'German' economics. This was the intellectual background of 1905, the year where the German edition of Marshall's *Principles* was published as *Handbuch der Volkswirtschaftslehre*. The translation was based on the fourth edition of the *Principles* and was prepared by two young economists, Hugo Ephraim and Arthur Salz from Leipzig. It was the first of many translations of Marshall's opus magnum. Since Marshall was a little baffled when two young Germans wrote him in 1902 that they already had translated three quarters of the book and wanted to complete the book in April 1904, he informed Lujo Brentano, with whom he had personal contact, and asked for assistance in and supervision of the project. The book was published in 1905 and for the first and only edition 1500 copies were printed. Brentano wrote an introduction which Marshall described as very 'flattering'. However, reading between the lines one cannot overlook the striking self-complacency of the members of the younger historical school. Brentano approved 'this opus of a foreigner' because the reader could learn what German economists (Brentano refers to the younger historical school), steadily producing 'new insights' into the subject, were necessarily apt to neglect: the old doctrines of the discipline. Brentano's message was almost identical with that of Schmoller, though much more polite.

So far our emphasis has been on the *Principles*. Other books by Marshall were not translated into German. However, it should be mentioned that *Industry and Trade* published in 1919 did not receive much attention in the German language area. This is the more perplexing because the themes of this book should have been of interest and relevance for the members of the historical school. Tschierschky (1921–22) observed in his review 'that Marshall describes the historical development not in a historical but in an analytical way'. And he concluded his review that 'in many respects it [*Industry and Trade*] is suggestive of Schmoller's universal representation'. We may speculate about the reasons for this neglect. One reason might be that the influence of the historical school was petering out. Furthermore, *Industry and Trade* was published three month after Keynes's pamphlet on the Versailles treaty. This unlucky coincidence might have diverted attention from Marshall's book. However it may be, *Industry and Trade* is up to now an almost unknown book in the German language area.

World War I was not only a decisive political but also an intellectual turning point in the German-speaking area. As already mentioned above, the discontent with the research programme of the younger historical school had appeared in outline already during the first decade of the twentieth century. According to Pribram (1983) two major antagonistic camps emerged after the war. On one side there was the historical school now becoming increasingly heterogeneous, and on the other side there was a group of theoretical economists which can be subdivided into the 'Austrians' and the 'Ricardians'. It should be mentioned that the 'Ricardians' referred to Ricardo's method of isolation and modelling and not to any theorem of Ricardo.

The leading textbook during this period was G. Cassel's *Theoretische Sozial-ökonomik* published in 1918 and written in German. In theoretical economics it dominated academic teaching till the end of the 1920s. From personal conversation I know that Adolph Lowe, a member of the 'Ricardians' used Marshall's *Principles* as a textbook in his lectures at Kiel and at Frankfurt Universities because he disliked Cassel's book. However, his was more or less an isolated case. In fact, Marshall's *Principles* were, according to Pribram, almost unknown during this period. At the end of the 1920s the influence of Cassel's book faded and in 1928 Adolf Weber's first edition of *Allgemeine Volkswirtschaftslehre* was published. The structure of this very successful textbook is similar to that of Cassel's with one exception: it also has parts on themes that were typical for the historical school, that is, the 'natural' and the social framework of the economy, stages of economic development and so on. Its seventh and last edition appeared in 1958. In this book, Marshall is, together with Cassel, Marx and Sombart, one of the most cited authors. Therefore, at least from the end of the 1920s, students of economics using this textbook were exposed to Marshall's contributions to economics.

After World War II the situation in economics in the German-speaking area presented itself as follows. Many leading economists of the pre-war period that had emigrated to the US or to the UK did not return to Germany or Austria after the war. Only a few, among them Erich Schneider, came back and took over chairs at economic faculties. Those emigrants had not been cut off from the international development in economics, and helped, therefore, in enabling German economics to catch up with the international discussion after the war. Most influential was Erich Schneider's *Einführung in die Wirtschaftstheorie* (1952), a four-volume textbook. Although Schneider was a student of Schumpeter he was an ardent Keynesian. It is quite obvious that macroeconomics was the dominant strand in Germany after the war. The 'new economics' had conquered many faculties except those where 'ordoliberalism' was predominant. In the 1960s Marshall had become a figure in the history of economic thought. Schneider dedicated a special chapter to him in the fourth volume (*History of Economic Thought*) of his *Einführung in die Wirtschaftstheorie*.

All in all, there is strong evidence that Marshall's influence on economics in German-speaking countries was not very significant. What may be the reasons for these findings? From Erich Streissler's (1990) research we know that Marshall's economic thinking was influenced by German economists, particularly by Roscher, Rau and von Mangoldt, all members of the older historical school. Streissler has demonstrated that these authors had developed a partial equilibrium approach which he characterises as 'proto-neoclassical' and very similar to Marshall's approach in the *Principles*. Since both the younger historical and the Austrian school had their roots in the older historical school, for both camps Marshall's approach may have seemed as an antiquated view, an approach which they had attempted to overcome.

A second reason, particularly on the Austrian side, might be that the 'shock' of Böhm-Bawerk's critique of Marshall's theory of interest was still reverberating. However, much more important is, in my eyes, that the Austrian school did not accept Marshall's concept of 'real' costs of production. According to the Austrians all costs can be traced back to the opportunity costs of the different uses of a factor. The different kinds of derived demand (uses) together with a given amount of a factor then determine factor prices and thus costs. Besides 'demand' there is no second determining force like 'supply' and it is the false metaphor of the 'pair of scissors' which the Austrians disliked. Since the Austrians neglected the supply side and the historical school did not share any interest in those problems anyway, the very important debate on 'the laws of return and the representative firm' – an eminent theme in Marshallian economics – was more or less ignored in the German language area. That this discussion became known in the German-speaking countries is entirely due to Oskar Morgenstern, who wrote a very detailed article, 'Offene Probleme der Kosten- und Ertragstheorie' ('Open problems in the theory of cost and return'), published in 1931 in the *Zeitschrift für Nationalökonomie* where he summarised the contributions by Pigou, Robbins, Robertson, Shove and Sraffa. Particularly with regard to increasing returns, Morgenstern mentions that this case which leads to decreasing (average and marginal) costs was completely neglected in the German literature and he wonders why even the 'three great Austrians (Menger, Böhm-Bawerk and Wieser) did not pay any attention to decreasing costs'. Moreover, Morgenstern agrees with Sraffa that perfect competition is compatible with constant returns and thus constant (average and marginal) costs only. He realises that from constant costs horizontal supply curves follow and that horizontal supply does not only disturb the symmetry between supply and demand in Marshallian economics but endangers the supremacy of 'demand' in Austrian theory too. Interestingly, one year later, in the 1932 conference of the *Verein für Socialpolitik* which was completely dedicated to 'Problems of the theory of value', there was no reference to this discussion. Even Morgenstern, who delivered a paper with the title 'Die drei Grundtypen der Theorie des subjektiven Werts' ('The three basic types of the theory of subjective value') did not even mention the problems he had emphasised one year previously.

REFERENCES

Cassel, G. ([1918] 1932), *Theoretische Sozialökonomie*, 5th edn, Leipzig: Deichert.
Katzenstein, L. (1893), 'Ein neues Lehrbuch der Nationalökonomie', *Jahrbuch für Gesetzgebung, Verwaltung und Volkswirtschaft*, n.s., **17**, 253–64.
Marshall, A. (1905), *Handbuch der Volkswirtschaftslehre*, with a preface by L. Brentano, Stuttgart and Berlin: Cotta.
Morgenstern, O. (1931), 'Offene Probleme der Kosten- und Ertragstheorie', *Zeitschrift für Nationalökonomie*, **2**, 481–522.
Philippovich, E. (1893), *Grundriß der politischen Oekonomie*, Tübingen: Mohr.
Pribram, K. (1983), *A History of Economic Reasoning*, Baltimore: The Johns Hopkins University Press.
Schmoller, G. (1897), 'Wechselnde Theorien und feststehende Wahrheiten im Gebiete der Staats- und Socialwissenschaften und die heutige deutsche Volkswirthschaftslehre', Speech at the entrance upon his Rectorat, Berlin.
Schmoller, G. (1900–04), *Grundriss der allgemeinen Volkswirtschaftslehre*, Berlin: Duncker and Humblot.
Schneider, E. (1952), *Einführung in die Wirtschaftstheorie*, 3 vols, Tübingen: Mohr.
Streissler, E.W. (1990), 'The influence of German economics on the work of Menger and Marshall', in B. Caldwell (ed.), *Carl Menger and his Legacy in Economics*, *History of Political Economy*, *Annual supplement* to vol. **22**, 31–68.

Tschierschky, S. (1921–22), '*Industry and Trade*', *Weltwirtschaftliches Archiv*, **17**, 422–5.

Wagner, A. (1891), 'Marshall's *Principles of Economics*', *Quarterly Journal of Economics*, **5**, 319–38.

Wagner, A. (1892–3), *Grundlegung der politischen Oekonomie*, Leipzig: Winter.

Weber, A. ([1928] 1958), *Allgemeine Volkswirtschaftslehre*, 7th edn, Berlin: Duncker & Humblot.

Zuckerkandl, R. (1891), 'A. Marshall's *Principles of Economics*', *Jahrbücher für Nationalökonomie und Statistik*, **3** (2), 45–53.

14. Alfred Marshall and economic theory in Holland

Arnold Heertje

Without any doubt the direct link between Alfred Marshall (1842–1924) and the development of economic theory in Holland is through the famous Dutch economist Nicolaas Gerard Pierson (1839–1909) (Heertje 1989). Pierson not only wrote many articles and several books before, during and after he was Professor of Economics at the University of Amsterdam from 1877 until 1885, but he also became a public figure. He was Director and President of the Dutch Central Bank and was Minister of Finance and Prime Minister. Pierson was well read in economics and knew all the great figures of his time in person or through their work, like van Böhm-Bawerk, Jevons, Walras, and both Marshall and his wife Mary Paley, with whom contacts were friendly and intimate. Pierson and his wife visited the Marshalls in Cambridge several times. They exchanged at least around ten letters, which are still available. Volume I of Marshall's *Principles* appeared in English in 1890 (Marshall 1890), and the translation of Pierson's textbook was published in English in 1902 by the same firm Macmillan (Pierson 1902).

Therefore, it is natural that I place particular emphasis on the relationship between Marshall and Pierson. I shall first outline the review of Marshall's *Principles* by Pierson, published in *De Economist* of 1891 (Pierson 1891, pp. 177–204). I shall then discuss the correspondence between both men. I continue with the references by Pierson to Marshall in the later editions of his textbook and in other theoretical publications. At the time of Pierson's death in 1909, Marshall's name was firmly established in the international arena. In order to grasp whether this was reflected in the Netherlands, I report on the references to Marshall in *De Economist* between 1910 and 1930 and in the work by C.A. Verrijn Stuart (1931).

PIERSON ON MARSHALL'S *PRINCIPLES*

In 1891 Pierson wrote the review of Marshall's *Principles* (first published in July 1890) in *De Economist*, the Dutch journal of economic theory, founded in 1852 by J.L. De Bruin Kops. Pierson himself was editor of the journal from

1887 to 1891 and again from 1901 until his death in 1909. In this review, Pierson acknowledges the great importance of Marshall as a major figure in the development of economic theory since the days of the classical school and pays much attention to the structure and contents of Marshall's *magnum opus*. He shows much appreciation for Marshall's exposition of economic theory, his modest style and scientific method, but is not without criticism. In particular, he is rather negative on the composition of Marshall's masterpiece. According to Pierson, Marshall's treatment of production, before the discussion of value, price and money, is incorrect. He describes to what extent Marshall deviates from Adam Smith, David Ricardo and John Stuart Mill, referring to the laws of productivity and rent and how Marshall introduces ideas of the German historical school on the social aspects of economic development. He declines Marshall's view that Ricardo's theory of rent is applicable to all products of agriculture. He regards Marshall as an optimist, who has confidence in the improvement of social conditions in society, despite the limitations of free trade, the market mechanism and economic freedom. It is striking that, in view of Pierson's contacts with, and knowledge of, the Austrians, Jevons and Walras on utility and all that, he does not refer to Marshall's rendering of the marginal utility theory, or the introduction of the term 'marginal utility' and the application of the subjectivist line of thought on labour, as is implicit from the term 'marginal disutility of labour' (Marshall 1890, pp. 155, 188). Pierson closes his review looking forward to Volume II of Marshall's work, which never appeared.

CORRESPONDENCE BETWEEN MARSHALL AND PIERSON

In a letter of March 1891, Marshall confirmed the receipt of Pierson's review of his *Principles*. Three weeks later he was able to read Pierson's observations, which Marshall considered useful in view of the second edition of the book (1891). Several misunderstandings between the two men emerged. However, Marshall expressed his misgivings about Pierson's review in writing:

> The only sentence in your generous notice which has hurt me at all is that in which you say my book has no one leading idea. I submit, with all respect, that the book was written to expound one idea, and only one: to this one idea almost every paragraph in the book is subordinate; it is the main product of my life's work, and the raison d'être of my appearing as a writer. That idea is that whereas Ricardo and co maintain that value is determined by cost of production, and Malthus, Macleod, Jevons and (in a measure the Austrians) that it is determined by utility, each was right in what he affirmed but wrong in what he denied. They none of them paid, I think, sufficient attention to the element of *Time*. When Ricardo spoke of cost of production as determining value he had in mind periods as to which cost of production is the determinant force; when Jevons emphasized utility, he had in mind shorter periods. The attempt to work all existing knowledge on the subject of value into one continuous and harmonious

whole, by means of a careful study of the element of Time permeates every book and almost every page of my volume. (Van Maarseveen 1992, p. 387)

This passage clearly reflects Marshall's own interpretation of his contribution to economic theory, in particular his distinction in price theory between a day market and the short and long run as periods of adjustment to changing demand conditions. It is of interest to note that in his review Pierson did not reproach Marshall with having no leading idea. What Pierson did was to criticise the composition of the book. However, it seems that the wording of his criticism has been translated wrongly.

On 30 April 1898, Marshall wrote a letter to Pierson, in which he reacted to a letter from Pierson, apparently concerning the translation of Pierson's *Textbook* into English. Marshall suggested several terms for Pierson's *Principles*. Marshall also announced the fourth edition of his Volume I (Van Maarseveen 1992, III, p. 89).

In April 1900, there was a further exchange of letters. Pierson wrote from his office in the Hague, informing Marshall about Dutch legislation on social and educational policy. He also appeared to be interested in Marshall's opinion on the Boer War in South Africa. Marshall was very concerned about this war (Groenewegen 1995, p. 604).

On 20 January 1903, Marshall thanked Pierson for his book, published in 1902. Marshall now accepted Pierson's treatment of production after the discussion of value and price theory. Marshall even saw in Pierson's book 'the model treatment on which the treatment of economics will be based hereafter. That will be rather bad for me: but it will be a good thing for the world, and I can rejoice at it' (Van Maarseveen 1992, III, p. 308). Pierson reacted on 15 February 1903. He asked Marshall's opinion on a few topics treated in his book, such as wages and interest, money and interest, and on his conception of the dispute regarding the 'currency' theory and the 'banking' principle. Pierson announced his visit to the Marshalls in May, a visit which in fact took place on 23 May 1903 (ibid., p. 314). The close relationship between the Piersons and the Marshalls can be observed again in 1904, as the couple stayed one week in August with the Marshalls in Cambridge. The occasion was a happy one. Pierson received an honorary degree of Doctor of Science (DSc) of the University of Cambridge (ibid., p. 344). When in Cambridge, Pierson met great men of the day, like F.Y. Edgeworth, A.L. Bowley, J.M. Keynes and H.S. Foxwell. John Maynard Keynes referred to meeting Pierson at Marshall's home, when young (Keynes 1933, p. 237).

Just before Pierson's death on 24 December 1909, Marshall wrote his final letter to him on 21 December 1909. Apparently, Pierson's wife had written to Marshall about Pierson's serious illness. Marshall wrote:

[A]nd the world will class you with Adam Smith, the thinker, the patriot, and the cosmopolitan; and with Turgot the statesman-economist. And it will always be one of my chief joys that I have felt justified in signing myself, yours affectionately, Alfred Marshall. (Van Maarseveen 1992, III, p. 542)

PIERSON'S REFERENCES TO MARSHALL

In 1896, the second edition of Pierson's *Textbook* appeared in Dutch (Pierson 1896). With respect to economic laws much attention is paid to Marshall. According to Pierson, Marshall's definition of economic laws is correct, but incomplete. Pierson mentions the term 'marginal utility' as an equivalent to 'final utility', but there is no reference to Marshall, though he adopts both terms himself. By 1896, three editions of Marshall's *Principles* had been published. As is well known, Marshall presented a thorough discussion of the price theory of products and factors of production, on the basis of marginal utility and marginal productivity. Pierson did not take the opportunity to revise his book in the light of Marshall's analysis. There is no trace of the concept of short and long run, of elasticity nor of a graphical exposition of demand and supply.

In other words, despite the intensive contacts and exchange of views between Marshall and Pierson, the actual influence of Marshall on Pierson's writing is less extensive and sophisticated than one would expect. One of the reasons might be that Pierson combined his scholarly work as an economist and writer of textbooks with a high-level political and public career.

AFTER PIERSON

After Pierson's death in 1909 Marshall's name hardly turns up in Dutch economics. In *De Economist* of 1921, I found a reference to Marshall in an article on wages by C.A. Verrijn Stuart (1865–1948), the prominent Dutch theoretical economist after Pierson with a bent for the Austrian approach (Verrijn Stuart 1921, p. 490). The reference is concerned with Marshall's law of substitution, applied to the factors of production (Marshall 1890, p. 401).

In 1927, W.L. Valk wrote an article in *De Economist* on the development of value and price theory, in which he reviewed a thesis of R. Van Genechten. His complaint is that not enough attention is paid to Marshall (Valk 1927, p. 844). In 1928, *De Economist* published the address by F. de Vries (1884–1958) to the Rotterdam school of economics, in which de Vries quoted with approval Marshall's opinion of quantitative analysis (de Vries 1928, p. 747). On the occasion of the centenary of *De Economist* in 1952, F. de Vries wrote an article on a hundred years of theoretical economics. He also noted that after Pierson the influence of Marshall and the Cambridge school is very moderate, while the Austrians took over (de Vries 1952, p. 844).

The former President of the Dutch Central Bank, M.W. Holtrop, wrote his thesis in 1928 on the velocity of money with H. Frijda, the specialist on monetary theory, as his promotor. In this book, which firmly establishes the Dutch contribution to monetary analysis, Holtrop deals with Marshall's observations on the velocity of money in *Money, Credit and Commerce* of 1923, which are in accordance with the Cambridge tradition on the subject (Holtrop 1928, pp. 68–9).

In his very successful textbook of 1931, C.A. Verrijn Stuart devoted much attention to Alfred Marshall. He discusses Marshall's proposal to introduce a fourth factor of production, organisation, Marshall's interpretation of the law of diminishing returns and the influence of wages on the quality of labour, exposed in the *Principles*. Verrijn Stuart also refers to two of Marshall's other books, *Money, Credit and Commerce* (Marshall 1923) and *Industry and Trade* (Marshall 1919).

Two other economists of the 1930s reflect a substantial knowledge of Marshall in their work, P.A. Diepenhorst in his *Principles of Economics* (Diepenhorst 1934) and H.W.C. Bordewijk in his *Principles of Agricultural Economics* (Bordewijk 1936).

CONCLUSION

We can hardly avoid the conclusion that the reception of Marshall's work took a long time in Holland. In particular, Marshall's synthetic approach to price theory – already spelled out in 1890 – took almost half a century to be digested in lectures and publications. In fact, we had to wait for J. Tinbergen (1903–94) in Rotterdam and in particular my teacher P. Hennipman (1911–94), who had a vast knowledge of the literature, in Amsterdam. Since Pierson, who did not pick up the concept of elasticity nor the mathematical formulation, there has been a setback in economic theory in the Netherlands. Dutch economists mainly devoted their time and analysis to monetary theory and financial problems of a national and international character. They neglected the general equilibrium theory of Walras, as well as the partial equilibrium approach of Marshall. None of Marshall's books has ever been translated into Dutch.

REFERENCES

Bordewijk, H.W.C. (1936), *Leerboek van de Landhuishoudkunde* (*Principles of Agricultural Economics*), 2 vols, Haarlem: Erven F. Bohn.
Diepenhorst, P.A. (1934), *Leerboek van de Economie* (*Principles of Economics*), 2 vols, Zutphen: G.J.A. Ruys.
Groenewegen, P. (1995), *A Soaring Eagle: Alfred Marshall 1842–1924*, Aldershot, UK and Brookfield, US: Edward Elgar.
Heertje, A. (1989), 'Nicolaas Gerard Pierson', in D. Walker (ed.), *Perspectives on the History of Economic Thought*, Aldershot, UK and Brookfield, US: Edward Elgar, pp. 167–90.

Holtrop, M.W. (1928), *De Omloopsnelheid van het Geld* (*The Velocity of Money*), Amsterdam: H.J. Paris.

Keynes, J.M. (1933), *Essays in Biography*, London: Macmillan.

Marshall, A. (1890), *Principles of Economics*, 1st edn, London: Macmillan.

Marshall, A. (1919), *Industry and Trade*, London: Macmillan.

Marshall, A. (1923), *Money, Credit and Commerce*, London: Macmillan.

Pierson, N.G. (1891), 'Economisch overzicht' ('Economic report'), *De Economist*, **40**, 177–207.

Pierson, N.G. (1896), *Leerboek der Staathuishoudkunde* (*Textbook of Political Economy*), 2 vols, Haarlem: Erven F. Bohn.

Pierson, N.G. (1902), *Principles of Economics*, 2 vols, London: Macmillan.

Valk, W.L. (1927), 'De ontwikkeling der moderne waarde- en prijsleer' ('The development of modern value and price theory'); review of R. Van Genechten (1927), *De Ontwikkeling der Waardeleer sinds 1870* (*The Development of the Theory of Value since 1870*), *De Economist*, **76**, 831–48.

Van Maarseveen, J.G.S.J. (1992), *Briefwisseling van Nicolaas Gerard Pierson 1839–1909*, 3 vols, vols II and III, Amsterdam: De Nederlandsche Bank.

Verrijn Stuart, C.A. (1921), 'De grondslag der loonbepaling' ('The foundation of wages'), *De Economist*, **70**, 455–505.

Verrijn Stuart, C.A. (1931), *Hoofdstukken van de Leer der Maatschappelijke Voortbrenging* (*Main Lines of the Theory of Social Production*), Haarlem: Erven F. Bohn.

Vries, P. de (1928), 'Institutionalisme' ('Institutionalism'), *De Economist*, **71**, 737–71.

Vries, P. de (1952), 'Honderd jaar theoretische economie' ('A hundred years of theoretical economics'), *De Economist*, **100**, 828–79.

15. Marshall in Belgium

Guido Erreygers

Probably the first Belgian economist who acknowledged the influence of Marshall upon his writings was Emile De Laveleye (1822–92). In the preface of his textbook *Eléments d'économie politique* – first published in 1882; English translation published in 1884 – he mentioned that among the elementary treatises which had been of great help to him was the one by 'A. and M.-P. Marshall', an allusion to *The Economics of Industry*, published in 1879 by Alfred and Mary Paley Marshall. In the book itself, however, De Laveleye did not explicitly refer to the publication of the Marshalls, and only a close reading of both texts would reveal the precise influence, if any. Although he lived just long enough to see the publication of Marshall's *Principles of Economics*, he never mentioned it. But it seems that he read and appreciated the book, at least if we believe Ernest Mahaim (1865–1938), who succeeded De Laveleye in the Chair of Political Economy at the University of Liège. In his obituary of De Laveleye he wrote 'that the labours of the Austrian school, and Professor Marshall's recent treatise had given him fresh food for thought' (Mahaim 1892, p. 196).

Perhaps De Laveleye had first learned of Marshall's work through his strong involvement in the international cause for bimetallism. Since the early 1860s De Laveleye had written scores of articles and books – in French, English and German – in which he advocated a monetary system based upon both gold and silver. He remained a staunch defender of bimetallism throughout his life, and in 1891 he reaffirmed his belief in the bimetallist case in his book *La monnaie et le bimétallisme international*. On the authority of Herbert Somerton Foxwell, De Laveleye considered Alfred Marshall to be part of the defenders of bimetallism in Great Britain (De Laveleye 1891, p. 246). But Marshall was only a lukewarm supporter of bimetallism, and moreover he propagated his own version of it.

In general one can say that there are fewer traces of a mutual influence between De Laveleye and Marshall than might have been expected. Emile De Laveleye was a prolific writer and a widely respected essayist, who entertained an extensive network of correspondents all over Europe. Yet no letters seem to have been exchanged between Marshall and De Laveleye. It also seems unlikely that they ever met, despite the fact that De Laveleye was well known in British economic circles. In 1872 the Cobden Club published a paper of him on the causes of war

(De Laveleye 1872) and praised his high reputation as a publicist (Cobden Club 1872, p. vi), and in 1876 he attended the Adam Smith memorial meeting of the Political Economy Club. In 1888 his name circulated as a possible candidate for the succession of Bonamy Price in the Drummond Chair in Oxford, as Marshall and John Neville Keynes observed in their correspondence (Groenewegen 1995, p. 683). Marshall was 'very much against that' (Letter to John Neville Keynes of January 1888, in Whitaker 1996, I, p. 256) and even wrote: 'M Laveleye is a man of warm & generous instincts, & has great knowledge of international public affairs. But I do not regard him as an authority on the strictly scientific side of economics. Please however not to repeat this' (Letter to an unknown correspondent of 20 October 1889, ibid., p. 303). Perhaps Marshall perceived De Laveleye as too much involved with the German historical school and as a sympathiser of socialism.

Another influential Belgian economist of the nineteenth century was Gustave De Molinari (1819–1912), one of the protagonists of the French liberal school. No discernible influence of Marshall upon his work can be found. This is in line with his aversion to economic theories that questioned the orthodoxy of the liberal tradition of Smith, Ricardo, Mill and the like (see Breton 1998).

On the whole, it might be said that at the end of the nineteenth and the beginning of the twentieth century, Belgian economists were not very receptive of the more mathematical approach of economics developed by Walras, Jevons and Marshall. (An exception is the group of economists and sociologists brought together by Ernest Solvay in his *Institut des Sciences Sociales*. Hector Denis, Guillaume De Greef and Emile Vandervelde studied the work of Jevons and Walras, and in 1898 managed to persuade Walras to write down his views on Solvay's 'social comptabilism'.) An example of the hesitant response of Belgian economists is provided by Victor Brants (1856–1917), who was Professor of Economics at the Catholic University of Louvain. In *Les grandes lignes de l'économie politique* – which was first published as the third (sic) edition in 1901, since it was based upon three other books each of which had had two editions – he did mention Walras, Jevons and Marshall, but he stopped short of a real discussion of their ideas. Their names, and that of Marshall in particular, are first connected to the law of diminishing utility in a chapter dealing with value. But Brants refused to go further than that: 'Several authors have sought to give a mathematical formulation to the rules of value. Here we will not analyse these calculations; they require special knowledge which the majority of our readers do not possess' (Brants 1901, p. 268). The second reference to Marshall occurs at the end of the book, in the part where Brants tried to classify systems of economic ideas. Menger, Jevons, Walras and so on are grouped under the heading of the 'Neo-theoretical school – mathematical school'. According to Brants, Marshall also belonged to this school, yet he somehow occupied a special position since he was more eclectic and tried to construct a theory whilst taking into account the diverse influences (in later editions he specified these as 'supra' and 'extra' economic) which act upon the economy (ibid., p. 605).

It is only after World War I that the attitude towards Marshall seems to change. This is clear, for instance, in the work of Maurice Ansiaux (1869–1943), Professor of Economics at the Free University of Brussels. Initially his research was focused upon labour issues and monetary theory, but in the 1920s he published an extensive three-volume *Traité d'économie politique* (1920–26). He frequently referred to both *The Economics of Industry* and *Principles of Economics*. An example of the influence of Marshall is Chapter v of Volume II, which deals with the elasticity of supply and demand. However, as economists before him, Ansiaux did not use any formulas or figures to illustrate the concept.

In view of the rather cautious attitude of Belgian economists towards Marshall and more mathematically oriented economists in general, it may come as a surprise that in 1920 the Royal Academy of Belgium awarded Alfred Marshall with the fourth Emile De Laveleye Prize. This prize was destined for the political economist or social scientist whose whole work had caused important progress in political economy or social science. The jury – consisting of Eugène Goblet d'Alviella, Arthur James Balfour, Guillaume De Greef, Edoaurd Descamps, Charles Gide, Benjamin Seebohm Rowntree and Ernest Mahaim – made it clear in its report that by giving the prize to Alfred Marshall it wanted not only to single out the eminent progress which economic science had made thanks to Marshall's work and the publication of the *Principles of Economics* 30 years earlier, but also to honour the English contribution to economic science (Mahaim 1921).

Later in the 1920s and 1930s the work of Marshall was increasingly recognised as of crucial importance for the diffusion of the subjective theory of value. A good illustration is the book on the development of the theory of value by Robert Van Genechten (1927). Van Genechten, an economist of the Austrian school, carefully distinguished Marshall's theory from those of Jevons and John Bates Clark, but also drew attention to Eugen von Böhm-Bawerk's critique of Marshall's notion of cost. Another contribution which is perhaps worth mentioning is the book on the history of economic thought published by Willy Cracco (1939). Cracco, an economist and demographer from the Catholic University of Louvain, emphasised Marshall's biological conception of economics and the role of time in his theories. He presented the work of Marshall and Maffeo Pantaleoni as belonging to what he called the theory of 'special equilibrium', in contrast to the theory of 'general equilibrium' represented by Walras and Vilfredo Pareto.

REFERENCES

Ansiaux, M. (1920–26), *Traité d'économie politique*, 3 vols, Paris: Giard.
Brants, V. (1901), *Les grandes lignes de l'économie politique*, Louvain: Charles Peeters; Paris: Victor Lecoffre; Leipzig: Otto Harrasowitz.

Breton, Y. (1998), 'French economists and marginalism (1871–1918)', in G. Faccarello (ed.), *Studies in the History of French Political Economy. From Bodin to Walras*, London and New York: Routledge, pp. 404–55.

Cobden Club (1872), 'Preface' to the 1st edn, in *Cobden Club Essays, Second Series, 1871–72*, 2nd edn, London: Cassell, Petter and Galpin, pp. v–vii.

Cracco, W. (1939), *Schets eener Geschiedenis der Economie*, Antwerpen: De Nederlandsche Boekhandel.

De Laveleye, E. (1872), 'On the causes of war, and the means of reducing their number', in *Cobden Club Essays, Second Series, 1871–72*, 2nd edn, London: Cassell, Petter and Galpin, pp. 1–55.

De Laveleye, E. (1882), *Eléments d'économie politique*, Paris: Hachette.

De Laveleye, E. (1891), *La monnaie et le bimétallisme international*, Paris: Félix Alcan.

Groenewegen, P.D. (1995), *A Soaring Eagle: Alfred Marshall 1842–1924*, Aldershot, UK and Brookfield, US: Edward Elgar.

Mahaim, E. (1892), 'Emile De Laveleye', *Economic Journal*, **2** (5), 193–6.

Mahaim, E. (1921), 'Prix Emile De Laveleye. Rapport du Jury', *Académie Royale de Belgique, Bulletin de la Classe des Lettres et des Sciences Morales et Politiques*, 5th series, **7**, 124–7.

Van Genechten, R. (1927), *De Ontwikkeling der Waardeleer sinds 1870*, Amsterdam: Elsevier.

Whitaker, J.K. (ed.) (1996), *The Correspondence of Alfred Marshall, Economist*, 3 vols, Cambridge: Cambridge University Press.

16. Marshall in France

Michel Quéré

For a series of related reasons, 'Marshall in France' is quite a difficult subject to deal with. First of all, although Marshall recognised the influence of earlier French economists in various areas, he did not regard the French economists of his own day as particularly significant. Secondly, for their part French economists were reluctant to consider Marshall's contributions to economics very central to the progress of the discipline. But, third, Marshall's prestige in France began to thrive after World War II, probably as an indirect result of the impact on the French economic community of the ideas of François Perroux and Giacomo Becattini concerning issues related to economic growth, inequality in development patterns and local development.

MARSHALL AND CONTEMPORARY FRENCH ECONOMISTS

Apart from Cournot, whom Marshall mentioned as one of his most influential masters and whom he placed on the same plane as von Thünen, and apart from appreciative references to Le Play, no other French economist of the past or of his own day seems to have impressed Marshall very much, still less to have played a significant role in the formation of his thought. In his notes on the development of economic science (both in early manuscripts and in Appendix B of the *Principles*) there is evidence of critical interest in Turgot and the Physiocrats, but this raises interpretative issues that we cannot develop here (see Cook 2009, pp. 204–6). Bastiat, too, seems to have caught his attention in the early years, but later references to this author are somewhat dismissive.

If Marshall showed no particular enthusiasm towards the French economists, however, it must be said that he was repaid in kind. On the whole, the French economists of his time did not pay much attention to him: either they were overly oriented towards practical issues aimed at influencing the State as a political apparatus, or they were overly oriented toward the 'formal route'. Whatever the reason, they were certainly not very sensitive to the Cambridge economist, whose influence in France, therefore, was very weak.

This conclusion is not at odds with the fact that most of Marshall's major works were regularly reviewed and commented upon in France. The *Principles* was reviewed by Jean-Gustave Courcelle-Seneuil in the *Journal des économistes* in 1890, and a four-page review appeared in the *Revue d'économie politique* by Richard Schüller in 1891, being one of around thirty reviews in the rather uninfluential bibliographical section. The tone of the latter review seems discouraging to potential readers: 'It should be indicated that what the author has accomplished is only a very small part of what is still to be done and of what should be done in the near future' (Schüller 1891, p. 406). Schüller also added that the *Principles* 'has to be thought of neither as an easy textbook for commercial schools, nor as a reference volume, but as a work destined to play an important role in the battle started from different sources for the acquisition of a deeper understanding of economic phenomena' (ibid., pp. 406–7). Courcelle-Seneuil, who, in addition to the *Principles* in 1890, reviewed also the *Elements of the Economics of Industry* in the *Journal des économistes* in 1892, was even more critical. On the one hand, he rejected Marshall's entire treatment of utility and theory of consumer rent, considering them to be but empty notions, 'une chimère qui file dans le vide' (Courcelle-Seneuil 1890, p. 463). On the other, in noting that the *Elements* was simply a summary of the *Principles* for beginners, he made the following scathing remark:

> [We hoped that] we would have understood this book better than the big volume about which we have entertained our readers some time ago. Our expectation has been deceived and we have not succeeded better than the previous time in understanding the exposition, which is still too rich in distinctions and minute remarks. (Courcelle-Seneuil 1892, p. 267)

Courcelle-Seneuil was not being entirely fair, for he concentrated the entire 1892 review on one chapter only of the book: 'We shall not engage in a full study of the present volume, which is only a summary of the previous one: better to report on a new chapter added to it and devoted to a practical issue, that of trades unions' (ibid., p. 267). And even then, he was reluctant to praise Marshall's method and 'les habitudes de son esprit': 'This method is honest, but it does not seem to us to be very scientific' (ibid., p. 268). Only Charles Gide (1919), in his review of *Industry and Trade* in the *Revue d'économie politique* in 1919, was sympathetic to Marshall and emphasised the rich content of Marshall's work.

In general, Marshall was perceived as an author who tried to establish a strong link between old and new economic doctrines. His modern use of the marginal method in the theories of utility and of value was not, as we noted, received with great enthusiasm. His theory of production, including as it did what appeared to be a traditional conception of labour and capital, was not considered as very original, although his emphasis on the social implications of production, especially through its effects on the working class, was considered remarkable by some French commentators (see Schüller 1891, p. 406). The general tone of the reception of his work in France confirms the impression that his influence on the development of the economic discipline in this country was insignificant.

We know from Groenewegen (1995) that Marshall sent copies of the *Elements of the Economics of Industry* to Charles Gide, to Paul Leroy Beaulieu and to Léon Walras. But the following quotation from a letter to Foxwell of 2 August 1903, is indicative of Marshall's actual scant regard for the first two French economists: 'You will notice that I have failed in the attempt to get good books in French Beaulieu is level headed, but prodigiously dull. Gide is, I think, quite empty' (Whitaker 1996, III, p. 42). The relationship with Walras, too, is remarkable for the contrast between Marshall's own private assessment of the value of Walras's work and the exterior expressions of praise contained in their correspondence. Thus, in a letter to Walras of 19 September 1889, Marshall rejoices 'that the pure mathematical route is being developed by [Walras with] great ability and energy' (ibid., II, p. 301), while the annotations in his copy of the *Eléments d'économie pure* are 'critical, and [reveal] a lack of appreciation for his colleague's work', which apparently he stopped reading at Lesson 12 (Groenewegen 1995, p. 478). This lack of consideration was probably reciprocal: as Groenewegen writes, 'Marshall would have been furious at Walras's approval of Rist's 1906 remark that both Pareto and Marshall had *continued* along lines which Jevons, Menger and Walras had *initiated*. Marshall always claimed his own niche of independent discovery in what was subsequently called the "marginal revolution" of the 1870s' (ibid., p. 778).

MARSHALL'S INFLUENCE ON ECONOMICS IN FRANCE

In light of the above remarks it is not surprising that Marshall is not considered as a major author in French histories of economic thought. French works on political economy typically distinguished between three major traditions when referring to the evolution of the discipline of economics: classical and neo-classical contributions, socialism and the German historicist tradition (Colson 1907; Landry 1908; Gide 1909; Gide and Rist 1909). Interestingly enough, the founders of the first tradition are considered to be Smith, Malthus, Ricardo and J.S. Mill. The name of Alfred Marshall is never included among those considered to be real pioneers. Moreover, if Marshall is acknowledged as the founder of the *école de Cambridge*, references to his views are infrequently found and appear mostly in end notes (see, for instance, Gide 1931, p. 54, on the theory of value). Usually, in these volumes the name of Marshall is not even included in the index.

Therefore, if Marshall is regarded in France as the founder of the Cambridge school, the influential role of that school is far from being easily identified and isolated. In my view, there are two main reasons why Marshall's influence on French economists has been so weak: language and economic method. When considering language, it is important to appreciate that, during the inter-war period, most French economists, such as for instance Brocard (1934), referred only to F. Sauvaire-Jourdan's 1907 French translation of the fourth edition of the *Principles* (Marshall 1907). This translation, however, is fairly inaccurate, which fact no doubt placed obstacles in the way of properly appreciating Marshall's place among those leading economists who established the neo-classical tradition. Not only did this weaken Marshall's influence in France, it also further added to the conviction that Marshall's arguments in the *Principles* lacked clarity. With regard to economic method, French economic thought in this period was dominated by a tradition of *ingénieurs-économistes*, whose conception of what economics should be was widely different from that of Marshall. Whereas the latter's methodological position was characterised by a reluctance to dissociate theory from facts, the French economists were on the whole in favour of making the dichotomy between pure and applied economics as sharp as possible: a demarcation fully in line with the French *esprit cartésien*. Due to such differing intellectual habits and customs, it is hardly surprising that Marshall's influence in France was insubstantial.

THE POST-WORLD WAR II MARSHALLIAN BOOM

The post-World War II period brought Marshall an unprecedented popularity in France. The role of François Perroux in propagating Marshall's doctrines and conceptual framework was central. In Perroux (1945), Marshall is presented as a remarkable pioneer, especially for his notion of internal and external economies (ibid., pp. 5–6) and for his theory of value. Perroux stressed the originality of the conception of utility in Marshall who, contrary to Jevons, Menger, Böhm-Bawerk and Walras, used it in order to develop a theory of prices as opposed to a pure theory of value. In other words, Perroux placed emphasis upon the fact that, in Marshall's framework, a demand curve was more essential than a utility curve. Marshall's central interest was in the way markets function, even though, of course, standing behind the demand side of the market are levels of utility. In Perroux's interpretation, the measurement of utility was not a relevant issue for Marshall (ibid., p. 25). It must be said that Marshallian themes were somewhat marginal with respect to Perroux's main concerns in economic analysis. But I think that the latter was in sympathy with the former's cautious attitude toward the status of formal reasoning and the risk of mathematical distractions. Perroux also stressed the presence of insights in Marshall's works that, by and large, would exert an influence upon economic thinking on the process of growth and economic development.

Another feature of French economics during the post-World War II period has arisen in response to an awareness of the importance of industrial districts in ensuring the competitiveness of the neighbouring Italian economy from the late 1970s onwards. Becattini's work (see Becattini 1987) has been very influential in calling attention to the importance of industrial districts in Marshall's analysis. A huge number of works by Italian scholars should be mentioned at this point. Suffice it to emphasise that this Italian line of research crossed the Alps quite substantially and resulted in significant developments in France. There are at least three major

French derivations, from this primary Italian derivation from Marshall's thought, that must be mentioned: the search to identify industrial districts in France, mainly developed in a series of empirical contributions from Grenoble University (from authors such as Colletis, Courlet, Pecqueur and Rousier); the 'innovative milieu' approach promoted by the GREMI research group (under the lead of Perrin, Maillat and Quévit); and investigations into the economic influence of proximity (see the special issue of the *Revue d'économie régionale et urbaine* edited by Bellet, Colletis and Lung in 1993, as well as all subsequent research on this topic). A further episode of Marshallian influence can also be seen in Rallet and Torre (1995). Each of these three major streams of research is evidence of current work in French economics that is more or less extensively inspired by Marshall's concepts of the industrial district and external economies.

On the whole, we may conclude that Marshall's influence in France has arisen quite indirectly (by way of Italy) and very late, after a long period of substantial neglect.

REFERENCES

Becattini, G. (1987), *Mercato e forze locali: Il distretto industriale*, Bologna: Il Mulino.
Bellet, M., G. Colletis and Y. Lung (eds) (1993), *L'économie des proximités*, special issue of *Revue d'economie regionale et urbaine*, **3**.
Brocard, L. (1934), *Les conditions générales de l'activité économique*, Paris: Sirey.
Colson, C. (1907), *Cours d'économie politique*, 2nd edn, Paris: Gauthier-Villars et Alcan.
Cook, S.J. (2009), *The Intellectual Foundations of Alfred Marshall's Economic Science*, New York: Cambridge University Press.
Courcelle-Seneuil, J.-G. (1890), 'Review of *Principles of Economics*', *Journal des économistes*, 5th series, **4**, 456–64.
Courcelle-Seneuil, J.-G. (1892), 'Review of *Elements of Economics of Industry*', *Journal des économistes*, 5th series, **11**, 267–9.
Gide, C. (1909), *Cours d'économie politique*, Paris: Sirey.
Gide, C. (1919), 'Review of *Industry and Trade*', *Revue d'économie politique*, **33**, 782–5.
Gide, C. (1931), *Principes d'économie politique*, 26th edn, Paris: Recueil Sirey.
Gide, C. and C. Rist (1909), *Histoire des doctrines économiques depuis les physiocrates jusqu'à nos jours*, Paris: Larose et Tenen.
Groenewegen, P.D. (1995), *A Soaring Eagle: Alfred Marshall 1842–1924*, Aldershot, UK and Brookfield, US: Edward Elgar.
Landry, A. (1908), *Manuel d'économique à l'usage des facultés de droit*, Paris: Giard.
Marshall, A. (1907), *Principes d'économie politique*, vol. 1, Paris: Giard et Brière.
Perroux, F. (1945), *Le néo-marginalisme*, Paris: Domat-Montchrestien.
Rallet, A. and A. Torre (eds) (1995), *Economie industrielle et économie spatiale*, Paris: Economica.
Schüller, R. (1891), 'Alfred Marshall, *Principles of Economics*', *Revue d'économie politique*, **5** (4), 404–7.
Whitaker, J.K. (ed.) (1996), *The Correspondence of Alfred Marshall, Economist*, 3 vols, Cambridge: Cambridge University Press.

17. Marshall in Italy

Mauro Gallegati and Riccardo Faucci

1885–1940

Marshall's works prior to *Principles* passed almost unnoticed in Italy: exceptions are the review of *The Present Position of Economics* (Dalla Volta 1885) and Maffeo Pantaleoni's use, by the author's permission, of excerpts from *The Pure Theory of Foreign Trade* and *The Pure Theory of Domestic Values* (Pantaleoni 1889), two works that were to be translated into Italian only in recent times (Marshall 1975).

Though Marshall's *Principles* did not meet with the same success in continental Europe as in Anglo-Saxon countries, it was immediately circulated in Italy. Riccardo Dalla Volta's timely review article (Dalla Volta 1890) is noticeable for the comparison with Jevons. It states that the principal merit of Marshall's volume consists in its presentation of an effective synthesis, a reconciliation between 'classical economics and the school of Jevons and Menger-Böhm'. In the same period the authoritative Luigi Cossa (1893) claimed Marshall to be the most important follower and scholar of the classical school. In the same years, Marshall was appointed as a member of *Accademia dei Lincei* (Becattini and Bellanca 1992).

Pantaleoni's correspondence with Vilfredo Pareto is important to clarify Marshall's controversial role in Pareto's 'conversion' to pure economics. Pareto's definitive acceptance of the mathematical method and the equimarginal principle on which the notion of economic equilibrium rests was intimately connected with acknowledgment of the accuracy of both Marshall's and Walras's methods. By November 1891 Pareto had not yet detected any significant difference between the two approaches. He noted certain differences between partial and general equilibrium, but seemed to attribute them more to different degrees of approximation to reality, or to the academic rivalry between the two economists, than to substantial methodological divergences. The U-turn came in 1893 when Pareto stated that Marshall had confused the price curve with that of total utility (Pareto 1960, I, p. 371). Two years later, he bitterly stated: 'Marshall translates the old ideas into modern language. The ideas of Walras have enabled economics to take a giant step forward, whilst Marshall has added nothing of great note to our understanding' (ibid., p. 418). In a letter of 1907, he criticised Pantaleoni for putting him 'together with' Marshall, in spite of many points of divergence concerning the concept of social laws, the demand schedule, the constancy of the marginal utility of money and, above all, the *cæteris paribus* assumption. In a subsequent letter, Pareto complained that Marshall prompted Wicksteed to write a unsympathetic review of his *Manuel* in the *Economic Journal* (Pareto 1960, III, p. 65). In 1909, Pantaleoni accused Marshall of being 'systematically silent about your [Pareto's] works, and servile towards Schmoller' (ibid., p. 379). For his part, writing to H.S. Foxwell in 1903, Marshall passed the following judgment on Pareto: '[T]he ablest [of the French-speaking economists], but very unreal and cranky' (Whitaker 1996, III, p. 42).

More sympathetic to Marshall were some Italian representatives of the historical school, as well as some neoclassical economists less influenced by Pareto and Walras. It must be recognised that Italian economists were much more elastic than is supposed by historians of economic thought accustomed to think in terms of 'schools'. Apart from a few extreme supporters of Pareto, most of them used either Marshallian or Walras-Paretian approaches, according to the problems they faced. This can be said, *inter alios*, of Enrico Barone, who followed Marshall on taxation and Pareto on planning. It is also worth noticing that, according to Gustavo Del Vecchio (1925, p. 573), Marshall was the 'primissimo' (very first) author who influenced Barone's research of a contact between abstraction and observation.

Pantaleoni's 'Di alcuni fenomeni di dinamica economica' (1909) specifically hints at decreasing costs industries, considered as factors of instability and progress (Pantaleoni 1925, II, pp. 121–2). He also writes that mechanical and bio-logical analogies in economics must not be considered antithetic (ibid., p. 78). Besides interpreting Marshall's contribution as a conciliation between the English classical school and marginalism, Pantaleoni attributed a fundamental role to partial analysis in interpreting the empirical evidence that the analytical rigour of Walras's method could not encompass. Nevertheless, Pantaleoni was not a Marshallian in his vision of society, in which contrast and friction prevail over the fruitful cooperation between individuals which characterises Marshall's perspective. Moreover, Pantaleoni's persistent hedonism (see Pantaleoni 1924), influenced by Jevons, distinguished him from Pareto and Marshall. His disciple Umberto Ricci worked on the demand curve utilising Marshallian tools (see Bruni 2004; Montesano 2004), but it would be misleading to regard him as a Marshallian in the proper sense.

It is possible to identify two distinct centres of spread of Marshallian ideas: Turin, with Salvatore Cognetti de Martiis's school and, to a lesser extent, Rome, with Pantaleoni himself, Barone and Ricci. Apart stands Marco Fanno.

Cognetti de Martiis's *Laboratorio di economia politica* (laboratory, as in experimental sciences, according to the positivist doctrines) consistently propagated an evolutionary vision of economics based on biological analogies. Cognetti emphasised the idea of organic rather than mechanical development of economic forces. The latter theory, though susceptible to rigorous analysis through systems of equations, is too mechanistic to represent a profitable analysis of empirical evidence.

Cognetti hosted the Italian translation of *Principles of Economics* in the series of 'Biblioteca dell'economista' that he edited. The preface, by Cognetti's disciple, Pasquale Jannaccone, is a clear exposition of the most peculiar features of Marshall's thought: the distinction between long and short period, rent as the difference between utility and cost, the non-hedonistic attitude towards economic behaviour, the role of increasing and decreasing production costs to decide on taxation of the various commodities (Jannaccone 1905). Jannaccone's previously published book, *Il costo di produzione* (1900), used the quasi-rent and decreasing and increasing cost apparatus and included some minor observations on Marshall.

Luigi Einaudi, another disciple of Cognetti, showed an early interest in the progress of the working class in a very Marshallian vein. His reportage on the wool industry strikes in Biella (Einaudi 1897) highlighted the transformation in the workers' 'character' due to better organisation and increasing self-confidence. In his full maturity writings, Einaudi underlined the importance of Marshallian externalities in evaluating the effects of public expenditure. However, he shifted from a partial equilibrium to a general equilibrium approach in his 'optimal tax' analysis.

Achille Loria, Cognetti's successor to the Turin chair, was a firm adversary of the Austrian school and by contrast praised Marshall's ability to penetrate the real working of the markets. He published a small book on Marshall (Loria 1924) and favourably reviewed *Industry and Trade, Money, Credit and Commerce* and *Memorials of Alfred Marshall* (Loria 1920, 1923 and 1926). In his correspondence with his disciple Augusto Graziani *sr*, Loria underlined Marshall's descent from Mill and, through him, the classics (Allocati 1990). However, Loria's general conception of economic progress, dominated by historical materialism (or rather determinism), was Marxian rather than Marshallian. Graziani's *Istituzioni di economia politica* (five editions from 1904 to 1936) also dedicated considerable room to Marshall's ideas.

Another historically-oriented economist, broadly connected with the Turin school, Francesco Saverio Nitti, was especially interested in labour and poor relief legislation and opened his journal, *La riforma sociale*, to these topics. Moreover, he shared Marshall's insistence on the importance of 'character'. Nevertheless, unlike Loria, neither he nor Cognetti had special interest in the analysis of Marshall's thought as such.

In Rome, Pantaleoni, Barone and Ricci appeared to be open to the theory of economic equilibrium, but they followed different approaches. As already said, Pantaleoni tried to reconcile Marshall with the classical tradition, while Barone and Ricci tried to reconcile him with the Walras-Pareto school. Barone (1894) maintains that, when dealing with dynamic or public finance problems, it is necessary to simplify the systems by the extensive use of Marshallian procedures ('the nearest approximation of dynamic phenomena, theoretically correct and very useful in a practical sense', ibid., p. 407), since the complicated 'calculation' that derives from Walras's entire system of equations could be avoided without altering the results in any significant way.

Between the two theories of equilibrium, the Italians strove to find an inter-mediate solution: a theory of 'connected prices'. Pantaleoni (1907, p. 201 illustrates the concept of 'families of goods' arguing that these relationships between goods, corresponding to the cases listed by Marshall in the Mathematical Appendix of *Principles*, Note XXI, enable the partial consideration of the supply and demand of goods, as function of a single price, to be abandoned. They only permit the description of the strongest links between goods, without arriving at the Pareto–Walras version, which is more general, but also more difficult to apply. This theory identifies a sector of collaboration between the two versions of equilibrium on which the Italian tradition would work at length.

The most analytically rigorous example consists of two contributions by the Padua Professor Marco Fanno on joint-cost supply (Fanno 1914) and on substitute goods (Fanno 1926). In these works the author highlights the functional relationship between the various families of goods. Fanno analyses only the relationships of primary importance between various goods; one must split up the system of correlations between prices into groups or categories, and then proceed to study each one separately.

The Italian contribution to the reconciliation between Marxism and margin-alism is also quite original (see Faucci and Perri 1995). In a nutshell, one might say that while there were some economists who tried to combine Marx with Walras or even with the Austrian school, others found themselves more in agreement with Marshall. The most authoritative *Marx-shallian* was Antonio Graziadei. His main work (Graziadei 1899), focusing on the mechanism of production of a surplus in macroeconomic terms according to a quasi-Physiocratic line of thought, introduced Marshall's distribution apparatus in order to analyse the division between the individual units of production at the firm's level (see Gallegati 1982). The unsatisfactory result of this work did not affect the treatment of the trade cycle, which Graziadei derived by mixing Marx's and Marshall's hypotheses and, above all, by constructing one of the most effective examples of the application of *cæteris paribus* to interpret a special market (Graziadei 1909).

By the time *Industry and Trade* (1919) and *Money, Credit and Commerce* (1923) were published, the diffusion of Marshall in Italy had already passed its peak. At the end of the 1920s, the Pareto school constituted the major component of marginalism, and, soon after, Sraffa was to contribute to the further removal of *cæteris paribus* from pure economics.

Sraffa's (1925) criticism on the relationship between costs and produced quantity did not cause the same devastating effect in Italy that it caused in England, since there was no 'Marshallian dictatorship' in Italy but, rather, a line of thought on the 'empty economic boxes' and the 'increasing returns and perfect competition' issues. Moreover, Sraffa's demonstration of the theoretical inadmissibility of *cæteris paribus* had been prompted by Barone (1894), while both the connection between variable returns and 'economic boxes', and that between increasing returns and perfect competition had been illustrated in two essays by Pantaleoni (1889, 1909). It is entirely possible, as Jannaccone (1914) pointed out, to find industries which, regardless of the sector, work for periods which are not well defined into operative intervals, under conditions of decreasing costs. After making an effective distinction between the increase–decrease of average and marginal costs along lines similar to those made years later by Sraffa, Jannaccone asserts that 'production with increasing or decreasing costs is not the prerogative of certain industries and certain categories of goods, but a *moment* in the life of every firm, no matter what industry it belongs to or the type of goods it produces' (ibid., p. 263). The increasing or decreasing returns are thus brought within the 'temporal cycles' that each industry passes through, going from the first to the second in shorter or longer periods for manufacturing industries or agriculture respectively. Jannaccone unsuccessfully claimed to have anticipated Sraffa's 1925 and 1926 essays (Jannaccone 1951, pp. 22–3), and his friend Einaudi (1950, p. 107) authoritatively endorsed this claim.

For all these reasons Sraffa's critique was not exhaustively discussed (and probably not well understood in all its implications) by Italian economists, but it contributed to signal the end of the favourable attitude towards Marshall in this country, and to bring to a close the period in which 'all Italian economists turned to the study of special problems, postulating *cæteris paribus*' (ibid., p. 104).

In a most balanced obituary of Marshall, Fanno sketches the merits of Marshall, especially in his representation of the markets and in his study of the money velocity of circulation (Fanno 1925). But one has to remember that Fanno followed Loria in his works on colonisation, and Wicksell as well as Hayek in his writings on the trade cycle. This was a feature of the eclecticism of many Italian economists in the inter-war years. They often preferred to adopt established theories, introducing amendments to them, than to follow new paths in search of original solutions.

In this general context of Marshall's reception into Italian economics, what Gustavo Del Vecchio wrote in his obituary of Marshall, published in the *Giornale degli economisti*, seems rather startling. In fact, he observes that all collaborators and even readers of that journal 'have to be considered as Marshall's disciples' (Del Vecchio 1924, p. 242), and presents Marshall as the economist who indicated the 'right way' to the profession; but soon after he raises some doubts about the future development of the science, implicitly manifesting his dissatisfaction with orthodoxy.

In 1934 the 'Nuova collana di economisti stranieri e italiani', a collection that succeeded to the 'Biblioteca dell'economista', published the translation of *Industry and trade* (without the appendixes) in a volume dedicated to *Industrial organisation.* The translator was Paolo Baffi, later Governor of the Bank of Italy (from 1975 to 1979). In 1936 the volume *Labour* of the same series included chapter xiv of *Elements of Economics of Industry* (1892). The editor, Celestino Arena, after underlining that Marshall had the merit of clarifying the limits of trade unions' power to obtain higher wages, triumphantly concluded that the corporative State founded by Fascism respected Marshall's warnings (Arena 1936, p. xxiii).

The most complete study on Marshall that appeared in Italy before World War II is probably Francesco Vito's *La concezione biologica dell'economia. Considerazioni sul sistema del Marshall* (1934). Vito observes that the time element introduced by Marshall destroys the marginalist symmetry between supply and demand; underlines the importance of the biological metaphor, that allows for the notion of external economies and representative firm; observes that Marshall does not follow Pareto's and Pantaleoni's value-free approach to economics; stresses that Marshall intends the relationship between individual and institutions as continuously changing; underlines the distinction between the static (*cæteris paribus*) method, which Marshall used, and the vision of society as a static system, which Marshall rejected. Vito finds some affinities between the Marshallian and the Schumpeterian notions of entrepreneur. Last but not least, he approves Marshall for preferring the notion of 'activity' to that of 'want'.

In 1937, in the 'Nuova collana di economisti' volume dedicated to pure economics, Sraffa's 1926 article and the 1930 discussion on the representative firm between Sraffa, Shove and Robertson were presented (Baffi's translation). The volume's editor, Del Vecchio, seemed to accept Sraffa's thesis that the concept of a firm operating at decreasing cost was incompatible with partial equilibrium analysis and that only a general equilibrium approach could generate a coherent theory (Del Vecchio 1937, p. xiv).

AFTER 1945

After the war interest in Marshall's economics declined throughout the world. The main reason is the rejection of Marshall by the Cambridge school itself, at that time dominated by Kaldor, J. Robinson, Kahn and Sraffa. In Italy too, Marshall was not popular among economists, but for quite different reasons. During the so-called reconstruction period (1945–55) all political parties, both centre and left, tended to assign the task of the country development to large private firms, concentrated in Northern Italy, and to State-owned firms, mainly located in the South (see Barucci 1978). An alternative path, relying on the development of small firms spread all over the territory, was not considered as feasible. Paradoxically enough, some efforts to revive Marshall's ideas in order to interpret Italy's industrial structure were made by a Marxist economist, Vittorio Angiolini (1957), who discussed the Marshallian concept of 'representative firm', without valuable results. A more influential Marxist thinker, the university professor and communist MP Antonio Pesenti, in part spared Marshall's teaching from the condemnation pronounced against 'subjectivist' economics, acknowledging Marshall's merits as far as concreteness and realism were concerned (Pesenti 1960; see Becattini 2002). Another of Marshall's merits, according to the Keynesian economist Ferdinando di Fenizio, was that his methodology seemed to anticipate that of 'positive' economics (di Fenizio n.d., but 1956, p. 14).

Many Italian economic historians, influenced by Gramsci's interpretation of the structural gap between Italy and the other West European countries, contended that the gap could be closed by a State- or banks-led energetic investment process (see Caracciolo 1963). Such concepts as 'big spurt' (Gerschenkron) or take-off (Rostow) were discussed and in many cases accepted. For this reason there was no room for the Marshallian approach based on economic continuity. Interest towards Marshall was therefore confined to historians of nineteenth-century British society, such as Edoardo Grendi, who in his study on the birth of the British labour party (Grendi 1964, p. 21) favourably reported Marshall's ideas on labour specialisation.

This situation was aggravated in the 1960s by the advent of the debate on planning (see Lombardini 1967), dominated by macroeconomic modelling, with no special attention to local industrialisation. The scientific climate was far from ideal for the appreciation of Marshall's ideas on small-scale, independent firms. However, the Russian-American economist Paul N. Rosenstein Rodan, influential among Italian planners and consulting economist at the Svimez (*Associazione per lo studio del Mezzogiorno*, Society for the study of the Southern economy), as early as 1943 had clearly indicated the role of the Marshallian concepts in the strategy for industrialisation through small firms in Southern and Eastern Europe (Rosenstein Rodan 1943; see Forte 1964). In 1971 Francesco Forte provided an extensive re-evaluation of Marshall's external economics, stressing their importance for economic development (Forte 1971). Some years later, E. Narni Mancinelli (1984) gave an interpretation of Vera Lutz's model of dualistic economy utilising Marshall's schemes.

Among the historians of economic thought, Umberto Meoli (1972) defended the Marshallian concept of industry as reinterpreted by P.S. Andrews. Two years later, in a paper given at a conference on Marshall and Keynes, Mauro Ridolfi (1974) insisted that Marshall's thought was very different from what Joan Robinson and Sraffa assumed. But these voices were isolated and came under the fire of the neo-Ricardian critics.

Soon afterwards, however, Italian economics underwent a decisive change. Because of the ineffectiveness of general planning to face the crisis of big industries in Northern Italy, attention shifted to the system of small and medium firms and its ability to export and grow. Moreover, the decline of trade unions after the 1969 so-called 'autunno caldo' (hot autumn) – a season of wage claims that the industrial structure did not tolerate – contributed to trigger rethinking of the industrial relation system, in search for more labour flexibility and less social conflict. Among fellow economists, the main champions of this revolution were Giorgio Fuà and Giacomo Becattini. The former, an Ancona professor, more and more dissatisfied with the misuses of macroeconomic policy, engaged himself in a territorially-linked training project for young managers and led several university research groups on local development through small firms (see Fuà and Zacchia 1983; Gruppo di Ancona 1999). The latter, a Florence professor, in his early work had stressed that the so-called dissolution of the Marshallian system was based on interpretive equivoques, mainly due to an imperfect understanding of Marshall's real complexity. The critics had erroneously identified Marshall's thought with his 'tool-box', while his vision of the economic system had been overlooked (Becattini 1962). Subsequently, Becattini became more and more unhappy with the mainstream aggregate techniques *à la mode* (especially export-led models) and decided to adopt a declared 'Marshallian' approach to empirical research on industrial economics, his favourite field of study. This brought him to reconsider, and often reinterpret, the various phases of Marshall's thought. He presented the Italian edition of *The Economics of Industry* (Marshall and Paley Marshall 1975), writing an important biographical, intellectual and analytical introduction. Later he provided a telling anthology of Marshall's texts, inclusive of methodological, ethical and political texts (Becattini 1981). Becattini's disciple Marco Dardi in a volume on the 'young Marshall' (Dardi 1984), focussed on Marshall's early search for a way out from the classical view of the mechanism of accumulation, a way out that did not lead to the neoclassical theory of interacting market mechanisms already under way in his time. The drift of Marshall's early work, instead, is seen to lie in the attempt to construct a dynamic framework of analysis in which evolutionary and sociological influences might find a place.

From 1979 onwards, Becattini and his industrial economics research team (M. Bellandi, G. Dei Ottati, F. Sforzi and others) have concentrated their efforts in highlighting the great potentialities of the Marshallian 'industrial district'. According to this group, the concept is particularly apt to explain the development of small scale industries in Tuscany, Marche and North-East Italy; that is, the regions in which the so-called *made in Italy* is concentrated. More generally, almost two hundred industrial districts have been recognised all over Italy, a phenomenon that counterbalances the decline of 'Fordist' large firms. Becattini lists the main features of such districts: a 'community' of citizens-workers who share the same fundamental socio-economic values of solidarity; a continuous flow of product and process innovations; the production of non-standard, well-recognizable commodities. Becattini comes to reshuffle the traditional concept of industry, considering it as liable to the critiques that were moved in the 1920s and 1930s, while the industrial district, with its conceptual flexibility, seems able to eschew them. In particular, it represents an attempt to overcome the traditional (and negative) contraposition between individual and system in economics, being an intermediate reality provided with an empirical dimension.

This line of research had the merit of producing interdisciplinary collaboration among economic sociologists (Bagnasco, Trigilia and others), business economists (Vaccà, Varaldo and others), economic geographers (Garofoli and others) and economic historians (Guenzi, Belfanti, Fontana and others) to highlight both the historical roots of the growth of several local industries and the perspectives of present Italian development. A favourite terrain of research is the well-known wool district of Prato, Tuscany, whose economic progress has been vividly described by Becattini as 'the caterpillar that became a butterfly' (Becattini 2001). But research on Marshallian districts has been carried on in other regions as well (see Belfanti and Maccabelli 1997). Historically, the origins of the Marshallian districts in Italy date back to the putting-out industry in the country or to the handicraft industries in the towns. The results of this kind of research are often very different from those of other more traditional lines, such as the 'primitive accumulation' approach typical of the Marxist historiography. It can be said that Becattini attempts to correct Marx with a considerable dose of Marshall (he is a declared Marx-shallian). These pro-district ideas that have successfully crossed the Italian borders (see Becattini 2004) have also peculiar political implications for our country. Namely, at least four Italian regions where industrial districts are most present are 'red' regions. The penetration of the ideas relating to the industrial district among post-Communist local leaders and town administrators may have the (unintended?) effect of encouraging the definitive abandonment of the old-fashioned anti-capitalist positions, in favour of more realistic programmes dealing with the expansion of labour flexibility, factor mobility, 'contextual' knowledge and a mix of self-help and solidarity at least at the local level. This political outcome could probably have been appreciated by Marshall himself.

Recent Marshall studies in Italy do not confine themselves to the practical implications and/or applications of Marshall's ideas. An original attempt to read Marshall with sociological glasses (under the example of Talcott Parson's well-known studies of the 1930s) is that of Trigilia (1998). Trigilia connects Marshall's attention to the 'substitution law' among productive factors to the broad sociological and institutional approach he followed in contrast with the at his time prevailing ideas on *homo oeconomicus* (ibid., p. 94).

Finally, we have to record the existence (since 1991) of a Florentine journal, *Marshall Studies Bulletin* (online: http://www.dse.unifi.it/marshall/welcome. htm). Edited by an international scientific board, it hosts original articles as well as archive material (see for example Raffaelli 1994a) and reviews. Tiziano Raffaelli's research on the philosophical background in Marshall's early writings has brought to the discovery that the Cambridge economist found very interesting parallelisms between the working of the mind and that of the firm: the processes of empirical data collection, elaboration and subsequent action, requiring open mind, 'willingness to do' and flexible organisation, are quite similar (Raffaelli 1991 and 1994b). The same author (Raffaelli 2003) has investigated and clarified the relationship between philosophy, psychology and economics in Marshall as well as his relationship with Keynes. Marshall is defined as an 'evolutionary economist' – a conclusion that only a few years ago would at least have been considered questionable.

REFERENCES

Allocati, A. (ed.) (1990), *Carteggio Loria-Graziani (1888–1943)*, Roma: Ministero per i beni culturali e ambientali.
Angiolini, V. (1957), *Contributo allo studio di una categoria neo-classica*, Padova: CEDAM.
Arena, C. (1936), 'Introduzione', in C. Arena (ed.), *Lavoro*, vol. XI of 'Nuova collana di economisti stranieri e italiani', Torino: UTET.
Barone, E. (1894), 'Sul trattamento di quistioni dinamiche', *Giornale degli economisti*, **8**, 407–35.
Barucci, P. (1978), *Ricostruzione, pianificazione, Mezzogiorno*, Bologna: Il Mulino.
Becattini, G. (1962), *Il concetto di industria e la teoria del valore*, Torino: Boringhieri.
Becattini, G. (ed.) (1981), *Marshall. Antologia di scritti economici*, Bologna: Il Mulino.
Becattini, G. (2001), *The Caterpillar and the Butterfly. An Exemplary Case of Development in the Italy of the Industrial Districts*, Firenze: Le Monnier.
Becattini, G. (2002), 'Il marxismo "applicato" di Antonio Pesenti', in *I nipoti di Cattaneo*, Roma: Donzelli, pp. 71–8.
Becattini, G. (2004), *Industrial Districts. A New Approach to Industrial Change*, Cheltenham, UK and Northampton, MA, USA: Edward Elgar.
Becattini, G. and N. Bellanca (1992), 'Marshall and the Italian Academies', in *Marshall Studies Bulletin*, **2**, 14–26. Online: http://www.dse.unifi.it/marshall/welcome.htm.
Belfanti, C.M. and T. Maccabelli (eds) (1997), *Un paradigma per i distretti industriali. Radici storiche, attualità e sfide future*, Brescia: Grafo.
Bruni, L. (2004), 'Gli "equilibri" di Ricci (fra economia e psicologia)', in P. Bini and A.M. Fusco (eds), *Umberto Ricci (1879–1946): economista militante e uomo combattivo*, Firenze: Polistampa, pp. 195–213.
Caracciolo, A. (ed.) (1963), *La formazione dell'Italia industriale*, Bari: Laterza.
Cossa, L. (1893), *An Introduction to the Study of Political Economy*, revised by the author and translated by L. Dyer, London: Macmillan.
Dalla Volta, R. (1885), 'Review of A. Marshall, *The Present Position of Economics*', *L'Economista*, 25 October, 682–3.
Dalla Volta, R. (1890), 'Review of A. Marshall, *Principles of Economics*', *L'Economista*, 28 September, 615–17.
Dardi, M. (1984), *Il giovane Marshall: accumulazione e mercato*, Bologna: Il Mulino.
Del Vecchio, G. (1924), 'L'opera di Alfredo Marshall', *Giornale degli economisti e rivista di statistica*, **65**, 642–5.
Del Vecchio, G. (1925), 'L'opera scientifica di Enrico Barone', *Giornale degli economisti e rivista di statistica*, **66**, 573–8.
Del Vecchio, G. (1937), 'Introduction' to *Economia pura*, 'Nuova collana di economisti stranieri e italiani', vol. IV, Torino: UTET, pp. vii–xxxi.
Di Fenizio, F. (n.d., but 1956), *Lezioni sul metodo dell'economia politica*, Milano: L'Industria.
Einaudi, L. (1897), 'La psicologia di uno sciopero', reprinted in *Le lotte del lavoro*, Torino: Einaudi, 1972, pp. 17–50.

Einaudi, L. (1950), 'La scienza economica in Italia. Reminiscenze', in C. Antoni and R. Mattioli (eds), *Cinquant'anni di vita intellettuale italiana, 1896–1946. Scritti in onore di Benedetto Croce per il suo ottantesimo anniversario*, Napoli: Edizioni scientifiche italiane, reprinted in Finoia (1980), pp. 94–115.

Fanno, M. (1914), 'Contributo alla teoria dell'offerta a costi congiunti', *Supplement* to *Giornale degli economisti e rivista di statistica*, **49** (October), 1–143.

Fanno, M. (1925), 'Alfredo Marshall', *Annali di economia*, **2**, 167–81.

Fanno, M. (1926), 'Contributo alla teoria economica dei beni succedanei', *Annali di economia*, **3**, 229–467.

Faucci, R. and S. Perri (1995), 'Socialism and marginalism in Italy, 1880–1910', in I. Steedman (ed.), *Socialism and Marginalism in Economics 1870–1930*, London and New York: Routledge.

Finoia, M. (ed.) (1980), *La scienza economica in Italia, 1850–1950*, Bologna: Cappelli.

Forte, F. (1964), *Introduzione alla politica economica. Il mercato e i piani*, Torino: Einaudi.

Forte, F. (1971), 'Le economie esterne marshalliane e la teoria contemporanea dello sviluppo', *Rivista internazionale di scienze sociali*, **42** (1), 117–60.

Fuà, G. and C. Zacchia (eds) (1983), *Industrializzazione senza fratture*, Bologna: Il Mulino.

Gallegati, M. (1982), 'Formazione e distribuzione del sovrappiù nell'"economia senza valore" di Antonio Graziadei (1894–1909)', in R. Faucci (ed.), *Gli italiani e Bentham. Dalla 'felicità pubblica' all'economia del benessere*, Milano: Franco Angeli, pp. 209–29.

Graziadei, A. (1899), *La produzione capitalistica*, Torino: Bocca.

Graziadei, A. (1909), *Saggio di un'indagine sui prezzi in regime di concorrenza e di sindacato tra gli imprenditori*, Imola: Galeati.

Grendi, E. (1964), *L'avvento del laburismo. Il movimento operaio inglese dal 1880 al 1920*, Milano: Feltrinelli.

Gruppo di Ancona (ed.) (1999), *Trasformazioni dell'economia e della società italiana. Studi e ricerche in onore di Giorgio Fuà*, Bologna: Il Mulino.

Jannaccone, P. (1900), *Il costo di produzione*, in 'Biblioteca dell'economista', IV series, vol. IV, Torino: UTET.

Jannaccone, P. (1905), 'Alfredo Marshall', in 'Biblioteca dell'economista', IV series, preface to vols IX and X, Torino: UTET.

Jannaccone, P. (1914), 'Il dumping e la discriminazione dei prezzi', *La riforma sociale*, **25** (March), 234–76, reprinted in Jannaccone (1936) and (1951).

Jannaccone, P. (1936 and 1951), *Prezzi e mercati*, Torino: Einaudi.

Lombardini, S. (1967), *La programmazione economica. Idee, esperienze, problemi*, Torino: Einaudi.

Loria, A. (1920), 'La nuova opera di Alfredo Marshall [*Industry and Trade*]', *Riforma sociale*, **31**, 1–13.

Loria, A. (1923), 'Marshall sulla circolazione', *Riforma sociale*, **34**, 234–40.

Loria, A. (1924), *Alfredo Marshall*, Roma: Formiggini.

Loria, A. (1926), 'I *Memorials* di Alfredo Marshall', *Riforma sociale*, **37**, 1–10.

Marshall, A. (1905), *Principii di economica*, trans. of 4th edn, in 'Biblioteca dell'economista', IV series, vol. IX, part 3, Torino: UTET.

Marshall, A. (1934), *Industria e commercio*, in G. Masci (ed.), *Organizzazione industriale*, vol. VII of 'Nuova collana di economisti stranieri e italiani', Torino: UTET.

Marshall, A. (1936), 'Le leghe operaie (Trade Unions) [chap. xiv of *Elements of the Economics of Industry*]', in C. Arena (ed.), *Lavoro*, vol. XI of 'Nuova collana di economisti stranieri e italiani', Torino: UTET.

Marshall, A. (1975), *Teoria pura del commercio internazionale. Teoria pura dei prezzi interni*, Milano: Feltrinelli.

Marshall, A. and M. Paley Marshall (1975), *Economia della produzione*, introduction by G. Becattini, Milano: Isedi.

Meoli, U. (1972), *Impresa e industria nel pensiero economico di Alfred Marshall*, Padova: CEDAM.

Montesano, A. (2004), 'Umberto Ricci, l'utilità marginale e la teoria della domanda', in P. Bini and A.M. Fusco (eds), *Umberto Ricci (1879–1946): economista militante e uomo combattivo*, Firenze: Polistampa, pp. 99–116.

Narni Mancinelli, E. (1984), 'Il dualismo industriale nel pensiero di Alfred Marshall', in *Moneta, dualismo e pianificazione nel pensiero di V. Lutz*, Bologna: Il Mulino, pp. 257–88.

Pantaleoni, M. (1889), *Principii di economia pura*, Firenze: Barbera, new edn Milano: Treves, 1931.

Pantaleoni, M. (1907) 'Una visione cinematografica della scienza economica', reprinted in Pantaleoni (1925), vol. 1.

Pantaleoni, M. (1909), 'Di alcuni fenomeni di dinamica economica', reprinted in Pantaleoni (1925), vol. 2.

Pantaleoni, M. (1924), 'In occasione della morte di Pareto: riflessioni', *Giornale degli economisti e rivista di statistica*, **65**, 1–19.

Pantaleoni, M. (1925), *Erotemi di economia*, 2 vols, Bari: Laterza.

Pareto, V. (1960), *Lettere a Maffeo Pantaleoni*, edited by G. De Rosa, 3 vols, Roma: Banca Nazionale del Lavoro.

Pesenti, A. ([1960] 1984), *Manuale di economia politica*, new edn, Roma: Editori Riuniti.

Raffaelli, T. (1991), 'The analysis of the human mind in the early Marshallian manuscripts', *Quaderni di storia dell'economia politica*, special issue on *Alfred Marshall's Principles of Economics 1890–1990*, **9**, 29–58.

Raffaelli, T. (1994a), 'Marshall on *Machinery and life*', *Marshall Studies Bulletin*, **4**, 9–22. Online: http://www.dse.unifi.it/marshall/welcome.htm.

Raffaelli, T. (1994b), 'Il ruolo degli studi psicologici di Marshall nella sua analisi dell'organizzazione dell'industria e degli affari', *Giornale degli economisti e annali di economia*, **53**, 499–523.

Raffaelli, T. (2003), *Marshall's Evolutionary Economics*, London: Routledge.

Ridolfi, M. (1974), 'Aspetti del sistema teorico di A. Marshall: una revisione critica di interpretazioni moderne', *Annali della Facoltà di scienze politiche*, Perugia, **12**, 122–204.

Rosenstein Rodan, P.N. (1943), 'Problems of industrialisation of Eastern and South-East Europe', *Economic Journal*, reprinted in A.N. Agarwala and S.P. Singh (eds) (1963), *The Economics of Underdevelopment*, Oxford: Oxford University Press, pp. 245–55; Italian trans. *L'economia dei paesi sottosviluppati*, Milano: Feltrinelli, 1966.

Sraffa, P. (1925), 'Sulle relazioni tra costo e quantità prodotta', *Annali di economia*, **2**, 277–328; English trans. 'On the relations between cost and quantity produced', in L. Pasinetti (ed.) (1998), *Italian Economic Papers*, vol. 3, Bologna: Il Mulino, Oxford: Oxford University Press, pp. 323–63.

Sraffa, P. (1926), 'The laws of return under competitive conditions', *Economic Journal*, **36**, 535–50.

Trigilia, C. (1998), *Sociologia economica. Stato, mercato e società nel capitalismo moderno*, Bologna: Il Mulino.

Vito, F. (1934), *La concezione biologica dell'economia. Considerazioni sul sistema del Marshall*, Milano: Vita e pensiero.

Whitaker, J.K. (ed.) (1996), *The Correspondence of Alfred Marshall, Economist*, 3 vols, Cambridge: Cambridge University Press.

18.   Marshall in Spain, 1890–1950

Lluis Argemí[*]

INTRODUCTION

Broadly speaking, from the second half of the nineteenth century until the 1940s economic thought in Spain was dominated by an eclectic approach, strongly dependent on the ideas of the French liberals, in the style of the *Journal des économistes*. In the last decades of the nineteenth century, Spanish economists also subscribed to a vision of their discipline rooted in the German historical school and named 'Krausism', after its originator, the legal philosopher Krause. Inspired by the German *Katheder Socialisten*, this vision was far removed from the neoclassical Marshallian school.

   In early twentieth-century Spain, the study of economics was dominated by the figure of Antonio Flores de Lemus and his pupils. Trained as a historian in Germany, Flores urged his pupils to study history, but encouraged them also to learn mathematics; some of his pupils rebelled against the historically-based training that was prevalent at the time and began to accept some marginalist principles. In general, however, the influence of German economics predominated and marginalist and neoclassical approaches made little impact (Malo Guillén 2001).

   Another explanation of this lack of influence may be the academic status of economics in Spanish universities before 1950, when the first faculties of Economics were created. Until then, political economy and public finance were taught in law faculties by lawyers with no mathematical training who regarded the mathematical aspects of economics as difficult and irrelevant. Though Marshall confined his mathematics to footnotes and appendices, he was often rejected for being a member of the 'mathematical' school.

TRANSLATIONS AND TRANSLATORS

Before Marshall, there were no translations of the marginalist trio – Menger, Jevons, Walras – nor did these thinkers exert any influence. A minor introduction to economics, Jevons's *Primer of Political Economy* of 1878, was translated as late as 1923 (Jevons 1923) but no translations of Walras or Menger can be found. So Marshall's thought reached Spain without any previous intercession on the part of the marginalists.

Marshall's ideas were introduced in Spain through the translation by Cossa, who reproduced several abstracts from his work (Cossa 1892). The first Spanish translation of Marshall's *Principles of Economics*, in 1922, was by a professor of Public Finance at the University of Madrid, Pio Ballesteros, not a member of Flores's group. He probably used the French translation by Sauvaire-Jourdain, thus eliminating the novel term of the title (*economics*) and reinstating the traditional name of political economy.

The second translation, published in 1931, was probably by a professional translator, Evenor Hazera, who also translated Ricardo's *Principles* shortly afterwards. Both books were part of a series that included Loria and others. Nothing is known of Hazera, though an idea of his professional ability can be gained from the fact that he wrote Cournet instead of Cournot not once but three times (which rules out the possibility of a misprint).

The third translator was Luis Vigil Escalera, who also translated works by Einzig and on the New Deal, but in this case the more interesting figure is the director of the series, Ramon Carande. A leading economic historian and a pupil of Flores de Lemus's, Carande was one of the few authors to represent a link between the group of economists who remained in Spain after the Civil War and those who were forced to leave the country. A socialist, he was protected by a fascist leader and became an internal exile. He made a name with his studies on the financial aspects of the reign of the emperor Charles V, mainly devoted to the Fuggers (*Carlos V y sus banqueros*). The translation in question, *Economía industrial* (*Economics of Industry*), is in fact a version of *Elements of Economics of Industry* (1892), and not of *The Economics of Industry* (1879).

A collection of papers by Marshall, selected by Guillebaud, was published in Mexico in 1949 (Marshall 1949), as *Obras escogidas* (*Selected Works*). This volume included Keynes's 1924 obituary and a selection from *The Economics of Industry*, *Money, Credit and Commerce*, *Memorials* and *Official Papers*. The publishing house, Fondo de Cultura Económica, was the main editor of economics books in Spanish, especially classics. Marshall's volume was included in the classics section alongside Mun, Cantillon, Smith, Ricardo and Marx.

None of these translations include prefaces or presentations by the translators. Indeed, the reason for the translation appears to have been their relevance to contemporary economics rather than their interest as landmarks in the history of economic thought. But this is not the case of the last translation, the canonical one published in 1954, and included in an important series alongside many classics of economic thought. The translator was Emilio de Figueroa, Professor of Economic Policy at the University of Madrid, and the book had an introduction by Manuel de Torres. Although these scholars are representative of the new Keynesian economics, the introduction highlights some key features of Marshall's work and pays special attention to the use of mathematics, in order to allay the fears of a readership largely unaccustomed to the discipline. The importance Torres attributes to Marshall in the history of economic thought is entirely appropriate, for at the time the predominant approach to economics still to an extent recalled corporatist economics and Marshall's work could be regarded as an instrument for modernising economic studies.

DIRECT INFLUENCES

Direct knowledge of Marshall's theories is evident in the works of only a few authors. Two of them, both outside mainstream economics in Spain, deserve mention here.

One is José María de Zumalacárregui y Prat, Grandee of Spain, Professor of Political Economy and Public Finance at the University of Valencia until 1937. After the Civil War he was appointed professor at the University of Madrid. His works before 1940 are mostly papers on applied economics, written from a social catholic perspective; only after the war did he enter the theoretical field. Against the ideas of Flores de Lemus, to a certain extent his opponent, he very soon became interested in mathematics as a tool for economics. Through his mathematical studies he discovered Walras, and above all Pareto. His works also reveal a direct knowledge of Marshall's works (Zumalacárregui 1946), which he often mentions in relation to specific topics such as elasticity. He died in 1946. The task of spreading Marshallian ideas thus fell to his pupils, Manuel de Torres and Castañeda. As professors at the recently created Faculty of Economic Sciences, they attempted to introduce a different, truly scientific approach, in order to fight the corporatist vision then predominant among the leaders of the fascist regime.

The other author who deserves mentioning here is Joan P. Fàbregas, a left-wing unionist intellectual. Author of an *Assaig d'economía política* (*Essay on Political Economy*) written in Catalan in 1932, Fàbregas starts from Marshall's definition of economics, but throughout the book discusses many aspects of social reform inspired mainly by Henry George and also Marx (Martín Rodríguez 2001). For Fàbregas, Marshall was the economist who rescued the classical vision; for this reason he ranks him alongside Marx and George. Fàbregas (1932) is an essay on the origin of economic societies rather than a treatise on economics or political economy since it was mainly directed at a non-specialist readership.

Finally, two of Flores's pupils, Rodríguez Mata and Castañeda, had some knowledge of Marshall. Their interest could be seen as a minor act of rebellion against their master, though Castañeda was also a student of Zumalacárregui, and so received his Marshallian leanings from one of the main proponents of the English economist's thought. But in the atmosphere of the 1940s and 1950s, the Hicksian approach predominated, and the introduction of Marshall was seen as an anachronism.

CONCLUSION

It comes as a surprise to see that Marshall had hardly any influence in Spain, but it is even more of a surprise that some of the people who knew his work, or helped introduce his ideas, adopted a heterodox approach; politically they were on the left, on the margins of the intellectual atmosphere of Spain. Most standard textbooks tend to see Marshall as the perfect representative of neoclassical orthodox economics, but in countries where orthodoxy was of a different kind he was regarded as an eccentric. He continued to be seen as such well into the middle of the twentieth century, when Spanish universities finally began a process of transformation.

NOTE

* We publish this chapter in the incomplete form in which Lluis Argemí left it at the time of his death. The reasons for this decision are explained in the introduction, which adds a few suggestions for further readings on Marshall in Spain.

REFERENCES

Cossa, L. (1892), *Introducción al estudio de la economía política*, Valladolid: Viuda de Cuesta.

Fàbregas, J.P. (1932), *Assaig d'economía política*, Barcelona: Bosch.

Fuentes Quintana, E. (ed.) (2001), *Economía y economistas españoles*, 8 vols, Barcelona: Circulo de Lectores.

Jevons, W.S. (1923), *Nociones de economía política*, Paris: Garnier.

Malo Guillén, J.L. (2001), 'El pensamiento económico del krausismo español', in Fuentes Quintana (2001), vol. 5, pp. 389–450.

Marshall, A. (1922), *Tratado de economía política (Principles of Economics)*, 3 vols, trans. P. Ballesteros, Madrid: La España moderna.

Marshall, A. (1931), *Principios de economía (Principles of Economics)*, 2 vols, trans. E. Hazera, Madrid: El consultor bibliográfico.

Marshall, A. (1936), *Economía industrial (Elements of Economics of Industry)*, edited by R. Carande, trans. L.V. Escalera, Madrid: Revista de derecho privado.

Marshall, A. (1949), *Obras escogidas*, México: Fondo de Cultura Económica.

Marshall, A. (1954), *Principios de economía (Principles of Economics)*, trans. E. de Figueroa, introduction by Manuel de Torres, Madrid: Aguilar.

Martín Rodríguez, M. (2001), 'La influencia de Henry George en España', in Fuentes Quintana (2001), vol. 5, pp. 525–55.

Zumalacárregui, J.M. de (1946), *La ley estadística en economía*, Madrid: Aguilar.

19. Marshallian industrial districts in Portugal: a conceptual solution for empirical analyses' pressures

José Reis

Moisés Bensabat Amzalak (1892–1978), Professor of Economics in the Technical University of Lisbon, was perhaps the first Portuguese scholar to pay particular attention to Marshall's work as the founder of the 'Cambridge school'. He considered Marshall a 'great professor and economist' and accorded a definite significance to the development of his work by successors like Pigou (Amzalak 1933).

It may be wondered whether Amzalak's attention was followed by an increased influence in classes and programmes of economics and economic thought. But little evidence is available to confirm such a suspicion. For that reason I will assume in this essay that the primary field by means of which we can analyse Alfred Marshall's (1946, 1988) influence in Portugal is to be found in the diffusion of the concept of the industrial district. Therefore, my subject is not how general economic theory received Marshall's ideas, an enquiry for which I think there are no reference points. My hypothesis is rather that, some few years ago, the Portuguese economy's material conditions invited analysis by means of Marshall's concept of the industrial district, which allowed for an interpretation of some crucial aspects of the national economy's development trajectory and structural features.

The argument below will be based on five points. It represents an interpretation of a problematic and an empirical context in which Marshall's vision, and Giacomo Becattini's conceptual development of this vision, appear as key elements in a solution that allows for a better understanding of economic complexity.

A SOCIO-ECONOMIC PROBLEMATIC: THE PRESSURE OF EMPIRICAL DATA

The diffusion of the Marshallian vision of industrial organisation must be interpreted in the context of the need to provide answers to the empirical research problems that emerged in the second half of the 1970s and the first half of the 1980s. Actually, in this period, socio-economic research in Portugal underwent a remarkable development. This was closely linked to the democratic revolution of April 1974, and to the subsequent modernisation of the country at all levels.

In the wake of such widespread and profound changes, it was necessary to identify and to give an interpretation to the role played by economic and material social structures, which themselves were much diversified. Discussion at the time was profound, with many doubts raised and questions opened. A pluralistic view was very useful, and a theoretical perspective based on innovative concepts was needed. In these perplexing times, the research agenda was forced to diversify and to engage with unexpected dynamics on the economic and social levels. Researchers had to work out how to deal with such challenges. They were facing a substantive reality hitherto ignored, with the situation further aggravated by the fact that the scientific community at that time was very small and marginalised. This environment was ripe for generating a 'conceptual demand' to which Marshallian ideas supplied one of many creative answers. The instruments of analysis of the various existing disciplines were able to capture only part of what was on the agenda and it was important to arrive at a theory that was global, interpretative and operational at the same time. And these are exactly the characteristics of Marshall's ideas on industrial organisation as the product of spatial agglomeration, local knowledge and relationships founded upon proximity. In Portugal, the new dynamic social and economic forces were both diffused and differentiated, but all of them were key elements of the national performance at that time, not least because no picture of the overall national dynamic was available. It is for this reason that, in the title of this section, I referred to the 'pressure of empirical data' which thus translated into a demand for new, adaptable and useful concepts. The evident usefulness of the Marshallian concept of the industrial district was the reason for its diffusion in Portugal at this time and its adoption by several researchers.

WHAT WAS ON THE AGENDA? TERRITORIAL-DIFFUSED DYNAMICS BASED ON PROXIMITY

What did this empirical reality consist of? Portugal, in the middle of the 1970s, as in our own day, was an intermediately developed economy (Reis 2005). As a European economy, it was the last to end its 'colonial empire' in Africa. During the 1950s and 1960s there had been a significant phase of industrial growth. This growth had been geographically concentrated, with the basic sectors and heavy industries the most important. Its potential for sustainable growth and social modernisation was, however, very weak. This weakness led to a sustained migration of labour to other European countries. As a result, internationalisation through workforce mobility was more intense than internationalisation through the trade of goods and services. There was, nevertheless, another side of the economy: its territorial systems and its systems of traditional manufacturing, the development of both of which were propelled by the internationalisation of economic relations. Local urban systems, where new forms of urban life grew through differentiation between activities, also became important and experienced a growing density. In these developments, the spatial factor was relevant, even crucial. Agglomeration, proximity, specialisation – these were the key elements of such emerging systems. These systems became clearly visible because in crisis situations they were the origin of different positive socio-economic effects. The transition from a closed economy to an economy that soon would be able to fast develop deep processes of integration – as was the case following Portugal's accession to the European Economic Community in 1986 – was closely bound up with all of these phenomena.

AN ANALYTICAL PLACE FOR PROXIMITY AND TERRITORIAL-INTENSIVE INTERACTIONS

Several studies used and diffused Marshall's vision throughout the Portuguese intellectual community (a review of these studies is beyond the scope of this essay). Economists, geographers and sociologists predominate in the research community that created the new Marshallian environment. Their common subject was a simple one: local productive systems, framed by a concrete geography of proximity and formed by differentiated social structures and material resources. Their presence within the national economy was illustrated by their contributions to employment, exports, innovation and economic and social diversification. Specific knowledge, accumulated during a long history and in both tacit and codified forms, was mobilised. Specialisation was the key to valuing them. Technical culture, proximity, specific sociability, and an organisational environment with a high propensity to autonomous entrepreneurship: these were the main specific assets of the phenomena now placed under the Marshallian rubric.

The common aim was to find an analytical place from which to view the dynamic interactions between economy and society, the emerging territorial-based relationships, and the way in which local cultures and traditions were active elements within economic performances. The result was a remarkable set of research outputs. Succinctly, we may say that the researchers achieved four objectives (Reis 2009, pp. 227–43). First, they came to understand territorial differentiation as a main structural condition of the economy and society (that is, they placed a complex notion of territory on the agenda). Second, they rebuilt conceptually, by means of the relational orders studied at the local level, the material and social fabric of each territory. Third, they made available a geography of industrial organisation and of the specific assets of each system.

Finally, they contributed to an ontological discussion concerning the relationship between the empirically-observed data and the existing knowledge capital.

AN UNEXPECTED NOTION EMERGING FROM A 'BLENDED' EPISTEMIC COMMUNITY

The diffusion of the concept of the industrial district was gradual. To begin with, it emerged into prominence from a relatively large set of convergent notions. The significance of the local as a phenomenological level was one of the first results reached. The understanding of the very idea of the 'local' occurred under Marshall's influence, and appeared as a result founded on the geographical study of the economies of agglomeration. A second and consequent outcome was an understanding that this level is not merely a description of the localisation of general geo-economic relations, but in fact has autonomy and is able to act as a creator of new relations and new phenomena. This second result was achieved under the influence of the interpretation of the 'industrial ambience' of some agglomerations in British regions conducted by Marshall a century ago. An understanding of the importance of proximity, as well as cultural and knowledge capital also arose under Marshallian influence. An interpretation of the relevant local productive systems as spaces where 'external economies' were created was the third outcome. In the sense given by Marshall, the very idea of 'external economies' points to a specific objective: to identify the advantages individual firms experience from their integration within a concrete territory, with its own structures, relations and environment. These conceptual propositions, developed by Becattini, thus helped to generate a synthesis that itself acted as an ultimate reference point for an epistemic community that until then had been diffused and unorganised. The notion of an industrial district, therefore, became the nuclear reactor fueling the research programmes, the group of researchers, and the theoretical ambiance within which innovative empirical studies have been developed.

A CONTINUING INFLUENCE: A LOOK AT THE MORPHOLOGY OF SOCIO-ECONOMIC REALITY

The influence of Marshall that I have tried to summarise here is beyond any single work on local systems or industrial districts. There is also a much broader significance that needs to be pointed to. Actually, Marshall's influence helps to foster, in contemporary debates, a way to support a complex interpretation of the morphology of socio-economic dynamics and relational intensities. After the contributions described above and the new conceptual building that resulted, such an interpretation became ontologically and epistemologically grounded. Crucial here was the Marshallian idea that economic and social space is not freely used by capitalism. For this insight, two issues were central. The first was the conclusion that we have to identify the relational orders upon which development and dynamics are based. The second was the realisation that if it is to be more useful and comprehensive, economics itself needs to build a *constitutional* approach. This means that social systems' performances are not sub-products (without their own qualities) of immanent relations. Such performances are, rather, pushed by actual structures, actual relations and actual and intentional orders.

REFERENCES

Amzalak, M. (1933), *A economia política em Inglaterra*, Lisboa: Instituto Superior de Ciências Económicas e Financeiras.

Marshall, A. (1946), *Princípios de economia: Tratado introdutório*, Rio de Janeiro: Editora Epasa.

Marshall, A. (1988), *Princípios de economia: Tratado introdutório*, revised version of 1946 trans., São Paulo Nova Cultural.

Reis, J. (2005), *State, Market and Community: The Portuguese Economy in the Networks of Contemporary Governance*, Coimbra: Oficina do CES. Online: http://www.ces.uc.pt/publicacoes/oficina/222/222.php.

Reis, J. (2009), *Ensaios de economia impura*, Coimbra: Almedina.

PART V

Marshall in Asian countries

20. Influence of Alfred Marshall on Indian economic thought

Nita Mitra

This chapter attempts to examine the influence of Alfred Marshall on Indian economic thought. It has been organised as follows.

In the first section, the syllabus of the Calcutta University is the initial point of reference. The inclusion of Marshall's major publications into its curriculum is examined, to be able to get an idea regarding the extent to which the students of the pre-independence era came into contact with Marshallian expositions, for this is where the initial influence of Marshall may be said to have reached the academic world. As to the logic of the choice of Calcutta University, it may be said that its extensive hinterland, its affiliating colleges spread practically all over the Asian subcontinent (see Figure 20.1) that included undivided India (now India, Pakistan and Bangladesh), Burma and Ceylon, served to help the spread of not only the syllabi but also the textbooks towards a wider body of students and teachers. That such influence did not remain confined just to the textbook/reference level may be seen by examining some of the publications of the Indian researchers of that period also. It is the objective of this section to see, from such a review, whether the Marshallian ideas entered into higher research works, which would be indicative of the extent of assimilation of Marshall into higher academic pursuits of the pre-independence Indian scholarship.

The next section will touch upon the research works of Indian economists of the post-independence period. The purpose is to see whether their reading of the *Principles*, *Industry and Trade* and the rest of Marshall's publications helped them to attain higher standards and maturity of inquiry as compared to their counterparts discussed in the earlier section. The strength and depth of Marshall's influence will become apparent.

The section following it will discuss the Indian economist Amartya Kumar Sen briefly, to look for the Marshall–Pigou welfare economics impact on him. The contributions of both Marshall and Sen to ethics and economics will be referred to. The aim is to find the direction in which they tried to realign the focus of the discipline.

We note that at the time when Marshall's works were being included in the academic curriculum in India, his views on important policy matters relating to

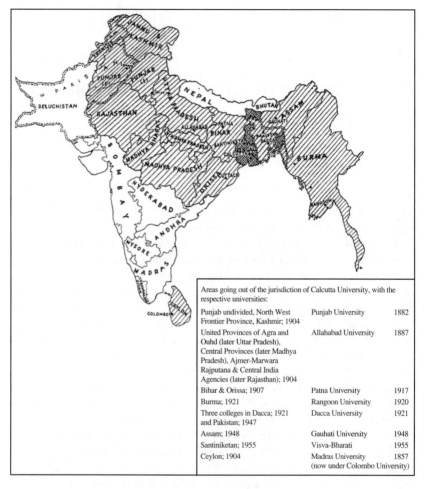

Areas going out of the jurisdiction of Calcutta University, with the respective universities:

Punjab undivided, North West Frontier Province, Kashmir; 1904	Punjab University	1882
United Provinces of Agra and Ouhd (later Uttar Pradesh), Central Provinces (later Madhya Pradesh), Ajmer-Marwara Rajputana & Central India Agencies (later Rajasthan); 1904	Allahabad University	1887
Bihar & Orissa; 1907	Patna University	1917
Burma; 1921	Rangoon University	1920
Three colleges in Dacca; 1921 and Pakistan; 1947	Dacca University	1921
Assam; 1948	Gauhati University	1948
Santiniketan; 1955	Visva-Bharati	1955
Ceylon; 1904	Madras University (now under Colombo University)	1857

Note: The map shows the names and the dates of birth of the universities that were carved out of the University of Calcutta's jurisdiction and the provinces, cities and countries they were meant to serve with the dates on which they attained independent status. The most thickly shaded area of the map denotes the residual areas that remained under the jurisdiction of Calcutta University.

Source: Asutosh Museum, Calcutta University.

Figure 20.1   Map showing extent of affiliating area of Calcutta University

the State and to Indian questions, were being sought by the British administration. India at that time was under the colonial rule, it may be noted.

Another group of Indians not belonging to the academic domain, the economic nationalists, examined many of his views on policy matters. For example, with respect to the currency question, his and Bowley's views on the impact of the falling rupee–sterling exchange on India's exports did not find acceptance on their part. On other issues too, the nationalists did not see eye to eye with him. A consideration of Marshall's views vis-à-vis those of the nationalists are excluded from the scope of this chapter however.

MARSHALLIAN ORIENTATION OF THE PRE-1950s INDIAN THOUGHT

The University of Calcutta was established in the year 1857, along with two other universities, of Bombay and Madras. It was from that time onwards that higher education in India came to be attuned to the standards of the best of British universities, of Cambridge, Oxford and London.

For an idea of the British influence in general, one may, for example, refer to the BA Honours and MA History syllabi for the year 1880, for the University of Calcutta. It is seen that at the BA Honours level, the candidates were required to be examined in Political Economy, along with several other papers. The questions at the graduate and postgraduate level included, among others, those on Mill's representative government, Adam Smith's maxims on taxation, Ricardo's theory of value and so on. Until the year 1885, Sidgwick, Mill, Fawcett and Adam Smith were included in the prescribed list of textbooks.

It was only in the year 1896, six years after its first publication, that Marshall's *Principles of Economics* was added to the History MA prescribed textbooks' list and was duly reflected in the topics that were set in the questions of the ensuing examination. A year later, in 1897, in the fifth paper of the MA History examination, the students were asked to write answers on how Marshall translated the law of diminishing utility into the law of diminishing marginal demand–price and so on. By 1898, Marshall's *The Economics of Industry* was incorporated within the BA Honours History syllabus.

It has to be noted that up to 1909, under the old regulation of this university, economics was not a subject to be studied exclusively for either the first- or the second-degree examination. Under the new regulations, framed under the Indian Universities Act of 1904, the University of Calcutta made provision for studies in economics both for the BA Honours and the MA examinations, but as the syllabi of studies in this subject included both economic theory and practice and political theory and practice, it was known as Political Economy and Political Philosophy. Marshall's evidence to the Gold and Silver Commission 1888 was incorporated into the syllabi of MA Political Economy and Political Philosophy in 1912, while the Mathematical Appendices of his *Principles* came to be included in the papers on Mathematical Economics. These references to the university's syllabi indicate the extent to which the ideas of Marshall and the analytical tools that this unquestioned leader of British orthodox economists familiarised in his textbooks, in particular, came to penetrate the academic disciplines in this part of the world.

As to the extent of influence of his theoretical ideas and the impetus that the Indian students got from such ideas, we may now refer to some of Marshall's former Indian students and other academics of the pre-independence era. Manohar Lal, who had been Marshall's student and had earned high Honours in Cambridge, may be mentioned. He came to occupy the first professorship of Economics at the University of Calcutta where he taught economics from 1909 to 1912. Although it was for a short period, his university association nevertheless helped him to give academic leadership and to pass on the torch to C.J. Hamilton, on being called to public life in his province of Punjab.

A brief reference to Manohar Lal–Marshall's correspondence may be made (Whitaker 1996).

In a letter dated 28 January 1909, Marshall wrote to his student regarding the notion that educated Indians held about the dignity of white-collar labour as opposed to manual-engineering shop work. Such a retrogressive outlook appeared not at all conducive to the nation's progress, he held. In fact Marshall wrote to Professor B. Mukherjee of Lucknow University, on 22 October 1910, that if India had a score or two of men like Mr Tata, and some thousands of men with Japanese interest in realities, and with no scorn for work on things, India would soon be a great nation. This idea appeared to the nationalists (see Chandra 1991 for British versus Indian views on development in colonial India) to be a very simple interpretation of actually a complex phenomenon – the outcome of an exploitative imperialist system. This has been discussed by many of them. We will not go into these.

We may now refer to Jehangir Coyajee (1930, 1932) who qualified for the Tripos in Economics in 1910, and got appointed as the professor of Economics in Presidency College, Calcutta. He served the said college for quite a long period from 1911 to 1930. This student of Marshall, from the very beginning, took up the task of nurturing the new generation of economists. Apart from familiarising his own students with Marshallian approaches to problems, the various academic lectures that he was invited to deliver at various institutions of higher learning in India helped diffuse further his teacher's viewpoints.

Marshall was aware of the extent to which his textbooks were instrumental in shaping Indian thought. His letter to one Jogis Chandra Sinha, a young scholar and professor of Economics who later became the principal of Presidency College, may be recalled. In 1920, Marshall was found responding to his query regarding the appropriate definition of 'representative firm' and suggesting a way out of his difficulties regarding representing adequately increasing returns–supply by a curve.

A brief review of some Indian research work of that time may now be considered to illustrate the theoretical impetus that was derived from his formulations. For example one could refer to Jajneswar Ghosh, whom Calcutta University had given, as early as in 1911, a PhD degree on his thesis on *History of Land Tenures in England, France, Germany and Russia and the Agrarian Question*. In the course of the literature review of his thesis, Ghosh pointed how Marshall had undertaken to free the Ricardian theory from vagueness and inconsistency with fact and to supply the necessary provisos and limitations. Similarly Amiya Kumar Dasgupta's LSE doctoral thesis on *The Conception of Surplus* is another example (Dasgupta 1942). Written around 1935–36 this book was in the Marshallian tradition. Most of the diagrams, it may be noted, were of the Marshallian variety used in *Money, Credit and Commerce* (1923). Dasgupta showed very lucidly how the concept of consumers' surplus under Marshall was used to play an important part as an effective tool either for understanding the mechanism of exchange or for purposes of guiding economic policy. This capable piece of work subsequently came to share along with Alfred Marshall's publications a place in Calcutta University's MA Economics text and reference list of the post-independence era (for example for the year 1957). This is just to indicate how through the university's curriculum and research activities, Marshall's influence was percolating in this part of the world. A third scholar, the case of Benoy Kumar Sarkar, may also be mentioned. He too, like all other academics, came under the influence of the master's major expositions on theory and policy concerns. Sarkar's publication on 'The theory of wages in the light of social insurance and public finance' (1936), discussed the Marshallian policy on high direct taxation including inheritance taxes for the relief of poverty. A policy that went beyond taxing for revenue and aimed at taxing in order to change or correct income distribution went against the spirit of Gladstonian finance no doubt.

MARSHALLIAN FOUNDATIONS OF THE POST-1950s INDIAN ECONOMIC INQUIRY

Indian economists of the new generation, many of whom it may be recalled were taught by Marshall's former students in this country or abroad (where they went for higher studies), have shown a maturity in advancing economic inquiry in its many facets and branches. One may start with Tapas Majumdar's (1958) studies on problems of utility measurement. As part of his review of the various utility hypotheses, he of course touched upon the hypotheses of Marshall, Pigou and other members of the Cambridge school along with those of Robbins, Hicks, Allen and others, as also those of the later approaches that had emerged in the debate. The *Economic Journal* of December 1958, in its review of the book, noted Majumdar's methodological sharpness in the terrain made familiar by Marshall and Hicks as compared to the other newer territories. This is quite understandable, given the thorough grounding that he received from Marshall's *Principles* and works of his other pupils.

In the field of microeconomics another scholar, Tapan Biswas, took up Marshall's concept of consumer surplus and the assumption of the constancy of the marginal utility of money. Biswas's (1977) alternative interpretation of the Marshallian consumer may be taken as an indication of how Marshall's theories were shaping the agenda of Indian academic research. In fact, how some of the best brains were overwhelmed with the theoretical impetus of the Marshallian methodology is perhaps accurately illustrated by the case of Krishna Bharadwaj.

One of the most eminent Indian economic theorists of the 1970s, Bharadwaj's analytical mind examined the impact of the methodological shift underlying the intellectual passage from classical political economy to supply- and demand-based theories of equilibrium (Bharadwaj 1976, 1978). For her, the effects of the transition to the Marshallian theory of value were of far-reaching consequences. She did note Marshall's attempts at weaving together the basically irreconcilable views of Ricardo and Jevons, by positing opposite but independent forces of supply and demand acting symmetrically to determine value in equilibrium. But she could not reconcile to the ultimate outcome of the shift of focus from the objective basis of the classical theory of value to individual subjectivity. The emphasis on prices and quantities to the neglect of production and exchange, she felt, was at the cost of excluding altogether the role of social classes, their conflict and alliances.

She took up Marshall's early writing on value and worked on the theme further. She also researched on his manuscript notes made in 1914, after the publication of Pigou's *Wealth and Welfare* (Bharadwaj 1972). The scrutiny of the notes led to her view that what appeared in Marshall as aberrations in the working of the competitive system, was actually transformed by Pigou (in generalising and extending Marshall's results) into failure of the competitive system to achieve maximum welfare.

She further drew attention to the Marshallian criticism of Pigou's conclusions in terms of the errors in the argument in case of decreasing returns. She noted how Marshall had also pointed to the limitations of the application of the statical approach to the problems of welfare (especially in the context of increasing returns) and to the theory of equilibrium itself. These are fairly well known. Our reference to her writings is towards pinpointing the strong influence of Marshall on Indian economic thought in the post-1950s period.

Not confined to the field of microeconomics and economic methodology, in international economics too, the Marshallian influence was significant. One of the outstanding contemporary authorities in trade theory and policy, Jagadish Bhagwati, in the 1960s began his early scholarly contributions to the field of international trade. He co-wrote with Harry G. Johnson (1960, 1961) on controversies in the theory of international trade. Obviously, Marshall was to be the point of reference with respect to the four disputed problems in the theory of international trade. His measure of the net benefit from foreign trade vis-à-vis Viner's position, his theorem regarding inelasticity of international demand and stability/instability of equilibrium points, Marshall and Graham's solution to the problem of impact of an autonomous shift in international demand on the net barter terms of trade and the volume of trade and so on are covered in the paper. Similarly, in Bhagwati's survey paper on the pure theory of international trade, the Marshallian view of the pure theory of international trade that applied the theories of value and welfare to questions of international economics and the growing new literature that attempted to bring the theory to the ground are given due importance (Bhagwati 1964). Marshallian influence and his methodology can be traced to his other papers also (Bhagwati 1957, 1971).

In another field too, namely with respect to the problem of equity and social justice in a mixed economy, a very renowned teacher of economics, Bhabatosh Datta, brought the Marshallian ideas under his scrutiny. He appears to have noticed some ambivalence in the economic reasoning of Alfred Marshall (Datta 1982). The contradiction related to Marshall's firm belief in the optimality of the equilibrium on the one hand, and the realisation of the influence of indivisibility and market imperfections, and also of the Sidgwickian divergence between private profits and social gains, on the other. However, he acknowledged how Marshall and Pigou were partially responsible for bringing in the welfare state which in turn brought the mixed economy into existence. In Datta's survey of the field, the liberal tradition from Marshall onwards, which rested on the moral recognition of the desirability of reducing disparities, combined with a distrust of socialised production, was examined. He noted how it was not realised or admitted that the problem of distribution cannot be solved without control over the production system.

We may also refer to N. Jha, an Indian economist who wrote a book entitled *The Age of Marshall: Aspects of British Economic Thought, 1890–1915*, that Guillebaud reviewed. His idea that the writings of the economists of that period laid the foundations of the welfare state was reiterated in later years by Datta (1978).

Thus, the theories of Alfred Marshall, the methodological implications of his theoretical contributions to the diverse fields of economics, his policy stance on critical policy issues, the effect of his liberal tradition on the concept of the welfare state and mixed economy, his times and so on, are some of the avenues through which this great economist reached out and traced the contours of Indian economic thought.

MARSHALL AND SEN'S CONTRIBUTIONS TO WELFARE ECONOMICS

In Marshall, welfare economics may be said to be of central importance, for his decision to take up economics originated in a moral purpose. He had held that inequalities of wealth were a serious flaw in our economic organisation and that their diminution would be a clear social gain. His stand was that the social and political dimension of human action should not be left out from the scope of economics because Marshall, it may be recalled, had studied Darwin's theory of evolution, Christian moral philosophy and Bentham's utilitarianism. His blending of these streams of thought into an original synthesis resulted in the philosophy of evolutionary progress. The implication of such a philosophical position was that, with progress, the whole society would tend to improve in material terms and not only the strong and courageous few, as the social Darwinists had argued. Marshall's philosophy led him to challenge the complacent attitude of 'harmony' economists, who saw in the natural working of economic forces, a 'divine order'. That such order led to the maximum good of mankind was not an unqualified truth, in his opinion. Their interpretation that the equilibrium position brought about by the free play of natural forces was the position of maximum satisfaction or social welfare was examined by Marshall, in the light of empirical social reality. Marshall's practical counsels pointed in the direction of possibilities of increase of social welfare through State intervention.

We may now consider the renowned Indian scholar Amartya Kumar Sen to locate the influence of Marshall on his thought, if any. Sen, too, had contributed to diverse areas of research ranging from inequality studies (1992, 1997), poverty and its measurement, standard of living, social justice and the distribution of income (2000), collective choice and social welfare, ethics and economics (1987), commodities and capabilities (1985), utilitarianism and beyond to freedom and justice. Given the expanse and depth of his scholarship, his search was directed towards finding a solution to the question of how it can be possible to arrive at a cogent aggregative judgment about society (for example about social welfare or the public interest or aggregate poverty), given the diversity of preferences, concerns and predicaments of different individuals within society. In this context it may be argued that notwithstanding the mutual intellectual stimuli arising from Sen, Arrow and Rawls's academic exchanges in later years, the ideas of Marshall–Pigou that he had initially encountered in his student days, at Presidency College, Calcutta and at Cambridge subsequently, may have nourished, to some extent, the ethical roots of his liberal mind.

Like Marshall, Sen saw in the distancing of ethics and economics, a major deficiency of contemporary economic theory. Economics could be made more productive by paying greater and more explicit attention to the ethical considerations that shape human behaviour and judgment. For Sen, it was not merely a problem of incorporating the lessons from the ethical literature into economics. In fact by using the approaches and techniques of economics to analyse some of the ethical issues, more meaningful insights may be gained. For example he set forth systematic suggestions as to how an adequate formulation of right and freedom could make substantial use of consequential reasoning of the type currently used in general equilibrium economics. The totality of his contributions appears to have enriched, in recent times, the old Marshallian tradition. Both economics and ethics thus gained depth and dimension as a result. Sen, by incorporating the ethical issues confronting economists, that got lost as the discipline matured, has elevated policy making to greater heights. In this sense, both Sen and Marshall considered realism and the exploratory power of theories no less important than their logical coherence and analytical elegance. But, while Marshall had called for the widening of the ethical base of economics, Sen indicated the possibilities of ethics and economics enriching each others' universe of discourse. As economics may gain by incorporating the ethical dimension, so ethics may appropriate suitably the procedures and approaches of economics.

Marshall has been described as the classic example of the right economist in the right place at the right time – of Victorian England that was sailing at full speed through the final years of the nineteenth century (Screpanti and Zamagni 2005). Sen, too, may be so described – of contemporary times and a world where the connection between the ideas of justice and freedom are used to arrive at an altogether new orientation, suited appropriately to the predicament of today's development, its indicators, and choice of intervention strategies and public policies.

MARSHALL'S CONTEMPORARY RELEVANCE

In modern trade theory, Marshall is again being revisited as a review of current research will indicate. Apart from the theoretical rediscovery of his ideas, in some of the policy debates in the developing word, one observes a re-examination of many of his earlier arguments relating to different policy issues. For instance, in the ongoing debates relating to industrialisation of the Asian economies in the post-globalisation era, where the question of acquisition of technological capability through special economic zones, that may be said to be the locomotives of export-led growth, are examined threadbare, Chapter x of Marshall's *Principles*, where he discussed the concentration of specialised industries in particular localities, comes to mind. These zones or areas within developing countries that offer incentives of a barrier-free environment to promote economic growth by attracting foreign investment for export-oriented production are fairly common now. Marshall's ideas on thickly peopled industrial districts or large industrial districts and explanations of the advantages of localised industries – the various forces on the geographical distribution of industries – bear some affinity to the recent phenomenon of the concentration of a large number of small businesses in special economic zones or industrial hubs or complexes. Similarly, the dilemma faced by local authorities in India, regarding the flow of foreign direct investment in retail trade or regarding massive indigenous retail trading versus the small retailers that may feel threatened, may call for a thorough re-reading of his *Industry and Trade* and its relevant chapters on services of wholesale and retail dealers, massive retailing and so on. The insights to be gained from his book may help to clear up much of the controversies encountered. The battles fought will rage on no doubt. However, the wide range of perspectives observed in many parts of the newly emerging economies of the world may gain from Marshall's texts.

The Indian experience with globalisation and trade liberalisation of recent decades that has been seen to break down the trade barriers and other distortions in international trade, the implications of transnational transactions and modern technological advances characterised by increasing returns appear to have again led some researchers of India to go back to the Marshallian views to be able to interpret the current scenario. Whether the benefits of such zones outweigh their costs is what is being looked into. With the leap into the information age, the context has changed dramatically no doubt. Liberal economic views have gained currency where the liberal tradition may find contemporary acceptance, reaffirmation, reorientation or rejection for that matter. The situation does call for research and critical assessment. The Marshallian texts may well be included among its primary reference list.

Technological development and growth models with increasing returns in the context of a theory of chaos may effectively represent the present scenario. An economic policy with a nudging hand is what the economic system showing chaotic behaviour tends to suggest. Marshall's ambivalence that Indian scholars had earlier pointed to, may perhaps be explained in this literature.

CONCLUSION

The Marshallian influence, it may be concluded, commenced with the inclusion of his major texts into the curriculum of university education in this country. Apart from the encountering of his ideas through the prescribed textbooks and references, Indian researchers could hardly avoid re-reading Marshall while working on diverse areas of economics. The influence of this authority permeated and the relevant concepts, definitions and explanations found proper reflection in their individual research outcomes. The diffusion of this influence strengthened as the theoretical exercises of scholars of India widened to diverse branches of economics. The research problems ranging from value theory and consumer choice, methodological issues, international trade theory and policy, equity and social justice, welfare economics and ethics, economic thought, to mention only a few that post-independent India took up and discussed in international journals, were mostly contextual to his analysis and viewpoints. Now, in this post-globalisation period, the value or relevance of Marshallian economics appears again to be gaining ground in the context of the experience of the opening up of hitherto closed economies.

Be it with respect to issues relating to the chemical hubs or export-processing zones, for example, or on questions pertaining to modern retailing under its different format, in the choice problems between the small shopkeepers/traders and the big giants, between the domestic and foreign firms, on questions relating to the allowing of the retail giants into cities or keeping them off city limits, the divergences on policy stance appear to present a rather confusing picture. The situation definitely calls for re-reading of Marshall (for Marshall on India see Raffaelli 2004) so as to be able to shed some light on the policy debates that are being held around these issues in different parts of the country. Then, the current Indian economic thought may perhaps be able to clear much of the undergrowth.

REFERENCES

Bhagwati, J. (1957), 'Immiserizing growth', *Review of Economic Studies*, **25** (3), 201–5.
Bhagwati, J. (1964), 'The pure theory of international trade: A survey', *Economic Journal*, **74**, 1–84.
Bhagwati, J. (1971), 'Generalized theory of distortions and welfare', in J.N. Bhagwati, R.W. Jones, A. Mundell and J. Vanek (eds), *Trade, Balance of Payments and Growth: Papers in International Economics in Honour of Charles P. Kindleberger*, Amsterdam: North Holland, pp. 69–90.
Bhagwati, J. and H.G. Johnson (1960), 'Notes on some controversies in the theory of international trade', *Economic Journal*, **70**, 74–93.
Bhagwati, J. and H.G. Johnson (1961), 'A generalized theory of effects of tariffs on the terms of trade', *Oxford Economic Papers*, **13** (3), 225–53.
Bharadwaj, K. (1972), 'Marshall on Pigou's *Wealth and Welfare*', *Economica*, n.s., **39**, 32–46.
Bharadwaj, K. (1976), *Classical Political Economy and Rise to Dominance of Supply and Demand Theories*, Calcutta: Orient Longmans.
Bharadwaj, K. (1978), 'The subversion of classical analysis: Alfred Marshall's early writings on value', *Cambridge Journal of Economics*, **2** (2), 253–71.
Biswas, T. (1977), 'The Marshallian consumer', *Economica*, **44**, 47–56.
Calcutta University (1957), *Hundred Years of the University of Calcutta, Suppl. 1857–1956*.
Chandra, B. (1991), 'Colonial India, British versus Indian views of development', *Review*, **14**, 81–167.
Coyajee, J.C. (1930), *Indian Currency System 1835–1926*, Madras: University of Madras Minerva Press.
Coyajee, J.C. (1932), *The World Economic Depression, A Plea for Co-operation*, Waltair, Madras: The Huxley Press.
Dasgupta, A.K. (1942), *The Conception of Surplus in Theoretical Economics*, Calcutta: Dasgupta & Co.
Datta, B. (1978), *Indian Economic Thought Twentieth Century Perspective (1900–50)*, New Delhi: Tata McGraw-Hill Publishing Co Ltd.
Datta, B. (1982), *Social Justice in a Mixed Economy*, Calcutta: Calcutta University.
Majumdar, T. (1958), *The Measurement of Utility*, London: Macmillan.
Marshall, A. (1923), *Money, Credit and Commerce*, London: Macmillan & Co.
Marshall, A. (1927), *Industry and Trade*, 3rd edn, London: Macmillan & Co.
Marshall, A. (1961), *Principles of Economics*, 9th (variorum) edn, edited by C.W. Guillebaud, London: Macmillan & Co.
Raffaelli, T. (2004), 'Marshall on India', in T. Aspromourgos and J. Lodewijks (eds), *History and Political Economy. Essays in Honour of P.D. Groenewegen*, London and New York: Routledge, pp. 156–66.
Sarkar, B.K. (1936), 'The theory of wages in the light of social insurance and public finance', published paper, 19th Indian Economic Conference, Dacca, January.
Screpanti, E. and S. Zamagni (2005), *History of Economic Thought*, Oxford: Oxford University Press.
Sen, A. (1985), *Commodities and Capabilities*, New Delhi: Oxford University Press.
Sen, A. (1987), *On Ethics and Economics*, New Delhi: Oxford University Press.
Sen, A. (1992), *Inequality Reexamined*, Oxford: Oxford University Press.
Sen, A. (1997), 'From income inequality to economic inequality', *Southern Economic Journal*, **64**, 384–401.
Sen, A. (2000), 'Social justice and distribution of income', in A.B. Atkinson and F. Bourguignon (eds), *Handbook of Income Distribution*, Amsterdam and New York: Elsevier, pp. 59–85.
Whitaker, J.K. (ed.) (1996), *The Correspondence of Alfred Marshall, Economist*, 3 vols, Cambridge: Cambridge University Press.

21. Alfred Marshall's ideas in China

Paul B. Trescott*

The introduction of Western economic ideas into China was just beginning at the time of the publication of Marshall's *Principles* in 1890. China had at that point no modern university, and China's intellectuals were unfamiliar with Western languages and the works expressed in them. Westerners had sponsored a few translations of mainstream Western economics books, principally Henry Fawcett's *Manual of Political Economy* (published 1867, translated 1880), and William Stanley Jevons's *Primer on Political Economy* (published 1878, translated 1886) (Trescott 2007, pp. 23–5).

A landmark in the process was the publication in 1902 of a Chinese translation of Adam Smith's *Wealth of Nations*. The translator, Yen Fu, had studied in England, and was literate in mathematics as well as English. In his preface, he wrote:

> Economics is a science of induction. Induction means that one observes the changes, understands the rules of change, then spells out economic laws. Works by people like Smith, Ricardo, Mill (father and son) all belong in this category. Recent works by scholars such as Jevons and Marshall gradually shifted to the method of deduction, using tools such as calculus and geometric presentation to infer the logic of economic phenomena. If readers want to understand economics in a more comprehensive sense, the works by Mill, Walker and Marshall must also be translated Although I understand the importance of this task, this is beyond my ability. (Lai 2000, p. 28)

China's humiliating defeat by Japan in the brief war of 1894–95 led to rapid development of higher education in China. Soon many Chinese went to Western countries to study, primarily to the United States. As they returned to staff Economics faculties in China, they typically used textbooks from the country where they had studied.

The Western economics textbook most widely used in China was *Outlines of Economics*, by Richard T. Ely, initially published in 1893 and translated into Chinese in 1910. His book contained much institutional-historical material and was often critical of unregulated capitalism. But it also presented a careful exposition of the principle of diminishing marginal utility (without the nomenclature). The book was brief and simple. There were throw-away citations to Marshall's *The Economics of Industry* (pp. 98, 102, 323).

Chinese students of economics were just beginning to attend Cambridge when Marshall retired from teaching in 1908. With the assistance of Mr Anthony Twist, we have identified 33 Chinese who studied economics at Cambridge between 1908 and 1950. A cluster of four attended in 1908–11, but only one of these, Zhang (Chang) Wei, returned to teach economics in China, and he concentrated on finance and banking. The most prominent Chinese economists from Cambridge were Fan Hong and Xu (Hsu) Yunan, both returning in the late 1930s to teach in Chinese universities. Fan was full of Marx via Maurice Dobb, and Xu brought enthusiasm for Keynes and Joan Robinson (Trescott 2007, pp. 85–6, 238–41, 251).

Although most of the more than 150 Chinese who studied economics in Britain attended the London School of Economics (LSE), we can safely assume that most of them studied Marshall. However, the much larger number who studied in the United States probably did not. Microeconomic theory did not typically play a large part in American graduate economics programmes prior to the 1940s.

In the following sections, we review findings from Chinese university course descriptions.

CHRISTIAN COLLEGES

Two of China's missionary colleges were among the first to assign Marshall's *Principles*. It appeared in the reading list for Canton Christian College (Lingnan) in 1922 for a course in Advanced Economics – but not in 1923 and after. Similarly, the book was assigned for the Principles course at Soochow University in 1924, but did not appear in the 1929 listing (next available) or after.

Yenching University in Beijing was the best of China's missionary universities. To complete a degree, each student was required to present a thesis. The thesis documents are preserved in the library of Peking University. In 1932, Wei Chi-ting wrote (in English) *A Study of Alfred Marshall's Theories of Value and Distribution*. Wei incorporated commentary and evaluation, chiefly derived from Homan (1928). The topic came around again in 1947, when Guang Jingwen (Kuang Ching-wen) wrote (in Chinese) *An Introduction to Marshall's Theory of Production and Value*. This was really a reprise of undergraduate micro theory. Neither thesis commented on the relevance of Marshall to China or discussions of Marshall by Chinese scholars.

OTHER CHINESE UNIVERSITIES

One British-trained Chinese economist who admired Marshall was Liu Binglin, who had studied at LSE in 1910–12. Liu was long a faculty member at

Wuhan University, reputedly the most heavily British-oriented of the Chinese universities. While on board ship travelling to Britain he translated Marshall's sections on distribution (Liu 1922). He wrote a widely used elementary textbook, and his teaching interests focused on applied areas rather than economic theory. Hu Jichuang's (1982) course and textbook listings for Wuhan University in 1933 and 1936 do not show any Marshall titles.

In 1931 Zheng Xuejia (Cheng Hsueh-chia) published a book entitled *Marshall's Economic Theories* (Cheng 1931). Zheng was on the faculty of Fudan University in Shanghai and probably used the book in his course on history of Western economic thought. In 1943 he produced *The Neo-classical Economics of Marshall* (Hu Jichuang 1982). Zheng had studied in Japan but not in the West. Marshall's *Principles* received a selective translation by Liu (1932), about whom we have no information.

A brief article entitled 'The paradox of the cost theories of Alfred Marshall' was published in 1934 in the *Nankai Economic Weekly*, a supplement to a very influential newspaper called *Ta Kung Bao* (*The Impartial*) (Yuen 1934a). The author was Yuen Wen-pu (Yuen Xiannen), then on the faculty of Nankai University in Tianjin. He summarised comments on Marshall by Paul Homan, Herbert G. Davenport and Edwin Cannan in regard to the degree to which cost and price would correspond to the 'efforts and sacrifices involved in its production' (Cannan [1929] 1964, p. 190).

Yuen had received a doctorate at New York University and was an intellectual dilettante and snob who published in the same periodical articles on the law of diminishing returns and on the monetary theories of the Vienna school. In another publication, Yuen (1934b) attached the label 'a well-known Marshallian' to Yeh Yuan-long. Yeh had studied at the University of Wisconsin and at LSE, and became head of the Economics Department at National Central University in the 1930s. He published a short book on *Modern Economic Thought* (1933). He later translated Marshall's *Money, Credit and Commerce* (see below).

By the mid-1930s, Marshall's books were appearing in the curricula of the indigenous Chinese universities. A prominent example was the distinguished Peking University ('Beida'). In 1933 Beida's course in Advanced Economics centred around Marshall's *Principles*, 'focusing on neoclassical basic theories to make preparation for contemporary thoughts' (*Peking University Catalogue* 1933, pp. 390–91). This was supplemented by Keynes's *Essays in Biography* and *Memorials of Alfred Marshall*. Paradoxically, the course was taught by Zhao (Chao) Naituan, whose 1930 doctoral dissertation at Columbia was en-titled *Richard Jones: An Early English Institutionalist*. In it, Zhao reported:

> [W]hile I was working in the National Bureau of Research in Peking from 1920 to 1922 I was greatly impressed by the abundance of historical documents on Chinese economic history, but at the same time I was disappointed to find that the English Classical eco-nomics had nothing in common with Chinese economic conditions. (Chao 1930, p. 7)

Zhao's introductory chapter on 'Institutional economics' observed that 'the economists of today are not so much interested in abstract economic theory' (ibid., p. 11). Beida's 1933 course in International Trade assigned Marshall's *Money, Credit and Commerce* (*Peking University Catalogue* 1933, p. 404).

By 1935, in addition to the two courses just described, Beida also assigned Marshall's *Industry and Trade* for a course with a similar title. 'The main point is to describe in order to provide historical and practical knowledge which can hardly be obtained from theoretical economics. First it introduces contemporary industrial technology and the origin of commercial organisation' (*Peking University Catalogue* 1935, pp. 47–8).

It may seem strange to the modern reader that Beida, with a faculty overwhelmingly educated in the US and with strong institutionalist leanings, would have featured Marshall's work. The most plausible interpretation is that, considering all three books, they recognised Marshall as a fellow institutionalist!

Returning students from the West were instrumental in boosting the component of theory in Chinese university Economics programmes. This process was muddled by the outbreak of war with Japan in 1937 and the consequent movement of major Chinese universities to new locations in South and West China. Li Chomin (Choh-ming) joined the faculty of Nankai University in 1937 after completing his doctorate at Berkeley. He soon upgraded the embryonic graduate programme into a sophisticated curriculum strongly emphasising theory and quantitative work. When he turned the graduate theory course over to Fan Hsiending (H.D. Fong) in 1943, it had become 'chiefly a critical study of the teachings by Marshall, Robinson, Chamberlain, Hicks and Keynes' (Ho 1945, p. 2).

Xu Yunan completed his doctorate at Cambridge and returned in 1938 to join the faculty of Southwest Associated Universities in Kunming. This campus combined the undergraduate programmes of three of China's top universities – Beida, Qinghua and Nankai. While Xu's chief enthusiasms were for Robinson and Keynes, he also incorporated a healthy dose of Marshall into his theory teaching.

Marshall's name was dragged into a slapdash criticism of Western economists incorporated in a book entitled *Chinese Economic Theory*, published in 1943 over the name of Generalissimo Chiang Kai-shek, but undoubtedly ghost-written. The reference claimed that 'the theories of mathematicians like Marshall displaced those of Adam Smith and Ricardo' (Chiang Kai-shek [1943] 1947, p. 260). This section of the book ended with the author's hope that 'Western economists will abandon their selfish individualism and materialism and, starting from human nature and aiming at the people's livelihood, will strive to attain the same goal as that prescribed in the economic theories of ancient China' (ibid., p. 263).

In 1947, Zhu Baoyi (Chu Pao-yi) published *Economic Theories of Marshall* (Hu Jichuang 1982). Zhu had received an MA from LSE in 1938 and was on the faculty of National Central University in Nanjing.

AFTER 1949

By the time of the Communist takeover in 1949, Western-educated Chinese constituted a large proportion of the university faculties of Economics (and other subjects). Over the next decade, the curriculum was restructured to focus on Marxism and on Stalinism. A startling confrontation between Marxism and mainstream economics erupted during the 'anti-rightist' campaign of 1957–58 (Trescott 2007, pp. 301–5). One set of targets were a group of supporters of Keynesian economics, including Xu Yunan. Another targeted group were advocates of birth control, stigmatised as Malthusians. A principal target in the latter group was Ma Yinchu (PhD Columbia, 1916), who had been appointed president of Peking University by Mao's regime. Among the vast numbers of publications denouncing Ma's ideas was one accusing him of bourgeois ideas derived from Cournot and Marshall (Walker 1963, p. 122).

The anti-rightist campaign was soon followed by the economic disasters of the Great Leap Forward in 1958–60. The obvious damage from excessive 'leftism' was followed by a thaw which permitted more acknowledgement of the possible merits of Western economics. In 1961 the Shanghai Society of Economics convened forums on Adam Smith, Ricardo, Marshall and Keynes (Goldman 1981, p. 23).

The same thaw initiated Yeh Yuan-long's translation of *Money, Credit and Commerce*, with Guo Jialing (Marshall 1984). In his preface, Guo added a poignant note:

> In 1964, Mr. Yeh was a Professor in Shanghai Social Science Academy and was invited to translate this book … In 1967, Mr. Yeh died of heart disease. Due to the Cultural Revolution, his lecture notes and materials … concerning Marshall's economic theory were lost. The translation became the only souvenir of his dedication to education … and to several decades of teaching Marshall's economic theories. (Marshall 1984, preface)

In the renewed leftism manifested in the Cultural Revolution, most universities were shut down, some for as much as a decade.

Following Mao's death and the overthrow of the Gang of Four in 1976, the atmosphere of repressive totalitarianism was steadily relaxed. Chinese universities moved to incorporate Western elements into their curricula. The Yeh and Guo translation could finally be published in 1984. A symbol of the new system was the publication of a respectful survey of the marginalist economists by Professor Yan Zhijie of Peking University (*Marginalism in Economics*, Yan 1987). Yan devoted a chapter to summarising Marshall, but did not attempt to survey Chinese responses.

OVERVIEW

Marshall's work did not receive much attention in China. The same could be said for economic theory in general. The Chinese who studied economics in the US were in programmes which stressed institutionalism and policy studies. China's most zealous economics writers and researchers were looking for clues to enhance China's wealth and power, to promote industrialisation and economic growth. Prior to the 1930s, few Chinese economists had the sophistication to appreciate the creative and innovative elements in Marshall's work, or to see in it any relevance to China.

To be sure, much of Marshall's work infiltrated China and the rest of the world through the intermediation of elementary textbooks which incorporated marginal utility, marginal cost, elasticity of demand and other Marshallian features. An example was Thomas Nixon Carver's *Principles of Political Economy* (1919) which was used in at least six Chinese universities. In his autobiography, Carver described how, during his graduate study at Johns Hopkins, he found Richard T. Ely's German historicism unrewarding, but was greatly stimulated by an informal seminar dealing with Marshall and Bohm-Bawerk (Carver 1949, pp. 97–8).

Economics students in Chinese universities were also exposed to a course in the history of Western economic thought, which normally included a small dose of Marshall. Standard Western textbooks were translated into Chinese, including Gide and Rist (1915), Ingram (1915), Haney (1922) and Homan (1928).

NOTE

*   The author thanks Lai Cheng-chung, Wu Minchao, and Gao Wei for valuable assistance.

REFERENCES

Archival references including course lists and catalogues are detailed in Trescott (2007).

Cannan, E. ([1929] 1964), *Review of Economic Theory*, New York: A.M. Kelley.
Carver, T.N. (1919), *Principles of Political Economy*, Boston: Ginn and Co.
Carver, T.N. (1949), *Reflections of an Unplanned Life*, Los Angeles: Ward Ritchie.
Chao Nai-tuan (1930), *Richard Jones: An Early English Institutionalist*, New York: Columbia University Press.
Cheng Hsueh-chia (1931), *Marshall's Economic Theories*, Shanghai: Shenzhou Guoguang Publishing House (Chinese language).
Chiang Kai-shek ([1943] 1947), *China's Destiny and Chinese Economic Theory*, New York: Roy Publishers, English trans. edited by P.J. Jaffe, New York: Roy Publishers.

Ely, R.T. (1893), *Outlines of Economics*, New York: Flood and Vincent.

Gide, C. and C. Rist (1915), *A History of Economic Doctrines from the Time of the Physiocrats to the Present Day*, trans. R. Richards, Boston: D.C. Heath.

Goldman, M. (1981), *China's Intellectuals: Advise and Dissent*, Cambridge, MA: Harvard University Press.

Haney, L.H. (1922), *History of Economic Thought*, revised edn, New York: Macmillan.

Ho, Franklin Lien (1945), 'Letter to M.C. Balfour, March 13, 1945', Rockefeller Archive: Record Group 1 Projects, Series 601 China, Box 52.

Homan, P.T. (1928), *Contemporary Economic Thought*, New York: Harper.

Hu Jichuang (1982), 'Basic economic theories of China from the 1920s to the 1940s', *Learned Journal of Beijing Institute of Trade and Finance*, September, 52–69 (Chinese language).

Ingram, J.K. (1915), *A History of Political Economy*, 2nd edn, New York: Macmillan.

Kuang Ching-wen (1947), *An Introduction to Marshall's Theory of Production and Value*, Senior thesis, Yenching University (in Peking University Library).

Lai Cheng-chun (ed.) (2000), *Adam Smith across Nations*, New York: Oxford University Press.

Liu Binglin (1922), *Distribution Theory*, Shanghai: Commercial Press (Chinese language).

Liu Chun-mu (1932), *Marshall's Economic Principles*, Shangai: Minzhi Book Bureau (Chinese language).

Marshall, A. (1984), *Money, Credit and Commerce*, trans. Yeh Yuan-long and Guo Jialing, Beijing: Commercial Press (Chinese language).

Peking University Catalogue (various years) (Chinese language).

Trescott, P.B. (2007), *Jingji Xue: The History of the Introduction of Western Economic Ideas into China, 1850–1950*, Hong Kong: Chinese University Press.

Walker, K. (1963), 'Ideology and economic discussion in China: Ma Yin-chu on development strategy and his critics', *Economic Development and Cultural Change*, **11** (2), 113–33.

Wei Chi-ting (1932), *A Study of Alfred Marshall's Theories of Value and Distribution*, Senior thesis, Yenching University (in Peking University Library).

Yan Zhijie (1987), *Marginalism in Economics. Historical and Critical Research*, Beijing: Peking University Press (Chinese language).

Yuen Wen-pu (Xiannen) (1934a), 'The paradox of the cost theories of Alfred Marshall', *Ta Kung Bao*, 6 June, 11 (Chinese language).

Yuen Wen-pu (Xiannen) (1934b), 'Review of *Contemporary Chinese Economic Thought* by Li Chuan-shih', *Nankai Monthly Bulletin*, **7** (11), 458–9.

22. Marshall in Japan

Mikio Nishioka

The science of economics was introduced into Japan in the latter half of the nineteenth century in response to the perception of an urgent need to modernise the country's military affairs, political system and industry. Alfred Marshall's economics, which itself was derived in the context of an advanced national economy, was uniformly accepted as one part of this modernisation scheme.

THE ECONOMICS OF INDUSTRY AS A DIGEST OF MILL'S POLITICAL ECONOMY

The Japanese translation of *The Economics of Industry* (1885–86) by Korekiyo Takahashi, who later became the finance minister and eventually the prime minister of Japan, is considered the basis of modern Japanese political economy. In this period, however, the dominant view among Japanese economists was that J.S. Mill's formulation of political economy still set 'the standard of economic ideas'. Marshall's economics was generally considered a digest of 'normal political economy in Britain and America', in which free competition based on the law of supply and demand was the fundamental principle, although there did exist a section of Japanese economists who paid attention to his ideas regarding the business cycle and entrepreneurship.

MARSHALL, MARGINAL UTILITY THEORY, AND THE GERMAN HISTORICAL SCHOOL

From a study of the archival material in the Marshall Archive (*Marshall Papers*, Cambridge), we know that more than ten Japanese students studied economics at Cambridge under Marshall during his tenure of the Chair of Political Economy (that is, between 1884 and 1908). Soyeda Juichi would become well known as the Japanese correspondent of the *Economic Journal*, and as the author of a biographical sketch and obituary of Marshall (1925) in *Kokka Gakkai Zasshi* (*Journal of the Association of Political and Social Science*). Juichi, however, was an able senior bureaucrat in the Japanese government, and not a professional economist. Marshall's criticisms of the German historical school notwithstanding, Soyeda adhered to German ideas of 'State Socialism'. In this context we should also mention Soda Kiichiro, who later became an economic philosopher, and wrote his famous books, *Geld und Wert* and *Die logische Natur der Wirtschaftsgesetze*, while studying in Germany and in Cambridge.

In August 1887, H.S. Foxwell was tempted to take up the post of a political economy professor or government advisor in Japan. Marshall, however, objected to the proposal: 'I think they [the Japanese] must take a German who knows a great deal & won't come to much' (Whitaker 1996, I, p. 247).

In these years Japanese economists primarily based their ideas on what was called the 'ready-made goods of German economics' (a term invented by Ouchi Hyoue, a Marxian scholar of public finance). The general idea was to use Marshall as a mediator between the old British school (Smith to J.S. Mill) and the new German historical school.

The concept of marginality was introduced to Japan in the translation of *Elements of Economics of Industry* (Marshall 1896, by Inoue). From this point onwards, a few economists began to understand Marshall's economics as a variant of marginalism or the Austrian school.

Fukuda Tokuzo, who tried to develop an economic analysis that would replace the system of the historical school, signalled the innovative stage in Japanese economics when, in the early 1900s, he adopted Marshall's economics. According to Fukuda, the ultimate purpose of an economic act is no more and no less than the creation of surplus utility, and such creation is thus the essence of economics. It is readily seen that the resulting concept of welfare economics was based upon Marshall's theory of consumer surplus. Fukuda considered the limit of exchange value to be determined by the subjective differences in evaluation between purchasers and sellers. He interpreted the core of Marshall's economics, not on the basis of the fifth book of *Principles*, as was done by Marshall himself, but rather tried to understand Marshall's economics from the standpoint of the Austrian school.

THE DECADE 1920–30 IN JAPANESE ECONOMICS

After Fukuda's study, translations of *Principles of Economics* (Marshall 1919, by Otsuka), *Industry and Trade* (Marshall 1923, by Sahara), *Money, Credit and Commerce* (Marshall 1928, by Matsumoto), and finally *Memorials of Alfred Marshall* (Pigou 1928, by Miyajima) were published in quick succession. In *The Social Science*, Nakayama Ichiro (1926) argued that through the tool of *cæteris paribus* and 'the principle of substitution', Marshall's economics managed to provide a synthesis of the different parts of the mathematical analysis of the general equilibrium theory.

Eiichi Sugimoto (1933), by contrast, emphasised the significance for Marshall of the time factor in economic processes, and also the fact that his economics was more comprehensive and dynamic than that of Walras. According to Sugimoto, Walras's economics was less powerful and less effective than Marshall's because Walras was unable to articulate the importance of either a dynamic economy, or the role of the entrepreneur within it. H. Aoyama (1937) tried to present Marshall's doctrines in terms of exchange equilibrium and the study of dynamic processes because he believed that this approach to Marshall's economics would aid the advancement of Japanese political economy.

From the latter half of the 1910s to the first half of the 1930s, then, there was a dramatic upsurge of interest in the Marshallian tradition of economics in modern Japan. Under the semi-war social system of the 1930s, however, the importance of Marshall's economics – which was now generally associated with the study of a dynamic economy and entrepreneurial functions – decreased gradually, as also did both mathematical economics (the Walras-Lausanne school) and Marxian economics. Economic studies in Japan now came to be based on established European economic doctrines, although in contrast to the Europeans, the Japanese focused on welfare economics not only as a means of improving the national standard of living and morality in general, but also as a means to social reorganisation. This was in keeping with the tradition of Japanese economic thought, which since the early eighteenth century had been strongly concerned with industry and 'the way to public welfare' (the *Keisei-ron*). More concretely, from the period of the *Keisei-ron* – the study of political economy in order to establish national governance that could achieve social stability – through to the early reception of Marshall's economics, Japanese socio-economic thought had been based upon recognition of the foundational value of the network of human life styles and morality. Moreover, this human school, which looked to learning to foster social stability by way of both material and moral means, was founded upon the moral principles and organisations that governed human lives and relationships, and in this way attempted to combine an interest in public welfare with political economy.

THE STUDY OF MARSHALL'S ECONOMICS IN THE POST-WAR AND CONTEMPORARY PERIODS

The study of Marshall's economics post-World War II falls under three main headings: (1) analysis of the historical meaning of Marshall's economics, (2) emphasis on the dynamic economy and potential growth, and (3) study of the significance of the 'double-edged scissors' metaphor from an axiological, methodological and historical perspective. Marshallian studies were consolidated in these areas, allowing for a steadier advance than had occurred in the pre-war period, which then arrived at a turning-point following the publication of

Guillebaud's variorum edition of *Principles of Economics* (Marshall 1961) and Whitaker's edition of *The Early Economic Writings of Alfred Marshall* (Whitaker 1975).

In discussions concerning the historical significance of Marshall's thought attention tended to focus upon the following topics: the introduction of Marshallian economics into Japan, the merits and demerits of his ideas on the institutionalisation of economics and on woman's professional education, and Marshall's original contributions to the theory of normal value and continuous time (from the early 'Essay on value', *Domestic Values*, and *The Economics of Industry*, through to *Principles of Economics* and *Industry and Trade*). Furthermore, Marshall's theory of the entrepreneur was now re-examined in light of the logic behind his description of the transitional process leading from disequilibria to equilibrium, his theory of innovation and standardisation, and his assumptions regarding different market systems. For Japanese scholars, Marshall underlined the role of economic chivalry, which they associated with entrepreneurship and the high standard of life brought about by workmanship based on a feedback process between the customs of economic agents (morality) and the style of activity (the economic system). In order to bring about continuous progress at the national level, Japanese economic studies have especially focused on the influences of the aforementioned factors on human capital and economic development. Marshall's interest in the economic evolution of human society is thus highly valued in Japanese economic thought.

Marshall's analysis of the theory of value in terms of the 'double-edged scissors' readily identifies him as an eclectic economist and places his economics within the dominant stream of the neoclassical school. Marshallian scholarship in Japan, however, has clearly rejected this interpretation. Japanese researchers stress that Marshall's economics was a continuation of the classical school in terms of both values and aims. Since the 1990s, moreover, they have begun to emphasise that Marshall's early shift in interest from ethical psychology to economics, and related aspects of his further early intellectual development, points to his distance from contemporary mainstream economics and calls attention to the significance in his thought of the role of knowledge networks in the community and the agglomeration economy.

Marshall's scholarship in Japan after World War II generally continued to emphasise the macro-dynamic nature of his economics, which thus places him as the orthodox successor to classical economics. Such a tradition of interpretation did not originate in the post-war period, however, but was already adopted by Japanese economists of the 1930s who were concerned with characterising the dynamic processes of industrial society. These features of Marshallian economics appeared new after the war only because factors such as the full-fledged introduction of Keynesian economics, the predominance of Walrasian general equilibrium theory, and the continued relevance of Marxian economics had generated a temporary lull in interest in Marshall's economic theory. In fact, it can be said that the enthusiastic reception of the dynamic aspects of Marshall's theory was actually deeply rooted in Japan's traditional economic thought, which emphasised industrial activities and 'the way to public welfare' (the *Keisei-ron*). Furthermore, a current research project attempts to assess Marshall's contribution to the theory of international trade in the context of his views on the leadership of Britain's industry and of the tariff reform controversy. The macro-dynamic characteristics of the economic theories of the Cambridge school, which range from those of Marshall to those of Keynes, as well as their evolutionary theories, insights into knowledge networks and the psychological basis of their economic thought, have all been especially useful in throwing new light on Japan's economic issues. Indeed, from the 1990s onwards, Japanese economic thought has focussed on Marshall's evolutionary economics and related fields (Hashimoto 2001), fostering international collaboration and promoting conferences whose proceedings have generated important publications (Shionoya and Nishizawa 2008; Raffaelli, Nishizawa and Cook, forthcoming).

REFERENCES

Aoyama, H. (1937), *Dokusen no Kezai Riron* (*The Economic Theory of Monopoly*), Tokyo: Nippon Hyoronsha.

Hashimoto, S. (2001), 'Marshall to Cambridge Gakuha' ('The present and future: Marshall and his circles'), *Annals of the Society for the History of Economic Thought*, **39** (May), 66–73.

Marshall, A. (1896), *Keizai Genron* (*Elements of Economics of Industry*, 1892), trans. T. Inoue, Tokyo: Tokyo Senmon Gastuko.

Marshall, A. (1919), *Keizaigaku Genri* (*Principles of Economics*, 7th edn, 1916), trans. K. Otsuka, Tokyo: Sato Shupanbu.

Marshall, A. (1923), *Sangyo Boeki Ron* (*Industry and Trade*, 3rd edn, 1921), trans. T. Sahara, Tokyo: Hobunkan.

Marshall, A. (1928), *Kahei, Shinyo oyobi Shogyo* (*Money, Credit and Commerce*, 1921), trans. K. Matsumoto, Tokyo: Jikyodo Shoten.

Marshall, A. (1961), *Principles of Economics*, 9th (variorum) edn with annotations by C.W. Guillebaud, London and New York: Macmillan.

Marshall, A. and M. Paley Marshall (1885–86), *The Kingyo Rizaigaku* (*The Economics of Industry*, 2nd edn, 1881), trans. K. Takahashi, Tokyo: The Editorial Bureau for the Ministry of Education.

Marshall Papers, 'List of Marshall's students registration card file', Marshall Library of Economics, **2** (5)(6), 1884–93, 1897–1908.

Nakayama, I. (1926), *The Social Science: The Special Issue of Alfred Marshall*, Tokyo: Kaizo-sha.

Pigou, A.C. (1928), *Alfred Marshall: Keizai Ronshu* (*Memorials of Alfred Marshall*, 1925), trans. T. Miyajima, Tokyo: Hobunkan.

Raffaelli, T., T. Nishizawa and S. Cook (forthcoming), *Marshall and Marshallians on Industrial Economics*, London and New York: Routledge.

Shionoya, Y. and T. Nishizawa (eds) (2008), *Marshall and Schumpeter on Evolution. Economic Sociology and Capitalist Development*, Cheltenham, UK and Northampton, MA, USA: Edward Elgar.

Soyeda, J. (1925), 'Marshall Sensei Shoden' ('The biographical account of Professor Marshall'), *The Kokka Gakkai Zasshi*, **39** (1), 54–72.
Sugimoto, E. (1933), 'The failure of static economics', *Chuo Koron*, **48** (10), 19–33.
Whitaker, J.K. (ed.) (1975), *The Early Economic Writings of Alfred Marshall, 1867–1890*, London: Macmillan.
Whitaker, J.K. (ed.) (1996), *The Correspondence of Alfred Marshall, Economist*, 3 vols, Cambridge: Cambridge University Press.

PART VI

Marshall in the views of some 'itinerant' economists

23. Pareto's 'third way' between Marshall and Walras

Marco Dardi and Alberto Zanni[*]

INTRODUCTION

This chapter contains a tentative assessment of the influence, if any, of Pareto on the diffusion of Marshallian economics during the course of the last century. Common opinion regards Pareto as essentially the successor to Walras, both in the Lausanne Chair and in the development of the mathematical theory of general economic equilibrium, hence as a principal representative of a competing tradition that had little to share with Marshall and the subsequent Cambridge school in its various tendencies. The hostility expressed by the mature Pareto towards Marshall privately and publicly on various occasions adds to the plausibility of the thesis of an irreconcilable intellectual split between two of the most important lines of development in twentieth-century economic thought. Since, for a part of the century at least, general equilibrium theory eclipsed Marshallian economics, it can be maintained that Pareto played a part of his own – different from Sraffa's, but concurring with it to the same effect – in bringing about a relative decline in Marshall's reputation.

We shall argue that such a thesis, although not refutable, needs qualifications. In a paper of a few years ago (Zanni 1991), one of the authors highlighted a less well-known side of the relationship between Pareto and Marshall, one that made it appear rather like a story of unreturned esteem followed by bitter disappointment. This side of the story focuses on the young Pareto and his fundamental consonance with Marshall on the idea of economics as only a part of the general science of society. At a certain point he even looked to Marshall as a model of methodological balance between abstract reasoning and factual observation. Afterwards, however, Marshall's aloofness, contrasts with Edgeworth, and increasing confidence in his own powers and originality pushed Pareto in a different direction. At first, he took sides with Walras, also out of gratitude for the pains that the latter had taken to have him granted the Lausanne appointment. But at the same time his esteem of Walras as an economist was rather tepid and qualified: 'Walras's great merit (perhaps the only one) is that of having found the [equilibrium] equations', he

199

wrote to his life-long friend and advisor, Maffeo Pantaleoni, in 1897. And in the same letter he did not fail to vindicate his independence of thought with respect to all of his illustrious forebears, including Walras:

> When you expound *my* theory you must not expound somebody else's theory! From Walras, I acknowledge having taken the idea of general equilibrium; to which I added the idea of successive approximations, and by this I have removed the excess of abstraction of Walras's doctrines. From Edgeworth and from Marshall, I do not think I have taken anything. (Pareto to Pantaleoni, 19 February 1897, in De Rosa 1960, II, pp. 35–6)

At this stage, Pareto had clearly found his way and did not want it to be confused either with Walras's or with Marshall's. But if we look at the divergences on the two sides, we find a meaningful polarisation. While totally adhering to Walras's formal representation of general equilibrium, Pareto disagreed with him in all matters of interpretation and purpose. His distance from Marshall was, instead, mainly one of method. Both saw economics as a small part of social science, a part in which it was still possible to maintain a certain amount of intellectual orderliness and precision in the face of ever-shifting and messy empirical evidence. But for Pareto this safe ground was to be relinquished quite soon for a plunge into the muddy waters of sociology, where instincts and sentiments, the sources of non-logical actions, reigned uncontested; instead, for Marshall, economics had to remain always at the centre of social explanations since, in his view, all kinds of historical changes were set in motion by forces having a more or less explicit economic rationale behind them. Pareto insisted on unconditional mathematical rigour in the limited field in which this was possible, and stressed the contrast with the inevitably rough methods and concepts to be adopted outside it. Marshall, instead, saw a continuous thread linking the loose practices of ordinary business and the rigorous methods of science and mathematics. Consequently, the former's economics was crystal clear but intentionally narrow; the latter's somewhat muddled but wide-ranging. Had Pareto been less driven by temperament towards exaggerating personal loyalties and distances, it might have been easier for later interpreters to recognise that, by the end of the nineteenth century, there were *three* distinct intellectual traditions in the making, and not the two – Walras's and Marshall's – that conventional historiography has emphasised. Besides, it might have appeared more clearly that, beyond formal differences, the two strands started by Pareto and Marshall had at least as much in common as Pareto's and Walras's, as they represented two different attempts at finding in an economics-based social philosophy the answers to many of the questions raised by late nineteenth-century historicism.

In the next sections we try to substantiate the above claims through an investigation of the relationship between Pareto and Marshall during the years in which Pareto, still an industrial engineer and manager, turned into an academic economist. In an ideal full-length essay on Pareto and Marshall this chapter would represent only an outline of the first part, limited to the period from approximately 1870 to the publication of the *Cours d'économie politique* (1896–97), with only a few anticipations of the sequel of the story. We have divided this part into three sections. The first one, covering the 1870–90 period in which the two *dramatis personae* ignored each other's existence, is perhaps the most important in order to fill in a persistent historical lacuna. The next two sections deal with the years from 1890 to 1893, from the meeting with Pantaleoni to the Lausanne Chair, and with the Swiss period, from 1893 to the two volumes of the *Cours*, with hints at the further steps towards the *Manuale-Manuel* (1906–09), Pareto's masterpiece as an economist. Short conclusions are provided in the final section.

PARETO AND MARSHALL, THE EARLY YEARS

In the years from 1870 to 1890 Pareto lived most of the time either in Florence or in nearby San Giovanni Valdarno where he worked as manager of an ironworks. He rarely travelled to England, where Marshall lived. Yet, although their lives had no chance of crossing, many parallel developments useful for understanding the follow-up have their origins in this period.

In his capacity as a manager, Pareto became an expert on speculative practices almost out of necessity, as he was involved in buying and selling warrants based on iron for insurance purposes. After Germany, followed by other countries, had adopted Gold Standard in 1873, both Pareto and Marshall took an interest in the speculation for a drop in the price of silver and for a rise in the price of gold. The two of them were thus well acquainted with a phenomenon, speculation, which has much to do with mass psychology, a common concern in their social philosophies. As to bimetallism, Pareto was convinced that silver was done for, while Marshall advocated a scheme of 'true bimetallism' designed with an eye to the particular position of India in the British Empire. It is also interesting to note that both had a reputation in their respective countries for being castigators of financial malpractices. Marshall antedated J.M. Keynes in his forceful condemnation of speculation as a form of corporation fraud (see Zanni 2006). Pareto famously accused the ruling class of post-Risorgimento Italy of being responsible for a fraudulent scheme by which the indigent illiterate masses were overburdened with indirect taxes, while the elites granted enormous profits to themselves by insider trading in stocks and public bonds.

But, of course, money and speculation were not Marshall's and Pareto's only common concern. Another one involved the recurrent crises in economic activity. Although the acceleration principle was not yet in view, Marshall built on the observation that the production of instrumental goods fluctuated more violently than the production of consumer goods. Pareto for his part had direct experience of what a crisis meant, having passed through the ordeal of being obliged to choose between closing an establishment during a slump period, with the attendant costs of inactivity and risk of definitive closing down, or to keep it in operation, thus incurring the expense of unwanted inventories. In reading Pareto's correspondence on this issue, with all his calculations for finding a way out of the dilemma (see Busino 1977), it is not only the value of that immaterial asset which Marshall calls 'business good-will' that comes to mind, but more in general Pareto's living acquaintance with the everyday uncertainties facing all those who are involved in the running of some economic activity. We emphasise this point because it is one of the aspects in which Pareto was much closer to Marshall than to Walras. It should not be forgotten that the first point of dissent between Pareto and Walras was related to the latter's delusion that a future age was forthcoming in which economic events could be predicted with certainty (Pareto 1894b, p. 162).

It is quite likely that during this period Marshall and Pareto read the same books on the same problems, starting from *The Wages Question* by F.A. Walker (1876). At the time, the English-speaking community was the most numerous foreign community living in Florence and English books had a wide circulation. The environment was one in which the English economic and political culture was enormously influent, and this may explain the presence of a Victorian streak in Pareto's intellectual formation. Darwin, Spencer and Buckle rated high among his early readings. One is reminded of Marshall's recollection of the early years in which 'a saying [of Spencer's] sent the blood rushing through the veins' (Whitaker 1996, III, p. 97): like Marshall, for Pareto it took years before he rid himself of this reverence for Spencer as a social philosopher. The publisher Barbera, one of several publishing houses then in existence in Florence, had put out Italian translations of W.T. Thornton's *On Labour* (1875) and J.E. Cairnes's *Some Leading Principles of Political Economy* (1877), thanks to the collaboration of Sidney Sonnino and Carlo Fontanelli, two political thinkers and (at that time) friends of Pareto's. Thornton's book had an important impact on the young Marshall as well; and the former's analysis of the peculiarities of the labour market was one of the sources of Marshall's and Edgeworth's interest in the problem of barter at variable rates of exchange, a problem that Pareto was to study in the early 1890s and that, as we shall see, would play an important role in the formation of his personal view of the theory of equilibrium.

Those who affirm that Pareto was born to economics after meeting Pantaleoni in 1890 overlook the fact that, as early as 1887, when Italy decided to join protectionism, Pareto had planned to write a book of economic theory. As he revealed in correspondence with Francesco Papafava, a young man who had contacted him for private tuition in economics (he later became an economic and political chronicler), what he had in mind was 'a treatise of *rational* political economy ... similar to what they do in mechanics, in the treatises that, in fact, are called of *rational* mechanics' (Busino 1977, p. 817). At that time, as he wrote to Papafava (ibid., p. 849), he had not yet decided whether or not to use mathematics, and if so to what extent. He turned for advice to a former fellow-student of his, the physicist Galileo Ferraris, who gave him the answer: mathematics *is* necessary. Yet Pareto's awareness of the potential pitfalls hidden in committing economic reasoning to mathematics was perhaps even keener than Marshall's. For not only would he in later years refer to Marshall as a guide in the way of exposition ('he puts mathematical propositions in the notes', Pareto 1892–93, p. 391), and share the latter's recommendation to keep to 'short deductive chains' (ibid., p. 399), but he was also to point out a potential source of trouble of which Marshall seems not to have taken any notice. This was the fact that, by introducing mathematics into an economic argument, one also risks importing unwanted assumptions that underlie the formulas, so that one may end up by obtaining 'answers that are not in tune with the questions' (ibid., p. 501). Here, we find a striking anticipation of recent concerns with the foundational set-theoretical axioms unwittingly imported into economics through the mathematical formalisation of its basic assumptions (see Vilks 2007). In any case, Pareto's reading suggestions to Papafava in the late 1880s made no mention of mathematics. Rather, they directed him to the chapters in Stuart Mill's *System of Logic* in which the method of social science is dealt with (Busino 1977, p. 820).

Two further facts from the pre-1890 period are worth mentioning. First, before reading Marshall, in a short paper of 1888 (republished in Pareto 1974, I, 275–88; see in particular 284ff.). Pareto had already conceived the idea of a generalised theory of rent as determined by the variable degree of difficulty of reproducing the underlying assets in either the short or long period. In the *Cours*, this embryo of a theory would resurface in the notion of the *rente acquise*, a general concept that only 'in a very particular case' corresponds to Ricardo's rent (Pareto [1896–97] 1964, II, pp. 105–8). Pareto was then able to establish a connection between this generalised *rente* and Marshall's quasi-rent, with a subtle distinction between a static (equilibrium) and a dynamic (transition between equilibria) interpretation (ibid. II, p. 108 n.). Secondly, Pareto was from the start, and would remain so until the end of his life, a free trader. However, he was also aware that the choice in favour of or against protectionism cannot be decided on the basis of pure theorems alone, and that for an overall evaluation of such issues one must have recourse to that complex of social disciplines which Mill (who, differently from Pareto, did not like the Comtian term 'sociology') called 'social science'. Pareto already held this position before 1890, and was to confirm it in the 'Proemio' to the 1906 edition of the *Manuale* (Pareto [1906] 2006, pp. 4–5; the Proemio was removed from the French edition of 1909).

We conclude this section by remarking on the similarity of the cultural influences to which Pareto and Marshall were subjected in their early years, above all Mill's idea of the unity of social science, and the interpretation of social phenomena in the light of the new evolutionary concepts. While they were to develop these suggestions in different directions, something of the common origin remains. To mention one particular aspect, they both resorted to analogies taken from biology and made it a point to keep them on a different plane from mechanical analogies. However, Marshall combined one with the other for purposes of economic clarification, while Pareto relied exclusively on the mechanical analogies in economics and reserved the biological ones for sociology. As we shall see, mixing or separating these two fields was to be the final bone of contention between them. But Marshall's celebrated trees of the forest find a worthy parallel in Pareto's cellular processes of growth and decay which he used to illustrate his theory of the circulation of the elites in the two volumes on *Les systèmes socialistes* of 1901–02.

THE FIRST THEORETICAL SKIRMISHES

Now on to the second period, 1890–93. In 1890 Pareto, who had just resigned as manager for the non-engaging position of engineering consultant, met Pantaleoni. In 1891, spurred on by this great friend of his who wanted him to join the 'New school of economics', he read Pantaleoni's *Principii di economia pura*, Walras's *Élements* in the 1889 edition, the second edition of Marshall's *Principles* and Edgeworth's *Mathematical Psychics*. Among the books in his personal library that Pantaleoni made available to Pareto there was also the Sidgwick edition of Marshall's chapters on the *Pure Theory of Foreign Trade/ Domestic Values*. There is no evidence that Pareto read other works by Marshall, in particular Alfred and Mary's *The Economics of Industry*.

It would be inaccurate to consider this period in Pareto's life as a mere bridge leading him straight away to the fundamental theorem of the optimality of competitive equilibrium (Pareto 1894a) and then to the *Cours*. These crucial years in the gestation of many of his most characteristic ideas give us a clearer understanding of how he came to define his position with respect to Marshall and Walras.

The theoretical contributions that Pareto wrote for the *Giornale degli economisti* between 1892 and 1893 give the impression of an attempt, conceived in a spirit of continuity with the classical economists, at showing in which way the new mathematical theory of equilibrium could help clarify a number of issues which the classical school, from Smith to Stuart Mill, had left open or had misunderstood. The use of mathematics was valued for its concision and as a guide to correct reasoning; however, Pareto made it clear that for him economics must search inspiration in 'the light radiated, as it seems to us, by the experimental method' (Pareto 1892–93, p. 395). Here, 'experimental' was intended in the qualified sense in which Mill, in Book VI of his *System of Logic*, talked of the application of scientific methods to social phenomena, that is, as that alternation of direct observation and *a priori* reasoning based on general principles to which he gave the name of 'concrete deductive method' (ibid., pp. 393 n. 2, 401, 406). Marshall, in Pareto's view, had already made great strides in this direction, as '[he] builds economic science on few principles; but Walras and the German school go even further. They create a whole science from scratch from one single postulate, the hedonistic postulate'. But Pareto also remarked that, at the hands of Walras, there was a danger that economic science might be driven towards a 'metaphysical concept of an absolute perfection': a tendency which was to be resisted, for 'the times of ontology are over and all the sciences now study the concrete properties of things, without caring much about their essence' (ibid., pp. 395–7). Thus, it was with great caution that Pareto followed Walras, enthralled by the absolute clarity of the equilibrium equations but repelled by what he saw as a fondness for *metafisicherie* ('metaphysical fancies'; see a letter to Guido Sensini of 8 August 1911 to which we will revert below, in Sensini 1948, p. 61), and determined not to lose touch with the reasoned empiricism that had inspired the classical economists.

Among the many analytical lines pursued by Pareto in those years, the two which indicate most clearly that he was moving to a middle ground between the concerns of the French and the British schools refer to the problem of the constancy of the marginal utility of money and to the theory of exchange with variable prices. He came into contact with the former issue in 1891 while studying the controversy between Walras and Auspitz and Lieben on price theory. In a critical note of 1890 Walras had rejected both the partial equilibrium approach of the two Austrians, and their development of Dupuit's idea of consumer surplus based on the constant marginal utility of money. Although the Dupuit–Auspitz–Lieben line and Marshall's seem to be independent of each other (see the 1906 exchange of letters between Marshall and Lieben in Whitaker 1996, III, pp. 138–41), Walras's strictures clearly applied to both. In an article written in order to elucidate the controversy (Pareto 1892) Pareto sided with Walras, and returned to the constancy of the marginal utility of money in the second and third instalments of Pareto (1892–93), in which he laid out the foundations of the modern analysis of price effects, paving the way for the decomposition now known as the Slutsky equation. His analysis implied a refutation of the hypothesis of constancy, but he also admitted that, while Walras was absolutely right in point of theory, if one were to follow him also in practice it would become impossible to solve any problem (Pareto 1892, p. 212; De Rosa 1960, I, p. 195). In Pareto (1892–93, p. 496) he discussed cases in which the hypothesis of constancy could be held with no great loss of realism, and contrasted them with others in which it was clearly out of place. This discussion was very much in line with analogous remarks found in Marshall's *Principles*, first of all with his explicit mention (in Book V, Chapter ii §3) of the labour market as a case to which the assumption cannot be applied, and seems to be an implicit acknowledgement of the virtues of Marshall's pragmatism in mediating between theoretical rigour and the compromises of applied economics.

This issue, which has a relatively minor importance in both Pareto's and Marshall's theories, provides a good illustration of how slight initial differences, with the help of personal idiosyncrasies, may amplify into intellectual divergences so wide as to appear irreconcilable. Both Walras and Marshall viewed the consumer as a total utility maximiser; but while Walras did not stop to consider how it is that the consumer manages to find the optimal plan of expenditure in the general case of many commodities, Marshall discussed the matter at length in Book III, Chapter v of the *Principles*. In his analysis of consumer decision money assumed a special role since it provided a common link between successive transactions. Thanks to the existence of this link the consumer does not have to reconsider the whole plan every time that he is faced with a new alternative, and uses money as mental shorthand for 'all the other alternatives', thus sparing intellectual effort. In normal circumstances, that is, barring exceptional expenses or important changes in prices or income, choice is actually restricted to the 'margin of expenditure', that is the limited bunch of commodities which the consumer may just as well buy or not buy, the more important needs having already been provided for up to the level at which any small adjustment in satisfaction would enter into competition with some marginal commodity. Insofar as the content of the margin does not change very much, a unit of money can be taken as a fixed standard of comparison. Saying that it has constant marginal utility is just another way of saying that different allocations of money represent substitutions between satisfactions of the same order (see Dardi 2008 for this interpretation). Thus, the constancy hypothesis is meant by Marshall as a hypothesis for normal individuals in their habitual circumstances. In fact, he warns repeatedly that reasoning on the market demand curve as if it were a collective utility curve is justified only within a limited neighbourhood of the situation considered because, among other reasons, there is no guarantee that, in situations far removed from the observed one, money would have the same meaning for all the people involved.

Pareto's consumer, like Marshall's, was not an abstract rational man but a social being with limited powers of foresight and reasoning. In Pareto's view, however, the instrument that aided this inadequate decision maker in the task of approximating a rational management of his resources was not the fact of using money in all transactions, but the very frequency with which he was faced with recurrent transactions, with the 'repetition of proofs' acting as a partial substitute for the lack of intelligence and culture (Pareto 1892–93, pp. 411, 417–20). As with Walras, therefore, money played no special role in Pareto's analysis of the consumer. The *numéraire* may be any commodity. If it happens to be money, nothing changes in the mathematical characterisation of the consumer optimum. Simply, since money is treated as a purely instrumental commodity having no direct utility, its indirect or notional marginal utility will coincide with the common value of the weighted marginal utilities of all the commodities that are included in the consumer's plan (see De Rosa 1960, I, pp. 375–6). The marginal utility of money cannot for Pareto be a constant, because the optimum conditions imply that this common value generally changes with each change in the given prices or endowments.

In a text of 1892, however, the mathematical demonstration of this point was preceded by an intuitive example for the non-mathematical reader, in which Pareto considered a case of perfectly divisible commodities, separable utilities, and marginal utilities as step functions of the amounts of each commodity (Pareto 1892–93, pp. 488–9). This example is notable for two reasons.

First, the representation of the consumer problem is very similar to Marshall's: commodities are ranked in order of the importance of the needs that they satisfy, and money is spent so that each unit of money goes to the most important need that is still unsatisfied. The example shows a 'margin of expenditure' in exactly the same sense as in Marshall: depending on the amount of money available, there is a set of ways of expenditure which are all indifferent, and their utility level defines the marginal utility of money. Now, for changes in the available amount of money or in commodity prices that leave the content of this margin unaltered, the marginal utility of money for the consumer remains constant, and the interval in which this holds is wider the richer the variety of marginal wants is. And here is the second point to be noted in the example. Almost as if misled by his eagerness to confirm the conclusion which he will reach in the mathematical demonstration, Pareto makes a curious slip and affirms that the marginal utility of money changes at any change in the amount of money or in prices also in the case of the example. The reason for his blunder lies in the fact that he calculates the marginal utility of money not by the utility purchased at the margin with one unit of money (which in his example is uniformly equal to one for a whole interval of values of available money), but by the ratio between the amount of money spent on the marginal commodities and their *total* utility (which in his example is a fraction that obviously varies with the amount of money available). Pareto did not realise that, had he calculated marginal utilities consistently with his own definition, the example would have supported Marshall's hypothesis within the limits of applicability that Marshall himself had made clear. Indeed, however restrictive it might appear in the case of continuous marginal utilities, the hypothesis is quite plausible in the realm of ordinary situations, that is, as a local hypothesis in a world where utility comes in discrete lumps. While Pareto, as we mentioned above, was uniquely alert to the traps hidden in passing from mathematics to facts, in this case he seems to have been hindered by his mathematics from seeing that Marshall's hypothesis *was* coherent with fact.

A second theoretical issue which intrigued Pareto in these years, namely the debate on exchange at variable prices, led him to diverge from the start from Walras's election of the *Bourse des valeurs* as the benchmark model of the functioning of markets, and to adopt a line nearer to Marshall's and Edgeworth's view of the market process as a sequence of false tracks and strategic moves. 'The rate of exchange, that for Walras is a constant, is assumed by Marshall to be liable to change, and this is a great progress' (Pareto to Pantaleoni, 25 December 1891, in De Rosa 1960, I, pp. 129–30). Earlier in 1891, Edgeworth's article on Marshall's theory of barter had come out in the *Giornale degli economisti*, followed by a critical note by the mathematician Arthur Berry, written at Marshall's instigation, and a rejoinder by Edgeworth. In a later letter to Pantaleoni, Pareto came back to this debate and gave a brilliant non-mathematical interpretation of the point at issue (De Rosa 1960, I, pp. 183–4). He saw clearly that the multiplicity of equilibria – the one which eventually occurs depending on the path of out-of-equilibrium transactions – makes it possible for market outcomes, and especially bargains struck on the labour market, to be manipulated by ruthless negotiators able to exploit any sort of inequality in power to their advantage. This was an implication that, with reference to the labour market, had been investigated by Marshall as well; but Pareto expressed it with his typical bluntness, and already pointed to the border where economic analysis goes no farther and sociology takes over. 'Marshall's famous problem of barter gives me little trouble because I can see a solution which is too simple' (ibid., p. 183). It does not take much formal elaboration to see that there is a problem of power, Pareto seems to say, but delving into it is a different matter and requires a different approach.

The theme of out-of-equilibrium variable prices resurfaces frequently in the papers of the early 1890s and in the *Cours*, but remains substantially marginal (Pareto 1892–93, pp. 300ff; 1894a, p. 48; [1896–97] 1964, I, p. 24 n.). It is only in the *Manuale* that it takes up a prominent position in the treatment of general equilibrium. We come back to it in the following section.

PARETO'S LAUSANNE YEARS AND FINAL BREAK-UP

When he accepted with enthusiasm, after initial hesitations, to join the 'New school', Pareto still felt as though he were indebted to everybody: Walras, together with Marshall and Edgeworth. On moving to Lausanne in 1893, his gratitude was particularly directed towards Walras for his part in procuring the appointment for him. As soon as he took office at the University he was faced with a ready-made outline, prepared by the *maître*, of the lectures he was supposed to deliver. Apparently he put up with this without argument (De Rosa 1960, II, p. 371). A few days later, however, he made it clear to Pantaleoni that he intended to organise his teaching in his own way: 'So far I get along well. I show the deference that I think I owe Walras by praising him all the time, but then I explain things so as to make myself understood by everybody' (ibid., p. 373). With time, Walras was to develop a hostility towards Pareto, or at least this was the perception that Pareto confided to Sensini in the letter of 1911 quoted in the previous section (Sensini 1948, pp. 61–2. For an assessment of the substance of Pareto's misgivings, see the endnotes by Busino to the reprint of this letter in Busino 1973, II, p. 737.) Walras seemed to realise that, from an intellectual point of view, Pareto had little or nothing in common with him; yet Pareto never receded from his habit of formal deference.

In the *Cours* a certain distance from Walras can be seen, but only implicitly, in the very layout of the volume. General equilibrium is treated sketchily in the first and sole chapter on pure theory, which is still presented in the style of Marshall with the mathematics confined to the footnotes. This theoretical core occupies less than one tenth of the work; the rest is taken up by themes that Pareto classifies as applied economics and by a general outline of social evolution with plenty of historical and statistical illustrations. Other features of the volume strike the reader for the certainly unintended similarities with Marshall's style of work. First of all, Pareto's equilibrium, like Marshall's, is a *virtual* state that is never actually attained since the conditions which define it are in continuous flow (Pareto 1896–97, I, p. 47). Pareto, again like Marshall, was fully aware of the mathematical difficulties involved in attempting a direct description of the dynamics of the system, and satisfied himself with static approximations, knowing full well what this implied (ibid., II, pp. 9–10; that Walras lacked such a clear perception of the gap between statics and dynamics is well argued in Donzelli 2006). As to method, while it is true that Pareto believed in maintaining pure economics up to a standard of absolute rigour – unlike Marshall, for whom the pursuit of rigour as such was a waste of time (Whitaker 1996, II, p. 393) – when he passed from pure to applied economics he accepted that one had to make do with essentially imprecise and imperfect concepts and procedures. His tolerance of all kinds of practical devices for solving problems of measure and aggregation extended to the use of averages, indexes, and representative individuals and firms. As he had written to Pantaleoni in 1892, this is 'a matter of life and death for the new theories. Economic science is a science of averages. If the final degrees [of utility] do not lend themselves to the use of averages, then they can find no place in science' (De Rosa 1960, I, p. 275). He shared the pragmatic attitude that Marshall had expressed in a letter to J. Neville Keynes, 'economics has to use every method known to science' (Whitaker 1996, I, pp. 299–300), to the point of asserting substantially the same concept in a letter to Pantaleoni: 'I don't know for how long I have been repeating that I am not in favour of the exclusive use of any *method*, that discussions on method are waste of time' (De Rosa 1960, III, p. 55). Lastly, the design of the work suggests that, like Marshall, he was obsessed with unlikely plans for gigantic treatises in which a kernel of economic theory was to be extended backwards and forwards to cover the entire universe of social phenomena. As is well known, Marshall occupied himself for years with the projected second volume of the *Principles* before admitting discomfiture and re-directing his efforts to the more focused *Industry and Trade*. In 1906–07 Pareto made ambitious plans for a second edition of the *Cours* in five volumes, two of which on pure and mathematical economics, to be preceded by one on sociology and followed by two on applied economics (see Sensini 1948, pp. 22–30). This project also fell through, swallowed up by the composition of the no less huge *Trattato di sociologia generale*, which drained all of his energies until 1916.

While on the one hand we find latent and unexpected concordances with Marshall, on the other Pareto's unshakable loyalty to Walras blocked all manifestations of dissent. It is because of this loyalty that Pareto's reservations on the Walrasian *tâtonnement* have passed generally unremarked in historiography (with the notable exception of Donzelli 2006), and the secondary literature on Edgeworth's recontracting and sequence economies has ignored him entirely. In the *Cours*, he referred in mild tones to Edgeworth's criticism of Walras's adjustment mechanism, but justified the latter as a representation which captured the essential part of the phenomenon (Pareto 1896–97, I, pp. 24–5). Saying more than that, in particular affirming that the theory should take into consideration the plethora of false prices that precede the equilibrium price, would have been ungenerous on his part. Nor could he have commented on the fact that the *tâtonnement* actually did away with that most salient characteristic of economic life, uncertainty. It was only in the 1897 letter to Pantaleoni quoted in the first section that he made his dissatisfaction with Walras's mechanism fully explicit.

> You say that you take prices 'given at random'. It may be a good expedient in order to solve the equations, but it has nothing to do with the way you *establish* those equations. Walras was wrong in confusing that artifice that determines equilibrium. Hence Edgeworth's *right* remark, that [Walras's way] is *one* way, not *the* way by which you reach equilibrium. 'Assuming n° 1'. Fine, but I am not assuming it! I must own up to my fault of not insisting enough in the first pages [of the *Cours*] on this disagreement with Walras. (De Rosa 1960, II, pp. 35–6, emphasis in original)

After Walras's death in 1910, but again only in private correspondence with Sensini, Pareto asserted that, had he wished to do so, he could have presented his theory of equilibrium in such a way that it would appear to have nothing in common with Walras's; but he was inhibited by his sense of fairness (Sensini 1948, p. 61). In fact, at a careful reading, the presentation of general equilibrium in the 1906 *Manuale* (and the French *Manuel*) seems in some way to go in the direction of the un-Walrasian formulation hinted at in the letter. Equilibrium is primarily defined as a matter of 'tastes' meeting 'obstacles', without recourse to the notion of price: prices enter only as 'auxiliary unknowns eventually to be abandoned to leave us with tastes and obstacles alone' (Pareto [1906] 2006, p. 150). The market process is geometrically described by a path in the commodities space which may assume various shapes, the linear or price-taking one being a special case, while the others point to the existence of situations of unequal power of the parties in the exchange, monopolies, combinations, and the like. The shape of the path determines the position of equilibrium and the distribution of the benefits from exchange (ibid., pp. 246ff.). To add to this generalised path-dependence, Pareto also makes provision for the possibility that the movement towards equilibrium is arrested by *punti termine* ('halting points', apparently derived from Cournot, see ibid., pp. 125, 590), types of barriers set across the paths owing to institutional or natural constraints, so that actual equilibrium is forced to occur in positions where not all the marginal conditions established by Walras's equations are satisfied (ibid., pp. 133–4).

In this final version, Pareto's equilibrium is a construction that is still statical but, even more so than in the *Cours*, is underpinned by a view of the economy full of dynamism and uncertainty. The concept of the market is that of a research engine liable to fail due to miscalculations on the part of market agents – the failures being at the origin of the periodic crises of the trade cycle – and always subject to the influence of the various powers in conflict with each other in society. At this stage, the general equilibrium of markets looks more and more like a blank canvas to be filled in by sociology and history. Even the theorem of the optimality of competitive equilibrium is now seen as simply a way to establish in a precise form the preliminaries for the further sociological problem of defining conditions for a maximum, not of subjective *ophelimity*, but of social *utility*, as he concisely explains in Pareto (1913). It is precisely as a preparation for the continuation of his research in the wider field of the general science of society that Pareto avoids anchoring equilibrium to specific hypotheses regarding prices and prefers the flexible framework provided by the notions of paths and halting points. He had emphasised his fondness for flexibility years earlier in a letter (9 July 1895) to Pantaleoni:

> [I]n our formulas there is room for all considerations, for all the hypotheses one may wish to make. You sent me a remark on the profits of gold mines, and I introduced it in the formulas. Edgeworth keeps repeating like a parrot that our formulas do not allow for 'non-competing groups'. I explained to him in detail and in print [in the 1895 paper on the mathematical theory of international trade] the way one may take them into account. That can be done in two substantially equivalent ways in Marshall's way and in my, and Walras's, way. Why quarrel about that? (De Rosa 1960, I, p. 425)

If this is Pareto's final product as a pure economist – afterwards he was to dedicate himself almost entirely to the *Trattato di sociologia* – we may well say that he managed to cast a number of Marshallian themes into a mould derived from, but not equal to, Walras's. But in 1906, while still in the grip of his personal obligation to Walras, Pareto's estrangement from Marshall had already precipitated. It may have been the fact that Marshall stubbornly refused to reciprocate, even with a simple calling-card, the off-prints that Pareto had sent to him at Pantaleoni's suggestion – had Pareto known that Marshall, in listing French books for the new Economic Tripos in 1903, referred to him as 'the ablest: but ... very un-real and cranky' (Whitaker 1996, III, 42), he would have had further reasons to be irritated; or possibly the universal acclaim reserved to the *Principles* while he would be unsuccessful in having his *Manuel* translated even in Calcutta; or may be the refusal, at the hands of Edgeworth and allegedly inspired by Marshall, of a paper by Enrico Barone for the *Economic Journal* (the episode is reconstructed in Zanni 1991, p. 418 n.). Whatever the reason, when Pantaleoni in a 1907 paper bunched him together with Marshall in a group of exponents of the new theories of general equilibrium, Pareto lost his temper: he would no longer acquiesce. The letters that he wrote to Pantaleoni in this occasion were vehement, yet well argued and illuminating.

> I divide economic theories into two categories: (α) those which, as you say, break up general equilibrium in so many particular equilibria; (β) those which consider general equilibrium and *don't* break it up. I claim ... that progress consists in passing from (α) to (β). I claim that the use of mathematics is justified only in (β), while it is useless, hence harmful, in (α). I say that the theories of so-called classical economy belong to (α); and so do also Marshall's theories and in addition I say that the so-called classical theories are better than Marshall's with all its mathematical flourish. (De Rosa 1960, III, p. 64)

Unlike the differences on points of detail, such as the hypothesis of the constant marginal utility of money, which a younger and less embittered Pareto considered of no great consequence, here the dissent is undoubtedly fundamental, but more as a matter of method than of concept or vision. The question is, where does the ultimate boundary of analytical precision lie? Pareto's answer is: in the representation of the network of interdependencies as a whole, in the general map. Marshall's answer is: no, *before* that – all you can do is break down the network into many small bits, and draw partial maps of each. For Pareto, the complications of ethics, sentiments, and politics, can be added to the map later. For Marshall, they must be there always: maps are never clean. This is why he thinks that the general map would be too messy to be of any use. In a later, lucid letter to Felice Vinci of 1912, Pareto summarises the argument neatly:

> Off with practical considerations – off with ethical considerations – total separation between economics and sociology – this is how I intended to characterize the *Manuale*. In Marshall practical, and particularly ethical considerations are powerful, it is difficult to sort economics from sociology. (Busino 1973, II, p. 759)

Yet both Pareto and Marshall agreed that, with reference to human societies, maps can only be provisional and unreliable, and that it is only when one starts exploring the ground that one learns how actual societies work. However, for Pareto this exploration was the object of sociology, a related but separate discipline which in his view still lacked scientific foundations, and he took it upon himself to construct them in his own way. For Marshall, instead, it was possible to keep everything inside economics, with no break in methodological continuity. Here, they definitely parted company.

TWO VIEWS OF SOCIAL SCIENCE UNDER THE SHADOW OF GENERAL EQUILIBRIUM THEORY

In conclusion, we have found many similarities in vision and general approach between Pareto and Marshall, but one big difference in method; and many differences between Pareto and Walras, but one big similarity in form. It seems reasonable to argue that the formal similarity is what mainly accounts for why, in twentieth-century economics, the gulf that divided Pareto from Marshall was immediately evident and perhaps even exaggerated in the common perception, while the equally wide – if not wider – gulf between Pareto and Walras passed unnoticed, and the two were merged into one single theoretical position opposed to Marshall's. Apart from the small number of economists who, in the period between the two wars, constituted the Italian Paretian school, but were barely known of outside Italy (see Pomini and Tusset 2009), it was generally not realised that, at the beginning of the century, in addition to the French and the Cambridge traditions, there was a third distinct line of thought competing for intellectual visibility.

John Hicks, who in the 1930s did much to bring Pareto to the attention of English-speaking economists, bore some responsibility for the rather partial account of Paretian theory that he gave in his influential *Value and Capital* ([1939] 1946). Hicks bunched Pareto, Walras and Wicksell all together, with little recognition of Pareto's independence of thought and with the somewhat damning remark that '[Pareto's] *Manuel* purports to be a sort of general *Principles*; but most problems are treated by it quite superficially, while its famous theory of General Equilibrium is nothing else but a more elegant restatement of the doctrines of Walras' (Hicks [1939] 1946, p. 12). The only point of originality that Hicks accorded to Pareto was the discovery that a quantitative notion of utility is not necessary for equilibrium theory, as well as the indication of how this could be developed on the basis of more general ordinal concepts. However, it is doubtful that Pareto attributed to this discovery of his all the importance that Hicks and others would find in it. For all his insistence on preference and mere choice as being the ultimate analytical foundations, Pareto never recanted his early belief in the *existence* of a virtually measurable utility (see Pareto 1892–93, pp. 136–7). Certainly he had other reasons for thinking that he was breaking new ground, and these are to be found in the link that he tried to establish between economics and his own version of sociology. But this has escaped notice, since economists have generally avoided venturing into a work as forbidding as the *Trattato di sociologia*, one that even sociologists have found it hard to digest.

It seems evident that the mathematical form has worked as both flattener and emphasiser of differences in the later economists' perception. We may let Pareto himself voice a posthumous protest against this:

> Talking of a 'mathematical school' is inappropriate. The use of mathematics is an accidental fact and cannot be the basis of a classification. There is greater difference between so-called mathematical economists than between them and those of other schools. For instance, I am nearer to Adam Smith than to Walras, although I derived the first concept of economic equilibrium from the latter. And I am more distant from Marshall than from many other economists who do not use mathematics. Thus, it is ridiculous to put me in the company of Walras and all such people, while the disagreement between us is fundamental. (Pareto to Vinci, 16 January 1912, in Busino 1973, II, p. 757)

Strangely enough for one who, as a sociologist, displayed such a keen understanding of the force of representations in directing human actions, Pareto seems to have misjudged the tendency of even a formal language like that of mathematics to bias the perception of the ideas entrusted to it. To revert then to our initial question – did Pareto have a part in bringing about the relative eclipse of Marshallian economics during the course of the twentieth century? – we think that we may answer: yes, certainly, but for reasons that he would not have approved, because the same reasons contributed to casting a shadow also on his claims to independent eminence as a theorist. If the Walrasian version of general equilibrium theory has dominated economics for most of the century, this is not what Pareto would have wished, and probably he would have considered it a sociological phenomenon rather than real scientific progress. Both he and Marshall suffered from this, each in his own way.

NOTE

* All translations from Pareto's Italian texts are ours. Comments from Aldo Montesano are gratefully acknowledged.

REFERENCES

Busino, G. (ed.) (1973), *Epistolario 1890–1923*, 2 vols, Roma: Accademia Nazionale dei Lincei.
Busino, G. (1977), *Pareto e l'industria del ferro nel Valdarno*, Milano: Banca Commerciale Italiana.
Dardi, M. (2008), 'Utilitarianism without utility: A missed opportunity in Alfred Marshall's theory of market choice', *History of Political Economy*, **40**, 613–32.
De Rosa, G. (ed.) (1960), [Vilfredo Pareto:] *Lettere a Maffeo Pantaleoni*, 3 vols, Roma: Banca Nazionale del Lavoro.
Donzelli, F. (2006), 'Walras and Pareto on the meaning of the solution concept in general equilibrium theory', *International Review of Economics*, **53**, 491–530.
Hicks, J.R. ([1939] 1946), *Value and Capital*, 2nd edn, Oxford: Oxford University Press.
Pareto, V. (1892), 'La teoria dei prezzi dei signori Auspitz e Lieben e le osservazioni del professore Walras', *Giornale degli economisti*, **4**, 201–39.
Pareto, V. (1892–93), 'Considerazioni sui principii fondamentali dell'economia politica pura', *Giornale degli economisti*, in five instalments: **4**, 389–420 and 485–512; **5**, 119–57; **6**, 1–37; **7**, 279–321.
Pareto, V. (1894a), 'Il massimo di utilità dato dalla libera concorrenza', *Giornale degli economisti*, **8**, 48–66.
Pareto, V. (1894b), 'Teoria matematica dei cambi forestieri', *Giornale degli economisti*, **8**, 142–73.
Pareto, V. ([1896–97] 1964), *Cours d'économie politique*, offset reprint of the original edn, prefaced by G.-H. Bousquet and G. Busino, Genève: Librairie Droz.
Pareto, V. ([1906] 2006), *Manuale di economia politica*, critical edn by A. Montesano, A. Zanni and L. Bruni, Milano: EGEA.
Pareto, V. (1913), 'Il massimo di utilità per una collettività in sociologia', *Giornale degli economisti e rivista di statistica*, **46**, 337–41.
Pareto, V. (1974), *Scritti politici*, edited by G. Busino, 2 vols, Torino: UTET.
Pomini, M. and G. Tusset (2009), 'Habits and expectations: Dynamic general equilibrium in the Italian Paretian school', *History of Political Economy*, **41**, 311–42.
Sensini, G. (1948), *Corrispondenza di Vilfredo Pareto*, Padova: CEDAM.
Vilks, A. (2007), *Axiomatization, immunization, and convention in economics*, European Conference on the History of Economics, Siena 2007. Online: http://www.econ-pol.unisi.it/eche07/PaperVilks.pdf.
Whitaker, J.K. (ed.) (1996), *The Correspondence of Alfred Marshall, Economist*, 3 vols, Cambridge: Cambridge University Press.
Zanni, A. (1991), 'Pareto's monologue with Marshall', *Quaderni di storia dell'economia politica*, **9**, 399–421.
Zanni, A. (2006), 'Price stabilization policies', in T. Raffaelli, G. Becattini and M. Dardi (eds), *The Elgar Companion to Alfred Marshall*, Cheltenham, UK and Northampton, MA, USA: Edward Elgar, pp. 435–44.

24. Schumpeter on Marshall

Harald Hagemann

New problems, ideas, and methods that are enemies to the work of other men, thus came to his own as allies.
(Schumpeter 1941, p. 237)

INTRODUCTION

As is well known, Schumpeter recognised progress in economics for the most part in improvements of its techniques of analysis, and he gave highest credit to Walras and his general equilibrium system. From that perspective of pure economics Schumpeter perceived Marshall's analytical apparatus as obsolete, pointing out that 'Marshallian economics has passed away already. His vision of the economic process, his methods, his results, are no longer ours' (Schumpeter 1941, p. 236). On the other hand, Schumpeter was full of praise for Marshall in whom he saw 'the greatest teacher that economists ever had, Alfred Marshall, whose pupils are ninety-nine percent of the English economists' (Schumpeter [1931] 1991, p. 290). For Schumpeter, Marshall's *Principles* constitute the classical achievement of the period 1870–1914, which he labelled the 'Marshallian Age' in England (Schumpeter 1954, pp. 829–40). It was Marshall who led English economics out of a valley on to a sunlit height' (ibid., p. 830), and in his semi-centennial appraisal Schumpeter compared Marshall's *Principles* with a Madonna who 'embodies to perfection the thought and feeling of her time' (Schumpeter 1941, p. 236). However, in his typical ambivalent style Schumpeter did not miss emphasising the long journey economics had made thereafter.

During his whole academic life Schumpeter's work and thought had been persistently inspired and challenged by the ideas of Marshall. Thus we find already flattering comments on Marshall in his Vienna habilitation thesis on *The Nature and the Main Content of Theoretical Economics* (Schumpeter 1908), which was published after the only time Schumpeter and Marshall had met in Cambridge in the year before, and in his early work on *Economic Doctrine and Method* Schumpeter (1914) classifies Marshall as the leading contemporary English economist. However, it took until the semi-centennial year of the first publication of Marshall's opus magnum for Schumpeter (1941) to give the first systematic appraisal of Marshall's work, which is succeeded and supplemented by long sections in his *History of Economic Analysis* (1954). Schumpeter acknowledges his debt to Keynes's 1924 biographical essay on Marshall which he regards 'as one of the outstanding masterpieces of biographical literature' (Schumpeter 1941, p. 236n. 1). Nevertheless, at the latest with the publication of Keynes's *General Theory*, of which he was a fierce critic, Schumpeter's way of thinking on Marshall 'became entangled with his attitude towards other members of the Cambridge school', as Backhouse (2008, p. 48) has argued.

MARSHALL AND THE CLASSICS

Schumpeter recognised Marshall's claim that his work, particularly the *Principles*, represented a continuation with classical economics in the line of Smith, Ricardo and John Stuart Mill and, no doubt, found 'the great loyalty of Marshall for his classic predecessors' (Schumpeter [1931] 1991, p. 294) excessive. Schumpeter attributed this loyalty to Marshall's insularity and to the solidarity among fellow liberals who were all strong advocates of free trade. However, there are certain qualifications concerning Schumpeter's statements on Marshall's assessments of the three great classical economists. Although he recognised certain similarities in the works of Marshall and Smith, notably with regard to their visions of economic evolution, Schumpeter appraised Marshall's esteem for Smith as boundless, repeatedly and ironically attributing the statement 'It's all in A. Smith' to Alfred Marshall and one of his favourite sayings (Schumpeter 1954, pp. 309, 835). Schumpeter noticed that Marshall's 'success was as great as A. Smith's, if account be taken of the facts that a science must inevitably grow less accessible to the general public as its techniques develop' (ibid., p. 830), but that abroad, Marshall's *Principles* were much less successful than Smith's *Wealth of Nations*. Schumpeter attributed this to the fact that 'Marshall's message was after all a message to the economics profession' (ibid., p. 834). In other words, the reason why Schumpeter appreciates Marshall more than Smith is exactly the same as why half a century later he found Marshall's analytical apparatus outdated, because Schumpeter made the advancement of techniques in pure economics the regression line of his judgements.

Schumpeter (1941, p. 239) noted 'Marshall's tendency to impute to Mill and Ricardo practically all that the reformers of economic theory had to say'. He had learned from Keynes's essay on Alfred Marshall that the latter had begun to study economic theory seriously in 1867, and that he first learned economics from John Stuart Mill's *Principles of Political Economy*. Schumpeter noticed that Marshall was driven to economics by the same ethical impulse to overcome the misery of the working class as some members of the German historical school, and that

Marshall 'retained a filial respect for J.S. Mill throughout his life though he was under no delusion concerning the latter's intellectual stature' (Schumpeter 1954, p. 837). Schumpeter, who had a low opinion of the 'loose statements' included in 'J.S. Mill's treatise, which hovers between Ricardo and Say' (ibid., p. 838), grants Marshall, who had an excellent training in mathematics, '*creative* achievement' in 'the transformation of the Smith-Ricardo-Mill material into a modern engine of research' (Schumpeter 1941, p. 240). This could hardly have been accomplished without mathematics, Marshall's 'great impersonal ally to which he owed so much' but 'never gave full credit. He hid the tool that had done the work' (ibid.).

Whereas Schumpeter agreed to give Smith and Mill a limited role as fore-runners of Marshallian economic ideas, this does not hold for Ricardo. Schumpeter made this very clear in his response to Shove's influential article 'The place of Marshall's *Principles* in the development of economic theory' (Shove 1942), published on the occasion of the centenary of Marshall's birth. Here Shove indicates that Marshall's opinion of Mill as an economic theorist was not very high, which is in agreement with Schumpeter's view on Mill but not with Schumpeter's interpretation of Marshall's view on Mill. Shove argues in particular that 'the analytical backbone of Marshall's *Principles* is nothing more or less than a completion and generalisation, by means of a mathematical apparatus, of Ricardo's theory of value and distribution as expounded by J.S. Mill' (ibid., pp. 294–5). Schumpeter, on the contrary, denies that the foundations of Marshall's work could be found in Ricardo and emphasises that, in contrast to Mill and even Smith, 'no really practicable bridge between Ricardo and Marshall' (Schumpeter 1954, p. 838 n. 11) exists. In his *History of Economic Analysis* Schumpeter points out the chasm that separates Marshall from the British classical economists, especially Ricardo. He makes this plain and clear when in the section on 'Marshall's attitude and real cost' he distances himself from Marshall's pro-Ricardian views on value theory. In this context Schumpeter not only refers to the fact that Marshall '*never* espoused the specifically Ricardian elements in the "classic" structure, such as, for example, the labour-quantity theory of value, which he quietly modified so that it is no longer what Ricardo had intended it to be' (ibid., p. 921 n. 4), but also emphasises that Marshall's famous analogy of the 'two blades of a pair of scissors', comprising the 'cost of production principle' for the supply side and the 'final utility principle' for the demand side, 'is thoroughly un-Ricardian. It is Malthusian' (ibid., n. 5).

MARSHALL AND MARGINALISM

There can be no doubt that Marshall had a very flexible interpretation of Ricardo's theory which permitted him to assert continuity with the great classical economists on the one side, without playing down the importance of modern economic analysis, in particular the marginalist approach, on the other. Schumpeter noticed Marshall's striving for a synthesis of classical economics, in the direct line of descent through J.S. Mill from Ricardo, with modern contributions but emphasised that the two blades of a pair of scissors, cost and utility, 'are both made of the same material, of utility', stating that '[i]f you know how to read Marshall you will find it is marginal utility analysis and nothing else' (Schumpeter [1931] 1991, p. 294).

Schumpeter recognised 'the twin facts that Marshall's theoretical structure is fundamentally the same as that of Jevons, Menger, and especially Walras, but that the rooms in this new house are unnecessarily cluttered up with Ricardian heirlooms, which received emphasis quite out of proportion to their operational importance' (Schumpeter 1954, p. 837). Whereas he can understand the widespread interpretation of Marshall as an eclectic synthesiser, he nevertheless sides with the Marshallians in rejecting this interpretation and points out that 'Marshall's powerful engine of analysis was the result of a creative effort and not of a synthetic one' (ibid.). Schumpeter had a high esteem for Marshall's technical skills. He was fully aware that Marshall was an excellent mathematician, with a much better training than Jevons and Menger, and even a better mathematical economist than Walras. However, he was irritated by the fact that Marshall relegated his mathematical analysis into appendices and his nice diagrams into footnotes in order to be read by businessmen and the general public. He concluded that Marshall was successful in this respect, that as a charismatic teacher and writer he created a genuine school leaving his mark on the next generation, comprising such outstanding economists as Pigou, Robertson and Keynes, and that he grasped contemporaneous business life better than most other academic economists. Although Schumpeter had a high esteem for Wicksteed among Marshall's British contemporaries and, above all, for Edgeworth, whose 'novel contributions (indifference curve, contract curve, decreasing returns, general equilibrium and so on) to the analytic apparatus of economics amount to as much as, *or more than*, do Marshall's *Principles*' (ibid., p. 831, emphasis in original), he had the fullest respect for the genius of Marshall as an author whose 'mathematical training disciplined even his verbal statements', although '[t]he precise nature of the performance is less easy to define' (Schumpeter 1941, pp. 241 and 238). However, Schumpeter credited Marshall for the fact that his realism helped to prevent the rise of an institutionalist approach in England, in remarkable contrast to American institutionalist economics, initiated by Veblen and Commons, which kept an important position for decades.

PARTIAL VERSUS GENERAL EQUILIBRIUM ANALYSIS

Whereas Schumpeter felt that Marshall was 'scrupulously fair to the classics, in particular to Ricardo and Mill', he thought that Marshall had taken up 'a position of armed neutrality against Menger, Jevons and the greatest of all theorists, Walras' (Schumpeter 1941, p. 239). It comes to no surprise that the comparison with Walras permeates all of Schumpeter's writings on Marshall. He explained Marshall's success with the neatness of the structure of his exposition relative to that of Walras. Schumpeter recognised that Marshall had advanced partial analysis significantly and that the *cæteris-paribus* clause, which had often been implied by classical economists, could be a proper device to analyse specific economic consequences provided indirect effects were negligible. He called Marshall 'the master of partial analysis' but discussed at length the shortcomings of that type of analysis (Schumpeter 1954, pp. 990–98; Duval 2002, pp. 79–81).

Schumpeter clearly considered Book V of Marshall's *Principles*, containing his theory of equilibrium of demand and supply, as the 'core of the analytic performance' and 'the classic masterpiece of partial analysis' (Schumpeter 1954, pp. 835–6). Although he sometimes equated partial equilibrium with Marshallian equilibrium, he nevertheless repeatedly pointed out 'that Marshall had fully grasped the idea of general equilibrium' (Schumpeter 1941, p. 241) and, despite the emphasis on the partial-analytic perspective identified throughout Marshall's work, concluded that it 'seems fair to list Marshall also among the builders of the general-equilibrium system as well as of the marginal utility analysis per se' (Schumpeter 1954, p. 836). Schumpeter was right in his view that Marshall was well aware of interdependencies in the economy and that therefore thoughtful attention to general equilibrium was often necessary, especially on issues of distribution and taxation. However, Marshall gave priority to empirical relevance and this fact directed him to the study of isolated markets, sometimes at the expense of analytical rigour. In contrast to Walras he was less concerned with the existence of overall equilibrium in an abstract decentralised economy. '*L'art pour l'art* had no place in his eminently Anglo-Saxon soul' (Schumpeter 1941, p. 244). Schumpeter regretted 'that though he [Marshall] grasped the idea of general equilibrium he yet relegated it to the background, erecting in the foreground the handier house of partial or particular analysis' (ibid., p. 246). According to Schumpeter this procedure contributed significantly to the earlier obsolescence of Marshall's theory compared to Walras's analysis of general equilibrium in the process of development of pure economics. Nevertheless, Schumpeter conceded that Marshall's achievements were unique in the sense that they were based on the mutual inspiration of the partial and the general equilibrium method, and the large set of handy tools devised, such as his substitution principle, elasticity coefficients, the concepts of consumers' surplus and of quasi-rents, the distinctions between external and internal economies as well as the short and the long run, the representative firm and so on (see ibid., pp. 241–2).

STATICS VERSUS DYNAMICS

From his first academic writings onwards Schumpeter made it clear that his theoretical system was based on the fundamental distinction between *statics* and *dynamics*. Thus in the introduction of his habilitation thesis Schumpeter (1908, pp. xix–xx) emphasised that dynamics in all relevant aspects is completely different from statics and that the most important results of pure economics up to his time were restricted to the static analysis of the economy on which he therefore wanted to focus attention. Despite his concentration on equilibrium analysis, from the very beginning he took up a dynamic perspective aiming at a theory of the business cycle and economic development. He considered his two books *Das Wesen* (1908) and *The Theory of Economic Development* (1911) as a unity, the former focusing on the pure logic of the interdependence between economic variables, with Walras as his great hero, and the latter comprising his vision of the long-run development of the capitalist economy challenged by Marx.

Whereas initially Schumpeter took the distinction between statics and dynamics as it had been elaborated by John Bates Clark, since 1929 he was strongly influenced by Ragnar Frisch's modern work on the clarification of the two concepts. In line with Frisch's precision, Schumpeter (see, for example, 1954, p. 1160) from then onwards distinguished between statics as connecting economic quantities that refer to the same point in time, and dynamic theorems which include in their functions values of variables which belong to different points of time (Hagemann 2003, pp. 54–7).

Schumpeter considered Walras's general equilibrium theory as strictly static in character and inappropriate for business-cycle theory. But he also regarded Marshall's theoretical apparatus in the *Principles* as 'strictly static' (Schumpeter 1954, p. 836). However, 'though it was essentially a static theory that he [Marshall] worked out, he always looked beyond it. He inserted dynamic elements whenever he could, more often than was compatible with the static logic he nevertheless retained' (Schumpeter 1941, p. 242). In his essay on 'The instability of capitalism' Schumpeter (1928) had already attacked the Smith–Ricardo–Marshall line of thought for not doing the dynamics properly, failing to provide the spark of motion to the economy. Schumpeter reiterated what he evidently regarded as a main point, for example when he quoted with approval Keynes's reference in the *Treatise on Money* to Marshall's occasional disposition 'to camouflage the essentially static character of his equilibrium theory with many wise and penetrating *obiter dicta* on dynamical problems' (Schumpeter 1954, p. 837), or when he alluded to Marshall's numerous 'extra-static considerations'. However, Marshall 'did not cross the Rubicon', that is, he

> left the main body of economic theory on the 'static' bank of the river; the thing to do is not to supplement static theory by the booty brought back from these excursions but to replace it by a system of general economic dynamics into which statics would enter as a special case. (Ibid., p. 1160)

EVOLUTIONARY ECONOMICS

As is well known, Marshall's *Principles* are full of evolutionary, biological arguments by analogy. He even went as far as to proclaim that biology and not mechanics is the 'Mecca' of the economist. Schumpeter, on the other hand, argued against the biological analogy which the use of the term 'evolution' can imply. He also made it clear that he wanted to protect himself against an unscientific mixing up of the term 'development' with value judgements of progress. However, whereas he kept the cautious attitude toward the biological analogy until his death and argued against the dilettante use of the term 'evolutionary' in economics in his *Theory of Economic Development* (Schumpeter [1911] 1934, pp. 57ff.), he seems to have changed his attitude towards the use of the term *evolution* shortly afterwards. In his *Business Cycles* the main conceptual chapters iii and iv take up the term evolution as a key ingredient. Schumpeter now defines *economic evolution* as 'the changes in the economic process brought about by innovation, together with all their effects, and the response to them by the economic system' (Schumpeter 1939, I, p. 86).

With regard to his bent for a theory of economic development/evolution and his dislike of biological analogies (see also Schumpeter 1928, p. 383) it comes as no surprise that Schumpeter became interested in Marshall's evolutionary economics but was also highly critical of it due to 'the clash between the two authors' evolutionary philosophies' (Raffaelli 2003, p. 119). Whereas in Schumpeter's view innovations are of a disruptive nature and economic development is endogenous, spontaneous and discontinuous, Marshall followed an organic and gradualist approach to the interplay of innovations and routine activities.

Schumpeter was fully aware that 'Marshall was one of the first economists to realise that economics is an evolutionary science, that he carried his "evolution-mindedness" into his theoretical work' (Schumpeter 1941, p. 237), and he also noticed that Marshall was conscious of the transitory nature of his own achievements. However, Schumpeter regarded Marshall's theory of economic evolution, for which he had not much sympathy, as unsatisfactory (ibid., pp. 242–3, 246–7). Schumpeter thought that Marshall's evolutionary economics did not go in the right direction because historical and biological arguments are constantly intermingled with static equilibrium analysis and the marginalist approach of pure economics. This point is restated by knowledgeable modern observers who are sympathetic to Marshall and Schumpeter. Thus, for example, Metcalfe (2006, p. 655) emphasises that 'Marshall is never completely clear as to how equilibrium and evolution are to be reconciled'. This point of critique points to the logical crux of the evolutionary method which lacks the stringency of the equilibrium method but is superior in its economic realism.

BEYOND THE *PRINCIPLES*

'The three volumes are all essential: nobody knows Marshall who knows only the *Principles*'. When Schumpeter (1954, p. 834) made this statement, besides the *Principles*, he was also referring to the two companion volumes *Industry and Trade* as well as *Money, Credit and Commerce* (1923). Furthermore, he mentioned Mary and Alfred Marshall's *The Economics of Industry* (1879), which he regarded as 'a most important stepping stone to the *Principles*' (ibid.). Despite his statement and although he knew Marshall's writings thoroughly, when discussing Marshalls's theoretical achievements Schumpeter almost exclusively focused on the *Principles*. From the perspective of modern pure economics, which is Schumpeter's decisive surveyor's rod, understanding the *Principles* and its analytical core is crucial for an assessment of Marshall's work as a whole.

Comments on Marshall's other works for Schumpeter are of secondary importance and scattered here and there. Schumpeter was one of the few contemporary economists who praised Marshall's *Industry and Trade* for its blend of theory and historical and statistical facts. Groenewegen (2007, p. 4) aptly refers to 'Schumpeter's (1941) praise of Marshall the economic historian'. In that context it should not be forgotten that in his own treatment of the development problem of capitalist economies Schumpeter had emphasised and combined the theoretical with the historical and statistical analysis, as comes out best in the subtitle of his monumental *Business Cycles* (1939). Nevertheless even in his praise of Marshall the economic historian a certain ambivalence creeps in when Schumpeter points out 'that to readers who neglect *Industry and Trade*, his treatment looks more "purely theoretical" than it is and much more so than does A. Smith's' (Schumpeter 1954, p. 835).

Schumpeter was well aware that Marshall was slow in publishing and that his teaching went further than and ahead of his published work. This holds in particular for Marshall's monetary theory. He accepted Keynes's claim that Marshall had developed his monetary theory already in the 1870s, but as a consequence of late publication '[u]p to 1914, monetary theory outside of Cambridge was practically untouched by Marshallian influences'. When finally *Money, Credit and Commerce* was published in 1923 'nothing in it seemed novel any more' (Schumpeter 1954, p. 1084). Furthermore, Schumpeter noticed Mill's analysis also as the starting point of Marshall's monetary theory, and that Marshall, like Wicksell, distinguished between the monetary and the 'real' rate of interest but criticised Marshall's failure to link up his treatment of aggregative quantities with money (Schumpeter 1941, p. 246). With regard to Keynes, Schumpeter recognised that the *Treatise* 'is a very good presentation of the Marshall type of monetary theory' ([1931] 1991, p. 296), but that in the *General Theory* 'allegiance to Marshall was formally renounced' (Schumpeter 1954, p. 1084). Schumpeter, who disliked the *General Theory*, in the 1940s sometimes fell into the habit of praising Marshall in order to criticise Keynes and his followers in Cambridge.

CONCLUSION

What was the role of Schumpeter in the diffusion of Marshall's thought in the various geographical areas in which he exerted some influence, that is,

Europe, Japan and ultimately the United States? The answer is a mixed one. In the German language area the main disseminator of Marshallian ideas was certainly Lujo Brentano who wrote the foreword to the only German edition of the *Principles* published in 1905 and made Marshallian thought a core element of his teaching at the University of Munich. Schumpeter's loyalty was to Walras, not Marshall, and he disliked Marshall's utilitarianism, his British insularity and embeddedness in Victorian culture. Furthermore, and most importantly, he found Marshall's work outdated at his time from the viewpoint of pure economics, which was the main reason why Schumpeter did not play an active role in the diffusion process of Marshallian economics. When he discusses the originality of Marshall's contributions, Schumpeter repeatedly distinguishes between *objective* and *subjective* originality in an unfavourable way for Marshall. Thus in his critical inspection of Keynes's emphasis on six major contributions by Marshall to economic knowledge Schumpeter came to the conclusion that '[n]ot one of them can be accepted without qualifying reference to the work of others, though in conjunction and as elements of a general treatise for a wider circle of readers, they were of course new enough':

> merit as there was in the rediscovery of the marginal utility principle is Jevons'; the system of general equilibrium is Walras'; the principle of substitution and the marginal productivity theory are Thünen's; the demand and supply curves and the static theory of monopoly are Cournot's; the consumers' rent is Dupuit's; the 'diagrammatic method' of presentation is also Dupuit's or else Jenkin's. If this had been always clearly understood, there would be no more to be said. (Schumpeter 1954, pp. 838–9)

So what remains on the positive side? First it may surprise readers how much space Schumpeter, in striking contrast to his diagnosed obsolescence of Marshall's analytical apparatus, dedicates in his *History of Economic Analysis* to Marshallian concepts and ideas despite the fact that his way of doing economics was not Marshall's. It can be explained only partly by the fact that, due to his didactic skills, Marshall's main treatise made the new economic concepts known and accessible to a wider audience. Despite his assessment of Marshall being inferior compared to modern technicians of economic theory, Schumpeter credited Marshall as 'a high-powered technician, a profoundly learned historian, a sure-footed framer of explanatory hypotheses' who '[u]nlike the technicians of today understood the working of the capitalist process' (Schumpeter 1954, p. 836). More than half a century later this statement seems remarkably modern and comes out still as a compliment for Marshall.

In his rational reconstruction of Marshallian economics Schumpeter (1940, pp. 246–7) Duval (2002) comes to the conclusion that Marshall paved the way to two important developments in modern economics: the theory of monopolistic (Chamberlin) or imperfect competition (Joan Robinson) and the emergence of modern econometrics. To Schumpeter (1954, pp. 1045–8, 1150–52) the first development was objectively connected to Marshall's work, with Sraffa's 'brilliantly original performance' (ibid., p. 1047 n.) in his critical inspection of Marshall's price analysis founding the English branch. Schumpeter considered Marshall's emphasis on the concept of substitution as fundamental for Marshall's analysis and 'as the main purely theoretical difference between his schema and that of Walras' (ibid., p. 246). He was convinced that '[e]conomics will never either have or merit any prestige until it can figure out results' (ibid., p. 247). Schumpeter, who was one of the co-founders of the Econometric Society, identified the openness and stimulus of Marshall's economic theory to statistical fact and econometric analysis as the decisive comparative advantage of Marshallian over Walrasian economics. Thus he recognised Marshall's role in stimulating the derivation of statistical (supply and) demand curves which became a prominent theme in the 1920s.

It is debatable how much Schumpeter's Walrasian interpretation of Marshall does justice to Marshall's work, or rather is the subjective originality of Schumpeter's explanation. Several characteristic features of Marshall's analysis lie outside the scope of the Walrasian system of general equilibrium. This holds characteristically for Marshall's evolution-mindedness which diffused into his theoretical work and which, on the one hand, attracted Schumpeter although, on the other hand, their evolutionary systems fell apart. There would not exist a genuine Schumpeter without major contradictions. Thus the economist to which he was closest in the United States was Taussig who was widely considered as 'the American Marshall', a term invented by Schumpeter himself. His mentor at Harvard might have been pleased that Schumpeter (1941, p. 248) in the year after Taussig's death concluded his semi-centennial appraisal of Marshall's work with the final assessment: 'Yes, he was a great economist'.

REFERENCES

Backhouse, R.E. (2008), 'Schumpeter on Marshall: a reconsideration', in Y. Shionoya and T. Nishizawa (eds), *Marshall and Schumpeter on Evolution. Economic sociology of capitalist development*, Cheltenham, UK and Northampton, MA, USA: Edward Elgar, pp. 48–61.

Duval, N. (2002), 'Schumpeter on Marshall', in R. Arena and C. Dangel-Hagnauer (eds), *The Contribution of Joseph Schumpeter to Economics. Economic Development and Institutional Change*, London and New York: Routledge, pp. 66–85.

Groenewegen, P. (2007), *Alfred Marshall*, London and New York: Palgrave Macmillan.

Hagemann, H. (2003), 'Schumpeter's early contributions on crises theory and business-cycle theory', *History of Economic Ideas*, **11** (1), 47–67.

Keynes, J.M. (1924), 'Alfred Marshall, 1842–1924', *Economic Journal*, **34**, 311–72, reprinted in J.M. Keynes (1972), *Essays in Biography*, in *The Collected Writings of John Maynard Keynes*, vol. 10, London: Macmillan.

Marshall, A. (1920), *Principles of Economics*, London: Macmillan.

Metcalfe, J.S. (2006), 'Evolutionary economics', in T. Raffaelli, G. Becattini and M. Dardi (eds), *The Elgar Companion to Alfred Marshall*, Cheltenham, UK and Northampton, MA, USA: Edward Elgar, pp. 651–7.

Raffaelli, T. (2003), *Marshall's Evolutionary Economics*, London and New York: Routledge.

Schumpeter, J.A. (1908), *Das Wesen und der Hauptinhalt der theoretischen National-ökonomie*, Munich: Duncker & Humblot.

Schumpeter, J.A. (1911), *Theorie der wirtschaftlichen Entwicklung*, Munich and Leipzig: Duncker & Humblot; 2nd revised edn 1926; English trans. *The Theory of Economic Development. An Inquiry into Profits, Capital, Credit, Interest, and the Business Cycle*, Cambridge, MA: Harvard University Press, 1934.

Schumpeter, J.A. (1914), *Epochen der Dogmen- und Methodengeschichte*, Tübingen: J.C.B. Mohr; English trans. *Economic Doctrine and Method. An Historical Sketch*, London: Allen & Unwin, 1954.

Schumpeter, J.A. (1928), 'The instability of capitalism', *Economic Journal*, **38**, 361–86.

Schumpeter, J.A. ([1931] 1991), 'Recent developments of political economy', lecture originally delivered in Japan, in R. Swedberg (ed.), *Joseph A. Schumpeter. The Economics and Sociology of Capitalism*, Princeton, NJ: Princeton University Press, pp. 284–97.

Schumpeter, J.A. (1939), *Business Cycles. A Theoretical, Historical and Statistical Analysis of the Capitalist Process*, 2 vols, New York: McGraw-Hill.

Schumpeter, J.A. (1941), 'Alfred Marshall's *Principles*: A semi-centennial appraisal', *American Economic Review*, **31** (2), 236–48.

Schumpeter, J.A. (1954), *History of Economic Analysis*, London: Allen & Unwin.

Shove, G.F. (1942), 'The place of Marshall's *Principles* in the development of economic theory', *Economic Journal*, **52** (208), 294–329.

25. Nicholas Georgescu-Roegen and the Mecca of the economist

Andrea Maneschi

When we consider the diffusion of Marshall's economic thought outside Britain, several well-known economists of the twentieth century come to mind whose approach to economics was critically influenced by Marshall (whether in positive or negative ways), but who developed their best noted contributions to economics outside their native country, sometimes in more than one other country. Aside from Pareto and Schumpeter, another significant example is the Romanian-born economist Nicholas Georgescu-Roegen, who studied first in Romania, then in France, and finally settled in the United States where he taught himself economics (mostly under the inspiration of Schumpeter, according to his own words) and carried out most of his research. Like Schumpeter and Pareto, Georgescu-Roegen was truly a 'citizen of the world': he spoke and published articles in several languages, travelled and taught in a variety of countries, and interacted with many international economists. In his formative years, he was subject to numerous intellectual influences only a subset of which emanated from economists: the others came from philosophers, scientists, statisticians, historians of science and other intellectuals (I traced the principal strands of the filiation of economic ideas to which he was subject in Maneschi 2006). That Marshall had an important effect on Georgescu-Roegen's economic thought is easy to document. Insofar as he was influenced by Marshall's philosophy, should its subsequent ramifications be measured by their impact on Romania and Mitteleuropa, on his country of immigration (the United States), or a wider group of countries? Although most of his work was done in the United States, Georgescu-Roegen's writings attracted greatest attention from European economists in France, Italy, Germany and a few other countries (eventually including Romania). While he had several admirers in the United States, he never had close disciples or attempted to create a school of bioeconomic thought to carry on his work. Indeed his relation to the American economics profession was somewhat prickly, especially after he started referring to most neoclassical economists (including some American winners of the Nobel Memorial Prize in economics) as 'standard economists'.

Georgescu-Roegen's attitude toward neoclassical economics can be briefly summarised as follows. One of his favourite targets of criticism was the mechanistic epistemology that inspired analytical economics since its beginnings and implies that economic processes are reversible. After any change that an economic system undergoes, the status quo ante can be restored by the simple expedient of running the process in reverse. Georgescu-Roegen claims instead that economic processes are unidirectional rather than circular, and characterised by an input of natural resources (low-entropy materials) and an output of high-entropy waste products. Only a fraction of the latter can be recycled, subject to cost and some degradation. He ranks himself among those economists 'who, like Marshall, have been fond of biological analogies and have even contended that economics "is a branch of biology broadly interpreted"' (Georgescu-Roegen 1966, p. 97, quoting Marshall 1920, p. 772). Georgescu-Roegen's interest gravitated toward biology and the nascent field of bioeconomics in the second part of his career after the mid-1960s. As was said of Marshall, '[w]hat took place later in his life was a progressive shift of interest from the mechanical to the biological side of social science' (Raffaelli 2003, p. 99). Marshall's early disenchantment with a statically-grounded representation of economic change arose from his realisation that 'an exclusively mechanical treatment was incapable on its own of providing a thorough understanding of economic movement' (Dardi 2006, p. 216). Dardi connects Marshall's focus in the *Principles* upon the analysis of partial equilibria to his strategy of breaking up the response to an economic disturbance into periods of varying length: the shorter the period, the more partial the resulting adjustment; and the longer the period, the greater the possibility to allow for more general, or even evolutionary developments (ibid., p. 220). In a similar vein, Georgescu-Roegen (1971, p. 203) observes that '[c]*æteris paribus* – the indispensable ingredient of every physical law – is poison to any science concerned with evolutionary phenomena'. Foster (2006, p. 285) concurs that 'it was clearly [Marshall's] long-standing interest in the problem of incorporating time into economic analysis that led him to consider an evolutionary perspective'.

BIOLOGY, IRREVERSIBILITY AND QUALITATIVE CHANGE

Georgescu-Roegen's viewpoint mirrors Marshall's contention that, in analysing economic problems, economists should not ignore

> the conditions of real life. In fact we are here verging on the high theme of economic progress; and here therefore it is especially needful to remember that economic problems are imperfectly presented when they are treated as problems of statical equilibrium, and not of organic growth. For though the statical treatment alone can give us definiteness and precision of thought, and is therefore a necessary introduction to a more philosophic treatment of society as an organism; it is yet only an introduction. (Marshall 1920, p. 461)

This reference to organic growth in chapter xii of Book V of the *Principles*, where Marshall examines the 'law of increasing return', recalls his often quoted dictum in the preface to the eighth edition that 'the Mecca of the economist lies in economic biology rather than in economic dynamics' (ibid., p. xiv). After citing this statement and Marshall's assertion that 'economic problems are not mechanical, but concerned with organic life and growth' (Marshall 1898, p. 44), Georgescu-Roegen comments that '[y]et even Marshall did not subordinate the analysis of his *Principles* to this epistemological position continuously' (Georgescu-Roegen [1974] 1976, p. 237). A sharper and more extensive critique of Marshall's alleged failure to live up to his promise to incorporate biology in economics was later made by Brinley Thomas (1991), according to whom '[o]ne must distinguish between biological analogies and biological analysis. There are sound reasons for concluding that Marshall was for the most part indulging in analogies or figures of speech. Economic biology remained promise rather than substance' (Thomas 1991, pp. 8, 11). Hodgson (1993) arrives at a similar conclusion. In considering the lack of development of Marshall's biological insights after his death, Hodgson (2006, p. 201) notes that '[b]iology was later purged with relative ease from the Marshallian system, to be replaced by a fortified metaphor from mechanics'. Metcalfe adds that

> [i]t was easy for Marshall's followers to reject the organic developmental view, because of the difficulties in casting it in definite form, and easy for them to find inconsistencies in the argument in relation to increasing returns and the partial equilibrium method. In so doing they failed to recognize the depth and subtlety of their master's argument. (Metcalfe 2006, p. 656)

The 'law of increasing return' has an important implication for the applicability of Marshall's postulated equilibrium between demand and supply, one of the foundation stones of Book V of the *Principles*. According to Georgescu-Roegen, 'it was Marshall who showed in the most incontrovertible way that even such a basic concept as the supply schedule of an "increasing returns" industry slips through the analytical mesh because "increasing returns" is an essentially evolutionary phenomenon, necessarily irreversible and perhaps irrevocable as well'. He praises 'the unique endeavor of Marshall to instill some life into the analytical skeleton of standard economics', as well as his desire 'to insist upon respect for relevance instead of succumbing to the temper of his age', and thus to transcend the static framework that characterises neoclassical economics (Georgescu-Roegen 1966, p. 107). Georgescu-Roegen applauds Marshall's efforts to view the economic system in evolutionary terms, citing Joseph Schumpeter's observation that '[Marshall's] thought ran in terms of evolutionary change – in terms of an organic, irreversible process' (Schumpeter 1951, p. 101). Like Schumpeter, Georgescu-Roegen laments the fact that Marshall's vision is no longer shared by the economics profession. Calling the irreversibility of long-run supply schedules a 'salient discovery', he argues that '[u]nfortunately, Marshall's teaching caused no lasting imprint and the fact that irreversibility is a general feature of all economic laws received no attention. Lacking Marshall's understanding, economists have seen no point in following the developments in biology and have thus missed many fertile ideas' (Georgescu-Roegen 1971, p. 11).

Consumer demand is subject to the analogous phenomenon of hysteresis, of which Marshall had become aware as early as 1869–73 when he was working on the appendix to a volume on international trade, privately published in 1879 (Marshall [1879] 1974) and eventually reproduced with minor changes in Appendix J of Marshall (1923). Raffaelli (2003, p. 44) cites this as an example of Marshall's unwillingness to 'embrace the standard view of equilibrium analysis'. As Marshall presciently noted well before the publication of the *Principles*,

> in economics every event causes permanent alterations in the conditions under which future events can occur ... every movement that takes place in the moral world alters the magnitude if not the character of the forces that govern succeeding movements. Where, for instance, any casual disturbance increases the amount of English wares of any kind that are consumed in Germany it leaves behind it a permanent effect in an increased familiarity on the part of German consumers with English wares; and in this and other ways occasions permanent alterations in the circumstances of demand. (Marshall [1879] 1974, p. 26)

In Appendix H of the *Principles*, that Raffaelli (2003, p. 113) describes as 'the *locus classicus* where he denounced the limits inherent in the statical method', Marshall returns to the phenomenon of hysteresis, connected to the irreversibility of changes in consumption following a change in price and return to the original price. Marshall (1920, p. 807) argues that a theory that ignores it 'is out of touch with real conditions of life'. Georgescu-Roegen ([1950] 1966, p. 173) highlights Marshall's clear anticipation of the hysteresis effects on consumption that he goes on to analyse in his paper. This article, together with others on utility, consumer choice and production theory of the 1950s, helped to establish his reputation as a first-rate economist, leading Paul Samuelson in his Foreword to Georgescu-Roegen (1966) (where many of these articles are collected) to characterise him as 'a scholar's scholar, an economist's economist'.

In commenting on irreversibility in more general terms, Georgescu-Roegen ([1974] 1976, pp. 244–5) adds that 'the irreversibility of economic development – on which Schumpeter insisted with even greater force than Marshall – is assured by the discontinuous novelty in the realm of commodities'. While he approves of Marshall's important insight that supply curves are subject to irreversibility, it is clear that irreversibility plays a different and more profound role in Georgescu-Roegen's economics than in Marshall's, since it is firmly anchored in natural phenomena such as the entropy law. Georgescu-Roegen argues that 'any economic change consists of two entirely distinct types of phenomena – *growth* and *development*' (ibid., p. 243). While using slightly different terms, Marshall preceded both him and Schumpeter in highlighting the same distinction:

'Progress' or 'evolution', industrial and social, is not mere increase and decrease. It is organic growth, chastened and confined and occasionally reversed by decay of innumerable factors, each of which influences and is influenced by those around it; and every such mutual influence varies with the stages which the respective factors have already reached in their growth. In this vital respect all sciences of life are akin to one another, and are unlike physical sciences. And therefore in the later stages of economics, when we are approaching nearly to the conditions of life, biological analogies are to be preferred to mechanical, other things being equal. (Marshall 1898, pp. 42–3)

When examining 'The scope and method of economics' in Appendix C of the *Principles*, Marshall (1920, p. 772) argues that 'economics, like biology, deals with a matter, of which the inner nature and constitution, as well as the outer form, are constantly changing'. Indeed, economics 'is a branch of biology broadly interpreted'. In comparing economics and biology, Georgescu-Roegen (1966, p. 106, emphasis added) goes even further than Marshall by asserting that '[e]volutionary elements predominate in every concrete economic phenomenon of some significance – *to a greater extent than even in biology*'. Yet he shares Marshall's scepticism toward the applicability of mathematics to economics. In discussing capitalism, he notes that '[s]ome aspects of its functioning lend themselves perfectly to mathematical analysis. Yet, when we come to the problem of its *evolution*, of its mutation into another form, mathematics proves to be too rigid and hence too simple a tool for handling it' (Georgescu-Roegen [1960a] 1966, p. 415). Georgescu-Roegen associates this rigidity with the narrow view of human nature that characterises standard economics and the fascination of neoclassical economists with 'arithmomorphic concepts', which he defines as those that can be expressed in numerical terms and used as variables in economic models (Georgescu-Roegen 1966, pp. 21–2). He contrasts arithmomorphic concepts with the dialectical ones espoused by Hegel and Marx, maintaining that the latter are often conceptually superior to the former, but are eschewed by neoclassical economists precisely because they cannot be expressed in quantitative terms:

> The obvious truth … is that the economic system continuously changes *qualitatively*. The most important aspect of the economic process is precisely the continuous emergence of novelty. Moreover, the novelty always represents a qualitative change. Nature thus has an infinite number of properties. It is because of this fact and because of the ever-present emerging novelty that the human mind cannot grasp actuality with the aid of analysis alone; it also must use dialectics. (Georgescu-Roegen 1979, pp. 321–2)

Similar views are expressed by Marshall who uses 'the term "contrivance" as synonymous with invention, creativity, innovation' in contrast to the 'routine' that characterises most economic processes, leading to a dialectical interplay between contrivance and routine (Raffaelli 2003, pp. 55–7). Because of this interplay and his awareness of the dialectical nature of many economic concepts,

Marshall advocates the associated 'principle of continuity' as symbolised by his (and Darwin's) motto 'Natura non facit saltum' (ibid., pp. 89–93).

Georgescu-Roegen's numerous references to Marshall's *Principles*, and the contrasts he often draws between Marshall's economics and that of the neo-classical school of thought, did not serve mainly as a pretext for him to lampoon neoclassical economics in order to draw attention to his own distinctly different research programme. Becattini (2004, pp. 142) lists Georgescu-Roegen among those economists who 'felt Marshall's thought held considerable unexpressed potential'. Georgescu-Roegen singles out Marshall for his zeal in alerting the economics profession to the dangers of relying exclusively on mechanical reasoning, which was already triumphing in the nineteenth century and whose victory became even more complete in the twentieth:

> The attachment of the Neoclassical forefathers to the mechanistic dogma led to the view of the economic process that characterizes the standard economic discipline of our time. *The mechanistic dogma was already solidly entrenched in economics when a solitary voice raised a protest against it. The voice was that of Alfred Marshall*, who in an 1898 article, 'Exchange and Distribution', argued that technological progress changes the coordinates of the economic process not only in a quantitative but also in a qualitative way. He recognized that economic dynamics (as he called the mechanistic economic theory) may serve some purpose in the first approach of facts. In this he was completely right. The qualitative changes usually reveal themselves only over a longer period of observation, hence, only at a higher level of analysis. But this does not mean that they can be safely ignored. (Georgescu-Roegen 1974, pp. 176, 179, emphasis added)

The biological paradigm that Georgescu-Roegen believed was better suited to portray the organic nature of phenomena such as economic development is sketched briefly below after his critique of 'economic man' is compared to Marshall's.

THE LIMITS OF *HOMO OECONOMICUS*

Georgescu-Roegen berates standard economics for its portrayal of *homo oeconomicus* as someone who measures welfare solely in terms of personal gains and losses. In addition to Marx, he cites Marshall as an economist who rejected this view. In his *Principles*, Marshall in fact criticised Ricardo and his followers because they 'regarded man as a constant quantity. The people whom they knew most intimately were city men; and they sometimes expressed themselves so carelessly as almost to imply that other Englishmen were very much like those whom they knew in the city'. This 'bent of mind led our economists to work out their theories on the tacit supposition that the world was made up of city men. They therefore attributed to the forces of supply and demand a much more mechanical and regular action than is to be found in real life' (Marshall 1920, pp. 762–3). Georgescu-Roegen observes that 'Marshall seems to be alone in reproaching the standard economists' for developing theories based on this presumption. Not only did it provide a false characterisation of most workers in Britain in the early nineteenth century: 'Still less can we expect it to be valid in all institutional settings. Actually, in *peasant* communities the satisfaction of the individual depends not only on the quantities of goods and services at his disposal but also on other economic variables, and gain depends on other factors besides money-profit' (Georgescu-Roegen 1966, pp. 109–10).

In a pioneering article of 1960 inspired by the nascent field of development economics, Georgescu-Roegen suggests a broader set of motivations underlying economic behaviour and the resulting income distribution in peasant societies such as that of his native Romania:

> For an economic theory to be operational at all, i.e. to be capable of serving as a guide for policy, it must concern itself with a specific type of economy, not with several types at the same time. As soon as we realize that for economic theory an economic system is characterized exclusively by institutional traits, it becomes obvious that neither Marxist nor Standard theory is valid as a whole for the analysis of a noncapitalistic economy, i.e. of the economy of a society in which part or all of the capitalist institutions are absent. Without institutional patterns concerning distribution, even the first human societies, small by necessity, could not have arrived at that modicum of stability which is the *sine qua non* condition of organic existence. Whether or not the faculty of 'sympathy' for his neighbor is part of man's original nature, that faculty must have evolved before the first viable communities could be formed. (Georgescu-Roegen [1960b] 1966, pp. 361–2, 385)

Both Georgescu-Roegen and Marshall recognise the positive role played by 'sympathy', a concept that Adam Smith made great use of in *The Theory of Moral Sentiments*, to ensure the viability and stability of human communities. In commenting on human evolution, Marshall (1920, p. 243) observes that '[g]radually the unreasoning sympathy, of which there are germs in the lower animals, extends its area and gets to be deliberately adopted as a basis of action: tribal affection gradually grows into a noble patriotism'. Elsewhere in the *Principles* he often refers to the fact that social forces, including altruism, shape individuals' conduct:

> [E]thical forces are among those of which the economist has to take account. Attempts have indeed been made to construct an abstract science with regard to the actions of an 'economic man', who is under no ethical influences and who pursues pecuniary gains warily and energetically, but mechanically and selfishly. But they have not been successful, nor even thoroughly carried out. (Ibid., p. vi)

After describing an individual's motives in taking actions on behalf of his family, Marshall asks:

[W]hy should they not include all other altruistic motives the action of which is so far uniform in any class at any time and place, that it can be reduced to general rule? There seems to be no reason; and in the present book normal action is taken to be that which may be expected, under certain conditions, from the members of an industrial group; and no attempt is made to exclude the influence of any motives, the action of which is regular, merely because they are altruistic. (Ibid.)

In his one and only indexed reference to 'economic man' in the text of the *Principles*, Marshall goes on to observe:

[E]conomists study the actions of individuals, but study them in relation to social rather than individual life. In all this they deal with man as he is: not with an abstract or 'economic' man; but a man of flesh and blood. They deal with a man who is largely influenced by egoistic motives in his business life to a great extent with reference to them; but who is also neither above vanity and recklessness, nor below delight in doing his work well for its own sake, or in sacrificing himself for the good of his family, his neighbours, or his country. (Ibid., pp. 25–7)

Besides his comments in the *Principles*, Groenewegen (2003, p. 115) points out that 'Marshall's hostility to "economic man" was strong and manifested itself on various occasions', starting with his inaugural lecture at Cambridge University on 'The present position of economics' where he 'discussed "economic man"' as one of 'the modes of expression adopted by the older economists' (ibid., p. 120) – from whom he clearly wished to differentiate himself. In commenting in the final chapter of the *Principles* on the rise in the 'standard of life' brought about by economic progress, where the latter is characterised by 'the development of new activities rather than of new wants', Marshall notes that this rise 'implies an increase of intelligence and energy and self-respect', and thus contains an important evolutionary dimension. For workers in any given trade it leads not only to an increase in wages, but 'will enable others to obtain their assistance at a cost somewhat less in proportion to its efficiency', thus benefitting the entire community (ibid., p. 689). Although they were not the first nor the last economists to adopt this view, it is clear that both Marshall and Georgescu-Roegen, for somewhat different reasons, reject the standard neoclassical portrayal of man as *homo oeconomicus*, and embrace a much broader range of motives in which unselfish personal actions taken on behalf of family members, associates and the community at large play an important role (Raffaelli 2003 elaborates further on Marshall's critique of 'economic man'.)

BIOECONOMICS: AN UNFINISHED PROJECT

Both Marshall and Georgescu-Roegen proclaim the need for economics to transcend mechanical analogies and the associated mathematical orientation characteristic of the neoclassical school of thought, in order to incorporate the insights of biology and (as Georgescu-Roegen argues in his 1971 book) those derived from the laws of thermodynamics as well as natural resource and environmental economics. Both authors did not live up to the promise of transforming economic theory and practice in light of these insights. As Thomas argues in Marshall's case,

> [h]e had come to realize more and more that the study of organic growth necessitated a break with his neoclassical system as definite as the break which he had made with the Ricardo-Mill system. By about 1900 he must have become convinced that, if Volume 2 [of the *Principles*] was to be true to his high standards, he would have to work out within him the foundations of yet another science – economic biology. If that was so, one could hardly blame him for regarding this as a task for his successors not for him. (Thomas 1991, pp. 11–12)

From the mid-1960s on, Georgescu-Roegen aimed like Marshall to devise a new paradigm for economic theory by grounding it in organic and evolutionary concepts. As well as providing a detailed critique of the neoclassical theories of consumption and production, he went further than Marshall in outlining the general features of what he referred to as 'bioeconomics', which goes beyond the 'economic biology' heralded by Thomas (Maneschi 2006 briefly describes bioeconomics and its antecedents in the history of economic thought). Inspired by the entropy law, Georgescu-Roegen proposed a novel flow-fund model of production that allows for the irreversible use of low-entropy natural resources available to humankind in finite amounts and the generation of high-entropy waste products (Georgescu-Roegen 1971, pp. 228–34). It highlights the need to replace the energy embodied in fossil fuels with the solar energy freely available on a daily basis. This is an aim with which Marshall would also have been sympathetic: 'The Marshallian concept of progress' – according to Caldari (2006, p. 485) – 'is very close to the more recent idea of sustainable development'. Marshall indeed anticipated Georgescu-Roegen's warning of impending worldwide shortages of energy and other resources: 'Nature's opportunities cannot long retain their present large generosity; for the world is small ere very many generations have passed, the limitation of agricultural and mineral resources must press heavily on the population of the world, even though its rate of increase should receive a considerable check' (Marshall 1919, p. 2). It is clear, however, that Georgescu-Roegen's project, initiated half a century after Marshall's death, goes well beyond anything that Marshall might have proposed, or for which he had even the requisite scientific background. While Georgescu-Roegen never claimed Marshall as an anticipator of the bioeconomic paradigm that was close to his heart, it remains true that he was significant source of inspiration and motivation for his own research.

Georgescu-Roegen was unable to follow through on his intention to gather and incorporate in book form the insights from the research that he doggedly carried out in the last three decades of his life until his death at the age of 88.

Although neither of his books of 1966 and 1971 uses the term 'bioeconomics', that term and its emerging features are clearly set out in articles such as 'Energy and economic myths' (Georgescu-Roegen [1975] 1976) that focus on the biophysical limitations on economic activity. As in Marshall's case, the new paradigm that he advocated for his fellow economists was a Mecca (or, to mix religious metaphors, a promised land) to which he wished to lead them, but was unable to reach in his lifetime.

REFERENCES

Becattini, G. (2004), 'New orientations in Marshallian studies', in T. Aspromourgos and J. Lodewijks (eds), *History and Political Economy: Essays in Honour of P.D. Groenewegen*, London: Routledge, pp. 142–55.

Caldari, K. (2006), 'Progress', in T. Raffaelli, G. Becattini and M. Dardi (eds), *The Elgar Companion to Alfred Marshall*, Cheltenham, UK and Northampton, MA, USA: Edward Elgar, pp. 483–7.

Dardi, M. (2006), 'Partial equilibrium and period analysis', in T. Raffaelli, G. Becattini and M. Dardi (eds), *The Elgar Companion to Alfred Marshall*, Cheltenham, UK and Northampton, MA, USA: Edward Elgar, pp. 215–25.

Foster, J. (2006), 'Time', in T. Raffaelli, G. Becattini and M. Dardi (eds), *The Elgar Companion to Alfred Marshall*, Cheltenham, UK and Northampton, MA, USA: Edward Elgar, pp. 281–7.

Georgescu-Roegen, N. ([1950] 1966), 'The theory of choice and the constancy of economic laws', *Quarterly Journal of Economics*, **64**, reprinted in Georgescu-Roegen (1966), pp. 171–83.

Georgescu-Roegen, N. ([1960a] 1966), 'Mathematical proofs of the breakdown of capitalism', *Econometrica*, **28**, reprinted in Georgescu-Roegen (1966), pp. 398–415.

Georgescu-Roegen, N. ([1960b] 1966), 'Economic theory and agrarian economics', *Oxford Economic Papers*, n.s., **12**, reprinted in Georgescu-Roegen (1966), pp. 359–97.

Georgescu-Roegen, N. (1966), *Analytical Economics: Issues and Problems*, Cambridge, MA: Harvard University Press.

Georgescu-Roegen, N. (1971), *The Entropy Law and the Economic Process*, Cambridge, MA: Harvard University Press.

Georgescu-Roegen, N. (1974), 'Mechanistic dogma and economics', *Methodology and Science*, **7** (3), 174–84.

Georgescu-Roegen, N. ([1974] 1976), 'Dynamic models and economic growth', in G. Schwödiauer (ed.), *Equilibrium and Disequilibrium in Economic Theory*, Dordrecht: Reidel, reprinted in Georgescu-Roegen (1976), pp. 235–53.

Georgescu-Roegen, N. ([1975] 1976), 'Energy and economic myths', *Southern Economic Journal*, **41**, reprinted in Georgescu-Roegen (1976), pp. 3–36.

Georgescu-Roegen, N. (1976), *Energy and Economic Myths: Institutional and Analytical Economic Essays*, New York: Pergamon.

Georgescu-Roegen, N. (1979), 'Methods in economic science', *Economic Issues*, **13**, 317–28.

Groenewegen, P. (2003), 'Alfred Marshall on *Homo oeconomicus*: evolution versus utilitarianism?', in J. Laurent (ed.), *Evolutionary Economics and Human Nature*, Cheltenham, UK and Northampton, MA, USA: Edward Elgar, pp. 114–33.

Hodgson, G.M. (1993), 'The Mecca of Alfred Marshall', *Economic Journal*, **103** (1), 406–15.
Hodgson, G.M. (2006), 'Economics and biology', in T. Raffaelli, G. Becattini and M. Dardi (eds), *The Elgar Companion to Alfred Marshall*, Cheltenham, UK and Northampton, MA, USA: Edward Elgar, pp. 197–202.
Maneschi, A. (2006), 'The filiation of economic ideas: Marx, Schumpeter, Georgescu-Roegen', *History of Economic Ideas*, **14**, 105–25.
Marshall, A. ([1879] 1974), *The Pure Theory of Foreign Trade and The Pure Theory of Domestic Values*, Clifton: Augustus M. Kelley.
Marshall, A. (1898) 'Distribution and exchange', *Economic Journal*, **8** (1), 37–59.
Marshall, A. (1919), *Industry and Trade*, London: Macmillan.
Marshall, A. (1920), *Principles of Economics*, 8th edn, London: Macmillan.
Marshall, A. (1923), *Money, Credit and Commerce*, London: Macmillan.
Metcalfe, J.S. (2006), 'Evolutionary economics', in T. Raffaelli, G. Becattini and M. Dardi (eds), *The Elgar Companion to Alfred Marshall*, Cheltenham, UK and Northampton, MA, USA: Edward Elgar, pp. 651–7.
Raffaelli, T. (2003), *Marshall's Evolutionary Economics*, London: Routledge.
Schumpeter, J.A. (1951), *Ten Great Economists*, New York: Oxford University Press.
Thomas, B. (1991), 'Alfred Marshall on economic biology', *Review of Political Economy*, **3**, 1–14.

Index

Pareto, V. 7, 13, 69, 72, 73, 147, 150–51, 199–214
Parsons, T. 69
partial equilibrium 6, 7, 24, 35, 70, 76, 102, 112, 113, 132, 139, 150, 155, 219–20, 228
path dependency 31, 211
Pearson, C. 83
peasant societies 233
perfect competition 9, 25, 68, 72–3, 75, 133, 154
Perroux, F. 145, 148
Pesciarelli, E. 13
Pesenti, A. 126, 156
Pethick-Lawrence, F.W. 18
Philippovich, E. von 130
philosophy 12, 34, 90, 120, 158, 179–80
Physiocrats 145
Pierson, N.G. 135–8, 139
Pigou, A.C. 3, 5, 6, 9, 17, 19, 20, 21–2, 25, 33, 47, 68, 88, 100, 133, 178, 179, 219
Pikhno, D.I. 120
planning/planners 151, 156
Plant, A. 72
Plumptre, A.F.W. 55
pluralism 75, 110, 123, 124, 167
Plutology 82
Poland 110–14
political economy 40–41, 42, 43, 114, 117, 118, 119, 123, 162, 191, 193
Political Economy (Lange) 114
Political Element in the Development of Economic Theory, The 99–100
population 121, 123, 127, 235
Portugal 166–70
positive economics 156
Positive Theorie des Kapitals 101
Posner, R. 72
Poznan school 110, 112
pragmatism 89, 91, 206, 209
Prendergast, R. 23, 26
Present Position of Economics, The 150
Pribram, K. 131
Price, B. 40, 142
Price, L. 40
price theory 5, 12, 18, 35, 69–71, 74, 76, 112, 120, 121, 122, 125, 129–30, 139, 148, 178, 186, 205

Price Theory 45
Prices 19
Primer of Political Economy 162, 184
Princeton University 74
Principles of Agricultural Economics 139
Principles of Economics 17, 18, 23, 24, 25–6, 28, 44, 45, 81, 205–6, 234
in Australia 82–3, 84, 85
in Belgium 141, 143
in China 185, 186
in France 146, 147
Georgescu-Roegen on 232
in German-speaking countries 129, 130, 131, 224
in the history of economic thought 3, 5, 6, 7
in Holland 135, 136–7, 138, 139
in India 175
in Italy 150, 152
in Japan 192, 194
in New Zealand 89
in Norway 105, 106, 107, 108
in Poland 111, 114
in Russia 116, 117, 118, 121, 122–3, 126–7
scholarship overview 9, 10, 11, 12, 13
Schumpeter on 216, 217, 220, 221, 222–3
in Spain 163
in Sweden 96, 99, 100, 101, 102
in the United States 60, 61, 62–6, 67, 70, 74, 75, 76, 77–8
Principles of Economics (Diepenhorst) 139
Principles of Economics (Taussig) 54, 56, 67
Principles of Political Economy (Carver) 189
Principles of Political Economy (Mill) 59, 62, 217
Principles of Political Economy (Shield Nicholson) 88, 100
Principles of Political Economy and Taxation (Ricardo) 7, 163
Prisbildningsproblemet och föränderligheten 95, 99
Problems of the theory of value 133
producer rent 112